Fog Valley

WINTER

Pioneer Heritage
Backroad Rambles
& Vintage Recipes

Frances Rivetti

A Fireside Companion : Fog Valley Winter

Pioneer Heritage, Back Road Rambles
and Vintage Recipes

The Tastiest Little Place on Earth

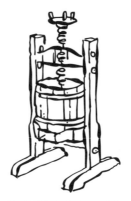

FOG VALLEY PRESS

Fog Valley Press
www.fogvalleypress.info

ISBN 978-0-9904921-0-8
"First Vintage" Edition 2016
Printed in China

For my mum and dad, John and Elaine, for letting me go
and for the people of Fog Valley for letting me in.

"The land flourished because it was fed
from so many sources — because it was nourished
by so many cultures and traditions and peoples."

Lyndon B. Johnson

Contents

Part Two: The People and Their Winter Celebrations

Part Three: Fog Valley Winter's Festive Food

Author's Note

Fog Valley, in my mind, is nothing less than a national treasure. It is a made-up name conjured in the mists of my imagination to capture the magic and mystery of the strangely beautiful place that I call home.

My first book, *Fog Valley Crush*, released in the fall of 2014, chronicled my perspective of "the good life" in the California farmstead frontier — 40 miles north of San Francisco.

I crafted the initial tone by transcribing from my pile of dog-eared reporter's notebooks onto to my laptop keyboard at the kitchen table. I'd spent several years romping around my adoptive Gold Rush-era city of Petaluma and surrounding Pacific coastal countryside in the guise of a food, wine and lifestyle writer.

My husband, Timo never knows where I'll be off to next. He calls my line of work "gallivanting" — and though it does, in actual fact, involve a lot of discipline and labor in its recount, these tasty and intriguing rambles of mine are not something I'd ever take for granted!

With this in mind, I passionately penned my first foray into Fog Valley's farm-to-table culture as a love letter to the micro-regional community of farmers, food innovators, artists and dreamers in which I live and work.

In the busy and exciting days and weeks that followed the book's release, a little voice in my newly minted author's head piped up, growing more vociferous each day. This persistent whisper gently nudged, prodded and pushed up the volume to the point of propelling me out of the door in search of yet more delicious adventures in the field.

With miles of coastal and country back roads to fully explore, I geared up for a new mission to peel back yet more tasty layers of this extraordinary place.

I decided to focus this second series of expeditions and research on my favorite season—wild and earthy, a largely untamed Fog Valley in winter. The peacefulness of this time of year proved the perfect time for challenging and changing the way I've considered the region I thought I'd come to know so well. When nights are long and days are short, the urge to batten down the hatches and isolate until spring keeps the crowds at bay. I found it a magical time to roam and better get to know the countryside, especially the week in between Christmas and New Year when time slows to a crawl.

My goal was, in exploration, to preserve this sense of place and to inspire. In doing so, I discovered a dynamic, interactive dialog between its sometimes surprising past and present. Though regional history books are amongst my favorites of reading material, I believe that in rescuing a more specific slice of a place's past, a more vibrant and vivid conversation emerges.

Human migration, its history and its future are close to my heart. I came to Fog Valley as an immigrant, a modern day settler, married in my early twenties to a globetrotting Anglo/Italian man whose idea it was to try our luck in California.

Old-fashioned west coast California country life wrapped its rolled-up sleeves around us and we stayed. I'd soon recognized the region's rich food culture a metaphor for family and community. It fed my deep, instinctive need for home and provided me a solid base in raising three American-born sons.

I grew up in a fairly remote farming region in the United Kingdom — the bleakly beautiful English Fenlands of East Anglia. The ancient past forms a vital part of my DNA. I think of my move over the pond a modern-day pioneer trail of my own.

Fog Valley is a place for hardy, grounded souls. Grit and determination, humor, grace and good neighborliness continue to set the stage for multi-generational casts of characters who've deeply rooted themselves within the footprints of the region's first people.

Come wintertime, holidays in Fog Valley bring a much-needed respite to all of this hard work and discipline, a communal slowing down, a time to reconnect, to give thanks, to look around at our landscape and be generous of spirit.

Home is where the heart is, especially in winter. Fog Valley family, friends and neighbors gather in toast of another year. Lives are well shared in this coastal ranchland realm, in close-knit, historic rural hamlets, remote coastal communities, a vibrant Victorian riverfront town bustling with holiday shoppers.

Winter season rolls in at a gentle pace. It creeps peacefully into the folds of Fog Valley. Inspiration for celebration and escape is conjured by its still and sacred landscape, a sea of ribald green, craggy coastal hills. Nature's perfect pasturelands, once home to great herds of herbivores, deer and elk today sustain grass-fed dairy cows, beef cattle, free range chickens and grapevines.

History holds in its hands so many lessons for our modern lives. Historians trace the candlelit evergreen of Pacific coastal holiday culture to an ancient belief in winter shelter for woodland spirits. I think of this as I gather fir branches, feathers and moss for fresh garlands and swags. A woodland spirit or two would be fine company by the fireside on a blustery winter's night.

Just as the first people of Fog Valley, the Coast Miwok marked Winter Solstice for more than five thousand years — the pagan-rooted practice of "bringing in the bough" continues to remind the farming region of earth's promise of renewal and a return to crops.

Fog Valley winter revelry is rooted in its pioneering past. At the end of the nineteenth-century, my adopted small city (then market town) of Petaluma was the largest shipping point for dairy products in California. A peculiarly potent cultural mix of people collaborated in the shaping of its history, much of which endures today through six generations and more. This is the flavor of Fog Valley.

Chinese, Danish, English, German, Irish, Italian, Jewish, Portuguese, Swiss and Welsh settled the area after early Russian, Spanish and Mexican influence gave way to the flood gates of the Gold Rush.

In travelling around this self-delineated Fog Valley map of mine, I set out on my panoramic journey in short bursts packed with fascinating backstory.

I discovered, to my delight, that although times have undoubtedly changed, a pioneer-spirit of integrity, creativity and honest food culture prevails.

For those who are discovering Fog Valley for the first time, I've taken great care to craft *Fog Valley Winter* as a stand-alone read.

And so, dear reader, I invite you to curl up in your favorite fireside chair, make yourself a cup of tea or something stronger and come along with me on my winter rambles through the region. Together, we're about to meet the region's early influencers and consider how their wintertime traditions shaped Fog Valley of today.

Traditional holiday meals have been tons of fun to research and select — evoking the fondest of memories — I'm reminded all the more how our favorite cultural recipes and customs serve as some of the strongest links between generations.

According to the Pew Research Center, eight out of 10 Americans celebrate Christmas in some shape or form. One third of people celebrating Christmas do so as a cultural holiday rather than a religious one. Whatever your cultural or religious beliefs, I hope you will enjoy the winter focus of this book.

Traditions of the mellow melting pot that is Fog Valley bind us together from coast to town during the shortest, darkest days of the year.

May you discover a new appreciation of winter season's "good life" — one that comes with a scaling back of the holiday seasonal spree in favor of uncovering the joys of regional heritage, of gifted meal time and experiences, coastal rambles and the natural splendor of the open road.

Vintage recipes featured within the following pages are intended to whet the appetite and to inspire. Most are fairly simple and straightforward to follow. Some, such as an authentic Fog Valley "Turkey Dinner for 250" serve as scene setters in the historic sense. Do let me know if you successfully replicate such a feast.

Take all reasonable caution, particularly when cooking meat and seafood. Make sure these delightful, old-fashioned recipes work for you in your contemporary kitchen. Check specific weights and measures and remember that meat thermometers and refrigerators are our friends!

Fog Valley's city of Petaluma under a winter cloak

ONE

the place

Children on Main Street, Tomales 1880
courtesy, the Tomales History Museum

Chapter 1

a journey back in time

Wintertime proved ideal as a brief incubation period, an essential starting point for research into short road trips around Fog Valley during the region's sleepy season. A series of Thursday afternoon visits to the Petaluma Historical Library and Museum provided me a framework in which to plot my route around its storied past and present.

Thursdays are designated as the hallowed day of exploration for eager Fog Valley historians, genealogists, students and writers such as myself to investigate collected tomes of old newspapers, maps, notices, cookbooks, journals and other remembrances stored in the museum.

Stacks of leather-bound annals of my adopted community reside there in splendid solitude, awaiting an occasional perusal by some particularly inquisitive soul or other.

Hoppy's place (formally The Hoppy Hopkin's Research Room) — named after one of the city's best loved historians is a compact and cozy partitioned space, positioned just far enough out of aimless arms reach of the casual visitor, located upstairs on the second story balcony of the Petaluma Museum, a specially sequestered spot for troves of historical documents.

Hoppy's legacy, amongst his many historical connections, was his focus on local history and lore. He was a charter member of the Petaluma Museum Association, prolific newsletter editor for the Petaluma Historical Society, Friend of the Library and a leading light of the city's Heritage Homes organization.

Not to be confused with 1960s British counter culture photographer, journalist, researcher and political activist of the same name, though the late Elbert H. Hopkins, a Fog Valley-raised U.S. Navy technician, did share a passion and talent for writing and detailed research.

One of his most colorful roles was co-hosting annual Halloween cemetery walks with former President of the Heritage Homes and Petaluma Museum Association, Deborah Riddle, to visit the graves of prominent, early Petalumans.

These days, Hoppy's graveyard tours are still a big deal in town, hosted by a spritely and enthusiastic Petalumans of Yesteryear group that leads regular walking tours in the city's historic downtown district.

Costumed guides or docents adopt detailed personas of Petaluma's most influential nineteenth or early twentieth-century citizens. And no one bats an eyelid as genteel Victorian ladies and gents stroll the city's bustling streets, to and from the museum. Tours are well worth taking if you'd like to learn more of old Petaluma's architectural and social history.

Petaluma's museum initially opened its doors in the form of a grand public library, its cornerstone laid in 1904 and funded in large part by American philanthropist Andrew Carnegie. It was one of a legion of more than 2,500 Carnegie municipal library buildings built in the English-speaking world during the late 1880s through 1919.

This beautiful building replaced libraries housed in the Independent Order of Odd Fellow's building on Main Street and in the old city hall.

Six Carnegie Libraries were built in Sonoma County alone. Sadly, only three remain today. Healdsburg's Carnegie Library is also a museum and the city of Sonoma's houses its Visitors' Bureau.

Architect Brainerd Jones designed Petaluma's Carnegie Library. In fact, he designed almost all of the city's most prominent Victorian buildings and was described by the *Petaluma Argus Courier* as: "The man who built a city."

One of Brainerd's crowning glories is a perfectly preserved, freestanding, leaded glass domed ceiling within the library's design. This stunning, yet subtle work of art is the largest freestanding glass domed ceiling west of the Rockies.

I found myself most comfortably entrenched in cozy winter afternoon forays into hallowed Hoppy's Place. Comfortably sequestered at wooden desk and chair, tucked into the shadows beneath the glow of the gracious glass dome, I basked in a time long passed.

It was here that I found my starting point in Fog Valley's lively, illustrious and colorful past — packed to the rafters on rickety, old shelving and within a fleet of wooden filing cabinets and draws.

I savored the tiny research room and its big, old, study table, more often than not, entirely to myself — Thursdays in winter are not peak season for a provincial museum.

Hours of desk chair travel ensued, notebook and pencil my charting tools. This was a journey back in time to more than a century past. With ease and enthusiasm, I surrendered any modern tech tools. I turned off my smart phone and willingly slipped into a bygone era of schooners and steamboats.

There, I wandered, freely, in my mind's eye, along familiar streets still under construction, submerging myself in the hustle and bustle of the blacksmith and wagon shop, peeking into the first hotel and its neighboring saloons, stepping aside for a flurry of horse driven buggies transporting optimistic and industrious folk of an early American frontier town.

I saw huts and shanties, primitive housing of the region's first arrivals giving way to grand, new iron front commercial buildings, banks, stores and homes. Early warehouses lined the creek bank, first conduit for incoming people and materials and the region's outgoing lumber and produce.

Journalistic thunderbolts struck early and frequently. Having worked for a variety of newspapers and magazines since my teens, I still believe in the magic of the printed word, the powerful profundity of the graphic image. It is the tactile feel of something permanent, the impression of newsprint on the fingers that I love. Ink-stained relics preserved over time, gifted page after glorious page of Victorian news, views, clever advertisements with their captivating graphics.

Barber shops, cigar and tobacco retailers catered to those making this their permanent residence and the many more who were passing through. The hotel lobby provided comfort for new arrivers and travelers. Livery stables were the service stations of their day along dusty, unpaved streets. Wagons, horses and buggies of farm folk caused Fog Valley's first mini traffic jams as settlers traded, conducted business and gossiped with neighbors.

Flat bottom scows, workhorses of the waterways, moved on wind and tide (before the internal combustion engine appeared), ferrying passengers, hay, fruits and vegetables, lumber, grapes for wine and hops for beer, some 14 notoriously twisting miles along the Petaluma Creek to the San Francisco Bay. These boats were specially designed for mudflats and sloughs — a good thing, as passage was frequently fraught and could take days in heavy fog.

Hardware stores sold stoves and ranges, cutlery, windmills, rudimentary plumbing materials. Long before the advent of the supermarket, "green thumb" farmers peddled fresh produce in the street from the back of their open-top wagons.

By the time the Christmas seasons rolled around in the late 1880s, stores put on their best and brightest appearance, with storefront windows and doors decorated with evergreens and window displays made picture-perfect with fancy goods in the gaslight.

Streets were crowded and trade was bustling until late into the evenings in December. A large, decorated Christmas tree took center stage in the lantern lit street.

Alongside newspaper clippings and books I perused handwritten holiday recipes and vivid mementos of founding families.

Petaluma's modern public library opened in 1976 in what had been known (prior to the arrival of a freeway) as the city's old, east side, on East Washington Street by the central fairgrounds.

I spent countless more hours at the library browsing for interesting background amongst the rows of bookshelves in the Sonoma County history section. Libraries are amongst my favorite places to hang out, especially when "a-buzz" with silent study.

En-route to the library, I pass, each time I visit, a large and vibrant wall mural depicting various stages of the city of Petaluma's evolution. Artist Steve Della Maggiora transformed the side of a former Goodwill store, an historic building at the crossroads of Petaluma Boulevard and East Washington, in 1988. For a whistle-stop tour through the ages, stop awhile across the street to take in this wonderful work.

The woman wearing full Victorian dress and hat painted on a stand-alone signal box in front of the wall is a depiction of costumed Debbie Riddle, Hoppy's co-host of the spirited first graveyard tours.

Sixteen miles out west, a visit to the Tomales Regional History Center proved a contrast in light to the dark wood and atmosphere of Victorian conservatism of its Petaluma counterpart.

This fully renovated, bright, open plan museum is housed in the coastal community's historic, former high school building. Winter hours, though posted, were somewhat unpredictable (given changeable weather) but, after a couple of attempts to visit, proved worth the wait.

Coastal heritage plays a most delicious part in the telling of a winter seasonal history of Fog Valley. Time spent in this small and informative museum was well spent — I considered it a second important portal into the region's rich heritage, its farming, dairy and fishing industries.

Before we launch into the illustrious Gold Rush boom or bust years in Fog Valley, a winter's visit further back in time is of paramount importance. In the next chapter we'll go where we ought to far more often — a visit to pay our respects to the region's first people.

Eucalyptus grove to Kule Loklo

Chapter 2

a Coast Miwok winter

December. Best to not plan travel days on a Monday or Tuesday, for most amenities out in the wilder western reaches of Fog Valley tend to take a day or two break at the beginning of the week, shutting shop when there's little more for company than stately Neolithic rock formations, eucalyptus, oak and redwood trees, dairy cows grazing by the Pacific Ocean at the edge of the world.

This bucolic scene was, more than 10,000 years ago, teeming with exotic wildlife. Senior State Archeologist for the California State Parks Association, Breck Parkman's 2006 hypotheses: *"The California Serengeti"* invites us to step back to the last Ice Age, where wide grassy valleys in the San Francisco Bay Area were home to herds of mammoth and mastodon, camel, horse, bison, llamas, elk and deer. Packs of wolf, saber-tooth cat, prides of California lion, bear and vultures were fierce predators in the Pleistocene Age, one of the greatest natural phenomena of all time.

Heading west towards Point Reyes from Petaluma on the D Street extension, somewhere along the way the same road out of town takes a notion to rename itself Point Reyes-Petaluma Road. In the nineteenth-century imperfect skeletons of several mastodons (distant relations to elephants) were found protruding from the Petaluma Creek, not far from downtown Petaluma. I take a lot of pleasure in putting life into perspective when I picture herds of mastodons grazing their way from the coast inland to Petaluma. It is something to think about when driving out to Point Reyes.

It's hard to think of a country road as a major artery in the region and yet this one certainly is and has been, historically, the direct route from Petaluma out to dairy farm communities and nowadays, the National Seashore at the farthest point west.

Heritage hues saturate the view, in town and out into open space. No matter how many times I've driven this scenic road with its shuttered, Victorian farmsteads and faded, brick-red painted chicken barns (some preserved, most not) a palpable sense of the past never fails to transfix.

Heading west towards my first destination — Bear Valley — I shed my everyday worries and woes. In stopping the clock, well, actually, by turning it back a century and a half, I drove out of Dodge and left the rest of my book writing to-do list on my desk.

In no time, vehicular horsepower kicked into gear, ramping up to climb a series of steep and curvy uphill turns before me. I looked ahead and then to my left as a giant olive grove unfolded across the hills of an historic, former dairy ranch.

The olive tree-studded majesty of 550-acre McEvoy Ranch is a sight to behold. It is nothing short of spectacular and right on my doorstep. I've stood on this site, in line under the morning mist along with hundreds of fellow backyard olive farmers come many a November's community crush.

Olive ranch founder Nan Tucker McEvoy passed away at age 95, in 2015, leaving her beloved ranch home for pastures even greener.

Nan was the last family member to run her grandfather's 150-year-old *San Francisco Chronicle* newspaper. A Peace Corps worker, reporter and vocal democrat, her early passions stood her in good stead for blazing an extraordinary (post-media career) pioneer trail of her own.

Nan's love for family, home and bold launch into California's first major olive enterprise transformed a rambling old farming property into a world renowned, private ranch. Scheduled tour visits and tasting room visits (estate wine as well as olive oil) are welcome by arrangement, but don't stop in here unannounced.

Cresting the hilltop beyond McEvoy Ranch land, Point Reyes — Petaluma Road drops down into a valley flanked by Holstein cows and a stately white Victorian farmhouse with big red barns that pop into the forefront of the panorama like a perpetual television commercial.

I've spotted multi-generational farmer Kitty Dolcini's distinctively positioned ranch as backdrop to more than a couple of TV ads over the past few years. It's a dreamy scene, whatever the season, but in winter, after the rains, the colors are sublime — a quintessential California country white farmstead with the red pop of barns set against an apple green valley.

A little ways farther along, historic Fog Valley Marin French Cheese Company (Rouge et Noir), founded in 1865, welcomes the weary passer-by for a brief but charming spot of rest or respite, whatever purpose of the journey. I never am able to resist a stretch of the legs around the Cheese Factory's pretty pond. Picnic benches perch under willow trees and rarely, except on weekends and holidays, are they full to the point of my being unable to scout one out.

There is a (newly remodeled) tasting room in the cheese factory that begs a visit for a sample or two or three from this historic first cheese making operation in the state. It's a good spot to stop and fill up your cooler or picnic basket with wines, beer, cheese and bread for the day ahead.

Back on the winding westward route, I looked for the glistening approach of Nicasio Reservoir, largest lake in north Marin County. Its 845 acres of flooded valleys, islands and coves was a heartening sight after four years of drought.

No boats, no swimming allowed, but lots of fishermen and fisherwomen parked along the roadside, out for a hopeful haul of Largemouth Bass, carp and catfish. Dog walking is OK, on leash and if you do stop off here, there's an easy trail around the shoreline for a waterside stroll. Its green hills and rugged terrain reminds me of the Scottish highlands. The reservoir's controversial beginning has not been forgotten.

Back in the early 1960s, Marin Municipal Water District essentially forced the sale of numerous historic farms to make way for an artificial reservoir. This was then created by the construction of Seeger Dam at Nicasio Creek. To the consternation of resourceful locals, the dam (that, ironically, does not provide water for those living in the immediate area) duly blocked spawning areas of a rich natural food source — salmon and steelhead trout — endangered species that had flourished in the creek.

A red tailed hawk hovered overhead as I drove on towards Olema, patiently plodding on behind a carefully contended convoy of horse trailers, en-route, no doubt for a brisk winter morning's coastal trail ride.

I figured I may as well pull over and stretch my legs in the quirky little hamlet of Olema, the name of which is Coast Miwok for little coyote. Olema is located a couple of miles south east of Point Reyes Station — an unincorporated community straddling State Route 1.

There's a lot more than meets the eye to the 1960s hippie hamlet that maintains its fair share of tie-dye and camping options to this day. A present population of 53, plus a few dozen overnighters in one of its several bed and breakfast establishments and campgrounds might sound somewhat uninspiring, yet visitors and locals alike find this one of the most alluring pit-stops for refreshment and lodgings in Fog Valley.

Unfortunately for me, it was too early in the day to take a coveted chair in the hallowed dining room of Sir and Star, formerly The Olema Inn, perched on the corner of Sir Francis Drake Boulevard and Star Route One.

This off-beat, atmospheric, quite fantastic brainchild of west country dining duo Margaret Grade and Daniel DeLong, chefs of nearby Manka's Inverness Lodge, is best in show when it comes to my idea of Fog Valley's most authentic farm-to-table dining experience.

There was, however, already a line out of the door of nearby Farmhouse Deli, a pint-sized emporium of a coast picnicker's delight. Espresso drinks are generally a hit when mustered in the middle of nowhere and a jostling line of ruddy-cheeked travelers from around the globe gathered at the java crossroads, last post of civilization, almost.

The Bear Valley Visitor Center sits a quarter mile from sweet Olema — the starting point for exploring the wonderland of Point Reyes National Seashore.

In the words of Secretary of the Interior (1961 to 1969) Stewart L. Udall: "No other area in the United States near a dense population center has been so unaltered by a man until now."

By the time the government moved in to preserve Point Reyes as a protected National Seashore wilderness area in the 1960s, only a mere handful of the region's indigenous people remained. This wild, Pacific coastal paradise was home to the Coast Miwok (Meewocs) for thousands of years — the earliest known date for human habitation in the region being about 1350 B.C.

More than one hundred and twenty Coast Miwok sites were once located within the 111 square miles of what would become the National Seashore parklands. This magnificent, dense and mystical 71,000 acre preserve provided then, as it does to this day, one of the richest natural food sheds in the country.

Tribal villages and smaller tribelets formed a large part of Fog Valley's native population. Over and above the 120 settlements within the National Seashore, some 44 more tribal branch villages were scattered along the coast north to Bodega Bay (Clamentko) and inland (Licatuit) to what we know now as the cities of Cotati, Petaluma, Novato and San Rafael to the south.

Tribal people were mostly peaceful and protective of the land and its natural resources. Their stewardship in villages typically of around one hundred men, women and children was in itself, a harmonious model of hunting, gathering and fishing, in tune with the seasons.

Many migrated inland during the coldest winter months, though the Coast Miwok were no strangers to the swirling mist and fog and brutal, unceasing winds that were frequent conditions, regardless of season.

Northern California coastal history does not begin with the Spanish Mission era. Nor does it start with the arrival of early Russian fur hunters, followed by traders and trappers and early Catholic missionaries. The Coast Miwok were the only people in this part of the world for more than five thousand years. They celebrated the winter season as: "The Season of Dreaming," "Buckeye Time" or even more evocatively: "World Sleeping Time."

The astronomical event of Winter Solstice marked the shortest, darkest days of the Coast Miwok year. Stand outside at Point Reyes on a midwinter's night and experience the elements yourself. For the first people, surviving winter was not a given.

The Miwok were not alone in early midwinter revelry. As far back as Neolithic times, humans recognized the impact and significance of Winter Solstice on wild animal mating and the management of winter reserves.

Winter was a time of acute shortage. Some years the Miwok's crucial acorn crop would fail. The California buckeye nut came into play as substitute and dietary mainstay during those leanest and meanest of months.

The ocean was a constant friend. It yielded a year-round supply of vital and nutritional crab, mussels, clams, limpet and oysters. The

Miwok fished in light, fast, easy to maneuver tule-grass boats built for eight to 10 people. They depended upon the sustenance of coastal duck, seafowl, otters, seals, sea lions, coastal greens of leaves and roots. Large amounts of dried kale came into play from careful winter storage.

Warriors gathered for a "Season of Dreaming Ceremony" in which the far-traveled Sun God was encouraged to return. Myth, ritual, spiritual song and dance transformed the bleak landscape.

Each village had a non-hereditary male elder (hoipu) and woman (maien) elected by the people who served as arbitrator of disputes, counselors and entertainment coordinators.

Medicine men cured diseases of the mind and body and winter ceremonies were arranged, using plants that induced spiritual-healing dreams, vision quests and cleansing.

Villagers constructed sweat lodges to rid the human scent by rubbing on mugwort and angelica before hunting. Meditation, particularly in wintertime promoted profound relaxation, journeys of self-discovery and reflection. A sacred time of silence befell the earth and its people.

I had designed my morning drive through Olema and out to the Bear Valley Visitor's center with the specific goal of revisiting a carefully recreated Miwok village named "Kule Loklo."

I'd toured the village several times over many years of elementary school field trips with one or another of my sons and their classmates, an important part of regional heritage that is so often overlooked. Though "Kule Loklo" stands, according to the National Seashore signage, "where no village ever was, but where one might have stood" — villages like this were scattered throughout the coastal region.

Opposite the trail to Kule Loklo from the visitors center is another important path worth its walk of a little over half a mile. This paved loop explores the infamous San Andreas Fault Zone. It begins at the southeast corner of the Bear Valley Picnic Area.

Shifting tectonic plates underneath the region are still moving today. According to the Marin Agricultural Land Trust: "Over millions of years, the San Andreas Fault zone averages about two inches of movement a year which is the equivalent of the growth of our fingernails." During the San Francisco Bay Area's historic 1906 earthquake, the San Andreas Fault moved a staggering 20 feet in less than one minute in Point Reyes.

Kule Loklo provides historians, hikers, school children and curious park visitors such as myself with as close to authentic an experience of a Coast Miwok village as to be found in these parts. Its isolation from the modern world is representative of the sorts of small villages that existed a few miles inland.

I planned to experience the place in the solitude and chill of a late December afternoon. In order to access Kule Loklo, its secluded approach lies beyond the bustling visitor's center parking lot, out into the depths of a heavily wooded, narrow trail, populated by a long line of (beautiful nuisance) non-native eucalyptus trees, swishing and swaying at best in the coastal breeze.

Wind indeed whipped through the creepy, creaking Tasmanian Blue Gum (the specific eucalyptus grove, planted with initial wanton abandon in a "get-rich-quick" scheme by misinformed 19th Century lumber industry investors). At one point, I ducked low in order to pass beneath a more modest by comparison, trunk of a fallen oak. Dropped acorn nuts crackled under foot. Strips of blue gum bark layered the isolated trail, blanket upon blanket, softening my solo serenade so that I might have easily surprised the people of Kule Loklo had they been waiting for me.

Included in my mission was the inevitable seasonal dodging of legions of poison oak, prolific, painful, more than an irritation to me, enormously reactive for others, within hours, if it comes into contact with the skin. My friend Houston, a local food-writer and lawyer, told me that his dad was one of the daring types I've heard of, who, like the native people of these parts, took a literal leaf from historical lore and often consumed a pinch of the dreaded leaves of three for immunity.

Several times a year this was the practice for the Coast Miwok — to pinch off a small part of poison oak, place it on the tongue, mince it into a pulp with the front teeth and duly swallow its potent mush. I'll take his and their word for it, but am not inclined to try it out myself!

Poison oak was used as poultices for healing wounds, its juice a sap to stop bleeding. I spend much of my time outdoors trying to avoid it. The notion of its native use in the wrapping of foods, stems for basketry and skewers, further astonishes. I remember to respect the dreaded leaves of three in their service to the ecosystem, protecting areas in need of renewed growth.

I pondered the mysteries of the forest floor as I walked that afternoon. Nearby ocean and marsh plant life nourished the Coast Miwok for generations. Each spring, streams of wild salmon ran by the thousands into their realm. They gathered clams and abalones. Not a part was wasted, once the white, meaty seafood was harvested, shells were used for ceremonial regalia and beads.

Several "kotcas" (Coast Miwok houses) stand sentry to the wind and fog. Extended families of usually five or six people lived in small, conical structures such as these, made from Tule grass or redwood bark. I wondered at the tight fit inside of these compact abodes, close quarters of multiple body warmth essential for conserving energy in the colder winter months. How calm and patient a people to cohabitate such a small space. Tule structures lasted a couple of years, redwood longer.

Frames of winter homes were built with peeled willow poles, tied together with willow bark. Bundles of tule mats were attached to the frame, with a hole in the center to allow for the safe passage of smoke. Sturdier homes were made of slabs of redwood bark on a Douglas fir frame.

I peeked inside for a better idea of willow and dried grasses interwoven through the poles, a roof of redwood bark or Douglas fir to keep precipitation out. Pine needles, dry grasses layered over with deerskin or rabbit blankets softened a dirt floor, the thicker the under-bedding, the greater the lap of relative luxury.

An acorn granary stored this staple of village winter fare, protecting the precious nut harvest from insect pests, deer (kacum) and elk (tante).

In her 2014 Native American food memoir *Enough for All* historian and storyteller Kathleen Rose Smith recounted the lay of the land of her Bodega Coast Miwok and Dry Creek Pomo people, who spoke of a time "not so long ago" when towering redwood trees (long before the eucalyptus) "stood like never ending sentinels" along the coastal range.

Kathleen wrote of her mother's reassurance that the family would never go hungry, with plentiful food all around. All they needed to know was when to gather food and how to prepare it.

There was not a single human soul, at least visible to the eye, other than me in the Coast Miwok model village at that hour, if at all on that chilly December day.

Although I knew the settlement to be a convincing recreation at best, my willing mind (sound tracked by a noisy pair of inquisitive ravens circling overhead), placed me in the primal heart of these ancient hunting grounds.

I half expected in turning a woodsy corner to cross paths with a startled Miwok woman, dressed in knee-length deerskins, tattooed slightly on the neck and breast, hair hung loose without a parting. What would she have made of me in my hiking shoes, jeans and sweater, backpack and camera in tow? She, on the other hand, would be better covered for the season — long, deerskin moccasin boots especially protective and warm. Given the chill of the afternoon and as evening approached, she'd be certain to have an extra layer of a rabbit-woven robe draped about her shoulders.

At that same time, a friend's young son was thrilled at his find of a perfectly preserved arrowhead on a family visit to Lake Tahoe, some 214 miles away. Whereas this wide-eyed little boy, in his small, round palm, held a piece of ancient history, a message from the past, I stumbled on little more than nature's own throwaways —seasonal reminders of a lost way of life.

Acorns serve as living charms of the spiritual ceremonies and healing rituals of the Coast Miwok. I took a look inside the deep dark, low-slung example of a sweat lodge, dug deep into a mound in the ground, though I didn't dare myself to crawl into its depth, alone.

Kathleen Smith has further lent her voice to informative signage for visitors to read at Kule Loklo. One sign attributed her people having lived on the coast for what she believed to be at least eight thousand years. They thrived amidst: "the spiritual and physical balance of the same small area for thousands of years without feeling the need to go somewhere else. This required restraint, respect, knowledge and assurance of one's place in the world."

Her ancestors had been adept at capturing and purifying water, pruning and digging to increase volume and health of plants for the benefit of humans and animals. Together they made sturdy stone mortars and pestles and built fires from the coals of slow burning hardwood manzanita or madrone.

Anthropologist/Archeologist Betty Goerke wrote compellingly of the Miwok in her account: *Chief Marin, Rebel and Legend.* She described the foundations of civilization. Their groupings: "provided physical, psychological and emotional sustenance, entertainment, education, safety and security.

Nightly story-telling around the fire imparted knowledge, inspired imagination, taught about the fire, taught about tribal connections and traditions, introduced expectations and ideals."

Milestones such as birth, coming of age, marriage and death were ritually celebrated. Children worked with parents and grandparents, hunting, gathering and on chores. These were a gentle, considerate people, who lavished attention on their young, did not believe in spanking their children, or, for that matter in the beating of anyone of any age. All members of the tribe cared for their elderly.

Not all was Utopia, all of the time. Tamallos and Ballanos tribes along the Marin shore spoke a different dialect from the Miwok and (allegedly, I've heard tell in local lore) were known, when tested to the limits of their patience to be pushed to the extreme of cutting off hands and feet or head of an enemy and displaying these various parts as trophies.

More peaceful medicine men were experts in their field of knowledge of thousands of medicinal herbs, trees, shrubs, flowers, ferns, grasses, nuts, fruits, forbs and vines. Hiking trails through the National Seashore today abound with the very profusion of these natural remedies.

How little most of us know or appreciate what we have at our fingertips. Herbs and plants were prepared by making infusions, tinctures, macerated (cold soaked) ointments, salves and poultices. Teas included Yerba Buena, a more narcotic version of mint tea and tea tree from the wetland evergreen bush.

I thought of the men who worked on foot drums, reed flutes, rattles and bone whistles during these same winter conditions. They hunted with bow and arrow and worked on their fishing boats and the double-ended paddles they constructed for deeper water.

Women focused on the creative (and practical) art of making essential tule grass baskets and mats with needles (awls) made from the leg bones of deer. Side by side, children and their mothers would be hard at work preparing animal skins for ceremonial clothing and winter capes. Dolls they made from dried twigs that had sat on the ground for a while. Twigs were snapped and twisted into shape.

They cooked acorn mush in waterproof baskets over heated rocks. Shellfish, fish, corms (stems) and bulbs were baked in underground ovens. Come springtime, abundant salmon came into play, wrapped in soap root leaves and cooked over hot coals or driftwood.

Though there is a resurgence of coastal foraging today, seaweed was and is considered widely nutritional, though not nearly as popular today in Western culture as it is in Asia — dried back in the Miwok days on big rocks abundant in the area and rolled for winter storage. The Miwok baked meat (though scarce in winter) underground or broiled over an open fire.

I stayed for some time in the center of the village, half hoping to conjure Coast Miwok spirits at rest, eating their warming acorn mush with two fingers (middle or index), sometimes watered down like a soup.

I contemplated their routine burnings of the landscape that encouraged new growth of native grasses, essential for the maintenance of healthy forage for elk and deer. September 2015's devastating 30-day Valley Fire in nearby Lake County burned 76,000 acres and thirteen hundred homes. Environmentalists lay part of the blame of these wild fires on the fact that ancient patterns of animal life and new growth have been thwarted in decades past by development in rural, wooded areas. It's a massive problem that won't go away.

We'd make good use of the Miwok's ancient prayer sticks today. Prayer sticks were of paramount importance for purification, rituals, rabbit hunts, feasts and blessings. These long, narrow, wooden sticks also known as spirit sticks or medicine sticks were made of brightly decorated (paint and feathers) cedar, willow or cottonwood.

"Everyday is our Christmas. Every meal is our Christmas" — spiritual interpreter "Looks for Buffalo" wrote of the (American) Indian culture in his book *Learning Journey on the Red Road.*

"At every meal we take a little portion of the food we are eating and offer it to the spirit world on behalf of the four legged and the winged and the two legged. We pray, not the way most Christians pray, but we thank the Grandfathers, the Spirit and the Guardian Angel."

Thanksgiving, Christmas, any time of year, whatever our culture, religious or non-religious proclivity, we would do well to heed the native American notion of hands held out to help the sick and needy, a notion of abundance, knowledge that we have everything that we need in fresh air, earth and water.

I did find it reassuring that same winter, to witness the coming together of communities around the San Francisco Bay Area in a rally of mass support in donations of goods and money to aid many thousands of people displaced by the devastating Valley fire.

The Miwok took not without asking, prayed over even the smallest gathering of herbs and asked each plant permission before taking even the tiniest of cutting. Every act was a spiritual one. This "intentional living" — is increasingly appealing as a way to live our modern lives and one that is much written about these days.

Though the Coast Miwok didn't own land in the way that we identify with, families passed down inheritances to key sources of food, such as hunting grounds, specific oak and buckeye trees.

I would have liked to wrap up my visit to Kule Loklo with this centuries-old image of calm and contentment and a wonderful Winter Solstice celebration, but the Coast Miwok story does not end here. It does not simply fade away.

Kotcas, Coast Miwok houses, standing sentry to the wind

Low slung example of a sweat lodge, dug deep into a mound in the ground

The Great Petaluma Mill today

Chapter 3

base camp —
Fog Valley's frontier town

It took considerable discipline for me to submit to the solitude of completing this manuscript. Every time I stepped out of the door I stumbled on yet another enthralling angle for rambling and research.

This is thirsty work for the body and soul. Whenever I felt myself heading into another tailspin, I'd turn back to the well.

The Petaluma Creek (changed in name only to River for dredging purposes, in 1959) was the conduit for economic prosperity for the settlers of Fog Valley. This winding, watery estuary retains a focal pulse in the region's identity, today.

One of my offline haunts for concentrated writing time away from my kitchen table or home office desk found me frequently seated at a wobbly bistro table overlooking the river, its turning basin and site of the former Golden Eagle Mill Company on the other side.

With a cup of tea, my notebook and pen for company, I found myself a quiet spot with a view and focused my attention on this pivotal, historic scene. The Apple Box Café's prime, waterfront location within the Great Petaluma Mill makes up for a motley collection of weather worn outdoor tables and chairs. A part of the Mill stands guard as one of the oldest structures in the city.

Home today to the café as well as neighboring (bustling) Wild Goat Bistro, several hair and beauty salons, Petaluma Chamber of Commerce, an independent publishing house and some state-of-the-art design and tech companies, the Mill, with its south-facing two-foot thick, insulating stonewall was built by one of the town's founding fathers, John A. McNear for grain, flour, hay and potato shipments to San Francisco, in 1864.

As I gazed out on the murky water of the tidal slough that gifted Petaluma its economic success, I pondered Maine transplant, John McNear's failed attempt to implement public bathing in the turning basin in the creek across the way. At that time, sewage was channeled into the waters with the general idea of tides conveniently carrying it away. Bathing beauties of the day surely vetoed plans for male and female bathing houses on the creek banks and swimming in the creek, not surprisingly, failed to take off.

Until the railroad arrived in 1870 (remarkably, the third in California) Petaluma's creek was the be all and end all as the sole avenue of commerce in and out of Sonoma and neighboring counties. The size and scope of the mill's location on the west bank reflects the bustling traffic the waterway experienced.

My main distraction in writing about the region's early days from this particular vantage point is an escalating alarm in the steady dilapidation of an historic 500 foot-long railroad trestle that continues to hang on for dear life about 20 feet from where I often sit.

This crumbling wooden structure, built in the spring of 1922 for trams to carry even more of the region's bounty and people to water transportation, has become a sorrowful sight indeed.

Its potential as an expanded 15,000 foot educational waterfront, walkway and park has been on the cards for years and yet little more than a chain-link fence to stop pedestrians falling in the river is all that has made its mark from a half-a-million dollar Coastal Conservancy grant to kick-start its renovation in recession era 2010.

The City of Petaluma struggled to find additional funding for the estimated $5 million project and plans are stalled. Grassroots efforts in the form of a "This Place Matters Campaign" and, hopefully, by the time this book is in print, a $5 million crowd-funding campaign might, I hope save this important trestle from collapse.

I couldn't take my eyes off this symbol of the region's past. Ugly duckling of the city's historic district, the trestle has the potential to be its crown jewel. If the trestle is saved and salvaged, its potential is to the region what the High Line urban parkway is to Manhattan.

In contrast to the trestle, the circa 1914 North Western Pacific Rail Depot, designed in classic Mission Revival Style, a couple of blocks to the east on Lakeville Highway, has been thankfully saved from obscurity. The Petaluma Arts Center makes a fine home in its renovated freight storage building — next door to the Visitors Center, housed in the former main depot.

Old photographs of downtown Petaluma depict a time of opportunity when anyone with any sort of inclination towards a life of farming held onto their hats and gravitated to the alluvial soil of Fog Valley.

Hunters and fur trappers were the first to arrive on the banks of the Petaluma Creek on the heels of rich Mexican rancheros who had first divided the land in Alta California (a then territory of independent Mexico) for a life fashioned on the Spanish Dons.

In his book *Historic Photos of Sonoma County*, historian Lee Torliatt summed things up nicely: "The climate was good and the people who came to this fertile area on the Pacific coast of America knew they had found a special place."

Half of the 300,000 people who flooded into the west, in a seven-year rush for gold from 1848 to 1855, came by ship. The other half traveled across the Great Plains by covered wagon. Meager fortunes and minefield misgivings were well spent by many on claims of stake on Fog Valley's appeal.

Homesteaders hit the ground running. A sign in Tomales Regional History Center serves as a poignant reminder of the bold culture of brilliance and ingenuity that prevails in the west: "Pioneers were mostly young and enterprising risk takers who are, in many ways, a part of our twenty-first-century lives."

According to the census of 1857, the creek town of Petaluma was one square mile in size. Its population consisted of 802 white males, 502 white females, 23 colored males, eight colored females and one Chinaman.

First arrivals were mostly in their 20s and 30s, single men, but some with wives and families — pioneering folk from the east, from Canada, from Europe. Most of the family-owned farms and ranches and many other businesses in Fog Valley have weathered the storms of time and survive into their fifth and sixth generation ownership today.

Tradition is well and good until it stifles creativity, ingenuity and freedom to fully express oneself. Early settlers were able to hold on to cultural ways while at the same time, letting go of many of the more stringent Old World traditions. They crafted purposeful, meaningful and joyful new traditions, particularly those centered around the winter season culture of their newfound home and American community.

Thanksgiving, winter solstice, Hanukkah, Christmas, New Year, Boxing Day and Chinese New Year played an important part in the shaping of the winter holiday landscape of the region.

The first unofficial Thanksgiving in Fog Valley likely fell on a random date as late as December, at the end of the year of 1848. Most who had found their way to the west had little or no concept of this holiday with its Puritan roots.

"Some of them ridiculed it and a few of the writers of the time objected to it as a piece of hypocrisy," reported the *San Francisco Call*. "But the pioneers were tolerant men as a rule and when the New Englanders determined to celebrate, they met with no obstacle."

Two years later, California would be named the 31st State in the Union. That year, 1850 —the state's first elected Governor, Peter H. Burnett issued a proclamation declaring Thanksgiving to be a legal holiday in California.

The west certainly was ahead of its time. It took until November 26th, 1863 — some 13 years later for U.S. President Abraham Lincoln to officially declare Thanksgiving a national holiday on the fourth Thursday of November.

First winter holidays in the region were in reality, working days for most on the farms and ranches. An hour or two of simple celebration — worship and a hot meal marked most religious observation.

"Christmas 1852," wrote a former Miss Weare of Independence, Missouri (widow of physician and state senator Noble Martin). "I was at Point Reyes, at the cabin of Dr. Crandell who owned land there. I was all alone that day, not a human being within 10 or 12 miles of me. It was raining."

As she stood within the cabin and looked out of the door across the ravine, a great mountain lion came about 300 feet away. "He looked toward the cabin and let out a frightful yell. I shut the door and put the crossbar in place."

Miss Weare, later Mrs. Martin's remembrance of an isolated Christmas in the wilds of west Marin County appeared in a *San Francisco Chronicle* report in 1900. Her memory of the murky, mysterious coastal wilderness in winter served her well. One of the six founders of the Association of Pioneer Women, she'd traveled by wagon train to Fog Valley from the mid-west with her family in 1849.

Petaluma is positioned some 30 feet above seawater. Its mild, Mediterranean climate was of big appeal as a frontier town to southern

European farm laborers looking for land of their own. For a short while, the settlement was bigger than that of Los Angeles at the time.

Hard to believe today, long before the opening of the Golden Gate Bridge (1938) and Richmond and San Rafael Bridges (1956), the twisting, turning, often troublesome Petaluma Creek was fast established as the main shipping depot not only for Sonoma County but for also for Napa and Mendocino counties, carrying more traffic than any waterway in California except for the Sacramento and San Joaquin Rivers.

A man named Garret W. Keller (also the city's first postmaster — it wasn't unusual for people to have two or three jobs) commissioned the first survey of the Petaluma area in 1852.

Garret's survey heralded rapid construction of lots, streets (named after prominent local citizens and their families) and a first hotel. Bridges, banks, schools, a cemetery, lumber and brickyards followed fast on the back of Petaluma's incorporation.

According to fellow Brit and former President of the Petaluma Museum Association, Susan Villa, it was an enterprising Garret who set up a wooden shanty by the creek where the Washington Street bridge now stands, complete with a set of wooden stairs from the waterway in order to entice newcomers through his small, dried goods store on first arrival in Petaluma.

It was the winter of 1851. Settlement of non-natives had begun earlier that year when two parties, Thomas Bayliss and David Flogdell and Lamarcus Wiatt and John Linus established creek services and a general store serving hunters.

"Garret was a squatter. He took a gamble on nobody upholding earlier Mexican land grants in the region," said Susan. "He knew that people being run out of San Francisco were making their way north and he made it his business to be the first person they met."

Such was Garret's influence, early consensus gave him the job of laying out plots in this new market town. "He employed a couple of men to help him go around with lengths of chain," said Susan. "In return for getting his hands dirty he was rewarded with as many plots of land as were allocated to others."

Petaluma's watershed drains almost 150 square miles with the city at its center and Sonoma Mountain at its peak. Seven streams that feed into the creek run through the city's residential neighborhoods today. Take a walk around McNear park neighborhoods and you'll cross several secluded bridges over fast flowing streams in winter months.

Historic downtown sits below water level, hence the need for sub pumps in the museum and in many neighboring homes and buildings. A branch of Wells Fargo Bank is positioned above what was an open watering hole used for quenching the thirst of horses pulling wagons and buggies into town.

Western slopes of the watershed drain into the river via several tributaries. One of these: the headwaters of Adobe Creek — served as the original water source for the fledgling city prior to the construction of a reservoir in 1910. Today, most of the region's water comes from the Russian River to the north.

Early residents relied on wells or cisterns fed by rainwater. Wooden pipes were run along roof eaves. In bigger, wealthier households, servants pumped water for laundry, pots, pans and tin baths, several times a day. Many homes in the historic neighborhoods of Petaluma (particularly in the vicinity of Petaluma High School) have wells on their properties that function to this day.

Spring Hill Road is a particularly scenic route to the west, when driving or cycling out of town. Several artesian wells exist in this area, hence its given name. An artesian well is fantastically, one that rises and falls with the phase of the moon, spurting cold, fresh water that flows underground from an aquifer trapped between layers of extremely porous rock and sandstone. This force of nature was a boon to early settlers.

Many of Fog Valley's earliest underground pipes are still in existence today. Modern requirements for sprinkler systems and water supply in the city of Petaluma's historic downtown district prevent expansion in the area — an antiquated affair that will have to be dealt with one day.

Little wonder beer has long since been in big demand in Fog Valley. According to J. P. Munro Fraser's 1880 *History of Sonoma County*, The Petaluma Brewery was the first recorded beer manufacturer in the area. It flourished amidst an atmosphere of: "pleasant gardens and shady arbors" on Main Street from 1855. This was two years before piped water would be introduced to city homes.

Given the popularity of craft breweries in the area today (with iconic Lagunitas Brewing Company leading the pack on a now international stage), it's interesting to note that the current wave of beer fever is nothing new. By 1880, the Petaluma Brewery's third owner, one George Roberson, was busy producing some 1,200 barrels a year.

Another well known Petaluma brewer, Frenchman George Griess and partner Charles Mitchell operated the Sonoma Brewery on Stanley and Upham Streets and, in 1866, The United States Brewery launched nearby, at Bodega Avenue and Upham.

Fog Valley, in my self-designed beat, extends west from the city of Petaluma through historic Two Rock and Chileno Valley to Bloomfield, Bodega and Bodega Bay. From there, the region runs south along the Pacific coast through Tomales and out to Dillon Beach, back onto Highway One, to Tomales Bay via the lost community of Hamlet, through Marshall to Point Reyes Station, Olema and out to the extreme west on the Point Reyes National Seashore peninsula.

For the purpose of this account, I pushed my exploration borders north to Fort Ross and east to the city of Sonoma to include the significance of Russian and Spanish missionary influence in the region.

On the road I kept note of my fellow travelers — turkey vultures, wild turkey, quail, red-tailed hawks, white tailed kites, kestrels, the wintering peregrine falcon, starlings, flocks of Hitchcock-worthy ravens and crows.

If you're not familiar with driving in Fog Valley and you find yourself inclined, prepare for dodging a rampant deer population. In fact, for thousands of years, duck, bear, geese, quail, elk, mule and black-tailed deer were the region's main food source. The slightly lesser-spotted jack rabbit was another popular game dish for growing families and a holiday menu mainstay, cooked whole, basted and turned on the hearth.

Wild turkeys (Meleagris gallopavo) were first introduced to California for hunting in the 1870s. According to the *San Francisco Call:* "The majority (of early settlers) didn't have turkey. Most would have been satisfied with a bit of fresh beef."

These are not the turkeys that roam our neighborhoods and ranches in Fog Valley today. It was the California Department of Fish and Game who we have to thank for that. The Texan subspecies Rio Grande (M. gallopavo intermedia) took to California like wildfire. An estimated quarter of a million turkeys roam the state today.

Shopping locally appeals to us today as do many of the old recipes of yesteryear. Vintage regional recipes for fish and game that I've chosen to include I consider every bit at home in the hands of a contemporary home cook.

Coastal pioneer Isaac Steele's words of wisdom describing life out west, sum up the sentiment of this untamed land of infinite opportunity: "There were no barriers to restrain our stock, save ocean, marsh and mountain crag, no roads except the old Spanish trail. But of wild, weird, beautiful grandeur, the appreciative soul could get his fill."

Dolcini Ranch, scenic Hicks Valley

Chapter 4

not so silent night —
a western country Christmas

One of my short forays out of town for Fog Valley Winter called for a leisurely 20-mile loop along Petaluma/Point Reyes Road through beautiful Hicks Valley and Chileno Valley and back to Petaluma. I drove out by picturesque one-room white clapboard Union School (1895) and just three miles on, the second of Marin County's historic, still-operational one-room schoolhouses, Lincoln District School, built in 1872.

In the early 1900s more than 120 of these lovely, little schoolhouses were dotted around the countryside in this rural ranching region. Swiss, Italian, Portuguese and Irish farming families were big and children walked to school across the fields. Roads into Petaluma and small towns in the region were developed with the advent of the motor car and today, only three one-room school houses remain in use in Marin County and three (in newer buildings) in neighboring Sonoma County.

Looping through Hicks Valley, up onto Wilson Hill Road and back down into scenic Chileno Valley Road, six miles, on, I passed a third small and charming country school, closed for winter break — Laguna School, built in 1906, and operational today with an only slightly expanded campus.

State of California requires six students each in average daily attendance to keep small schools such as these operational. Although there have been some close calls with closure or potential consolidation in recent years, school communities have so far rallied to attract just enough enthusiastic newcomers to keep kids at desks in the traditional American schoolhouse.

To visit or to live in Fog Valley and be deprived of "The Big View" on Wilson Hill Road is to have missed out on one of the most spectacularly unspoiled inland vistas in the region — especially in winter when the rolling hills are a velvety, emerald green unfolding as far as the eye can see.

Earlier that week, I'd stumbled upon some intriguing, old newspaper "society" reports chronicling early goings-on out in remote Hicks Valley during a Victorian era holiday season. Clearly those who settled in the countryside this far from town knew how to celebrate despite being stewards of the land for so many hours of the day and night.

Secluded Hicks Valley certainly enjoyed its moment of regional spotlight as the unsuspected center of print-worthy seasonal revelry. According to a report in an early January 1885 edition of *The Sausalito News*, hills had been covered with a rare blanketing of snow.

"There was a good supply of mud on hand yet to be dried up," clarified the unidentified, though on-the-spot correspondent of this odd little report. "The grass is growing finely and dairymen fell happily." In love, I wondered? Down a hill? In a state of festive inebriation?

Festivities may have run amuck! Readers were informed that a number of books were stolen from the library of Lincoln Schoolhouse. And yet, despite such criminal activity — as I'm sure the newspaper's entire North Bay readership was relieved to hear: "Everybody (managed to have) an enjoyable Christmas and New Years."

This intrepid correspondent had more to add, assuring all that turkey had been plentiful in the area over the holidays. Furthermore, a number of Hicks Valley luminaries attended a (presumably costumed) grand, masked ball in Petaluma. "Sophus, Washington and the Princess were there."

Without naming names: "A committee of one," the report concluded, "appointed to select a suitable site for the Florentine statue, got lost, broke his cart, lamed his horse and says it was all account of the moon being full."

The main change to the landscape in Hicks Valley and along this scenic loop today is the volume of road bikers that circuit this extraordinarily pretty, peaceful loop. Though it was curious to learn that an active road biking group was in fact, in existence in the Petaluma area in the late 1800s.

Hicks Valley then and now boasts a small population of no more than 100 residents of ranches and farmsteads. Nowadays, as in its early days, most everyone knows his or her neighbors on a first name basis. Many of the last names have graced the mailbox and gatepost for generations.

Our nameless correspondent of 1885 further illuminated his or her inside scoop on Hicks Valley seasonal shenanigans in an odd little footnote to the festive recap: "Bob says he is willing to challenge Benjamin P at a bread making match, miner's flap jackets or anything else."

This exciting challenge was to take place two weeks into the New Year at: "Bob's new oven in the north end of the valley." This was fun stuff to chew on while making my way through Hicks Valley. I wondered where was Bob's new oven?

I signaled, just in case a random road biker appeared around the corner and I pulled over for a closer look at a large old Victorian farmhouse, tucked into the hillside. I imagined myself at home there in relative rural splendor of the day. How was it to be so cut off from the community at large, with only a horse and wagon for transportation?

Old-timers speak of "an idealistic life — all about the fabric of family" and "visiting" as the sole leisure activity every high day or holiday. I've asked octogenarians and nonagenarians in the area about their fondest memories of growing up in Fog Valley and more often than not, favored recollections are of time spent at the table with elders, parents, siblings, immigrant ranch hands and neighboring families. Breaking bread in simple celebration shares the same sentiment whatever the cultural background.

What sort of welcome would I receive if I knocked at the door of the farmhouse, unannounced? Today, when someone shows up who we're not expecting, we tend, regrettably, towards wariness. Who might it be and what do they want?

During the holidays there is a slight exception to this rule. The American custom of hand delivering cookies and other holiday treats to friends and neighbors enjoys a robust seasonal revival between Thanksgiving and New Years.

Needless to say, I had walked out of my kitchen that morning without prerequisite home baked cookies in hand and so I refrained from making a surprise visit to a stranger's appealing home, empty armed. I moved on with my journey and made a note to self to be more prolific with impromptu visits, all year round.

A dog lounged on the porch of the farmhouse, barn cats wandered in and out of sight, ducks splashed in a small pond. I'd read about the children of these rural areas having been given lots of animals as pets in the Victorian era (not unlike today). Wild caught squirrels, rabbits, deer, reptiles and larger dogs were considered suitable companions for boys, while girls (generally assumed back then to be of a genteel nature), were gifted caged birds, cats and smaller dogs.

Cats were popular for their service as ratters. Rural homesteads, mostly differentiate still between their "inside" and "outside" cats.

Specially selected farm animals served double duty out on the ranches, first as pets, later for more practical means. Farm kids certainly were given far more scope in the learning of animal husbandry than their counterparts in Victorian town homes. Today, the terrific 4-H Youth Development Program flourishes throughout Fog Valley, home-from-home for hundreds of young people passionate about dairy, livestock, forestry, gardening, the rivers, coast and environment.

Thirst for knowledge of the outside world was great in the early days of settlement in the area. Newspapers and periodicals were held in the highest regard. *The Petaluma Weekly Journal* and *Sonoma County Advertiser* rolled off the presses for the first time in 1855. Publications from around the country carried the sorts of news, views and cultural reports that Fog Valley's fairly isolated community relied upon as a vital connection to the outside world.

Likewise, curious happenings and holiday galas in the region were important enough as social events to be chronicled as far away as the state capital.

Civilized society stuck together, swiftly establishing service organizations and civic groups, gathering places and social activities. Winter holidays were the highlight of the year.

Two years after the earlier report on the first grand, masked ball in Petaluma, *The Sacramento Daily Union* reported in 1878 that: "Christmas Day is (finally) being observed as a holiday (in Petaluma) by almost everyone. Those religiously disposed are holding a service in the churches of this city. The day will be appropriately (once again) terminated by a grand masquerade ball."

By January 1884, settlers had peopled Fog Valley's ranchlands for over two decades. An early January edition of the *Daily Alta California* reported on what was one of the first social holiday gatherings of scale. The occasion was a holiday ball at the Petaluma

Center for German Traditions (known as Turn Verein — gymnastics club). Aerobics and vaulting were all the rage at such centers in the Fatherland, but here in Fog Valley, the concept of seasonal merry making was ramped up an Americanized notch or two.

"A large Christmas tree, bearing 250 presents, was the feature of the occasion," according to the report. "The crowd gathered to dance the old year out and the New Year in."

Over at the American Hotel, genial host, proprietor J. H. Roberts took advantage of an apparent suspension in business to throw an invitation-only party of which the newspaper report dutifully noted: "The ladies, taking (early) advantage of Leap Year, were doing the calling and the gentlemen, forming one club, the receiving."

Let's assume those who joined in on the fun of a subsequent shooting match the following afternoon had rested sufficiently in-between!

For most hardworking souls who were devoted to 18-hour days on the land, keeping regular company extended to little more than a visit to church. Long before the telephone, radio and television, newspapers and periodicals served as trusted friend and informant, read by the fireside during scant hours of rest. Local and national politics and society affairs went hand-in-hand in a rapidly developing American west.

During the American Civil War (1861 to 1865) the influx of settlers who had dug their roots into the isolated oasis of the Wild West Frontier found themselves building barns such as those that I passed on my route through Chileno Valley, far from the battlefields and warring factions of the east.

Half a million Americans, including many literate Fog Valley newcomers avidly subscribed to *Harper's Weekly* throughout the Civil War years. News articles, illustrations, cartoons, novels and editorials traveled the length and breadth of the country, depicting the atrocities of war.

New Year 1870, several years after the Civil War ended, "Margaret" of Petaluma wrote the editor of *California Farmer and Journal of Useful Sciences* (the state's beloved farm magazine for more than a century). Margaret wished to send him the sort of Christmas greeting and a happy New Year to melt the heart of any dedicated newspaperman or woman in today's ultra-competitive multi-media world.

"As the old year draws to a close and you feel that your pages will soon open a new record, it must be pleasant to you to receive the congratulations of your friends and their hearty thanks, for all that you have contributed during the past year to their happiness, as well as instruction and merriment," this most loyal reader so generously enthused.

These were heady days indeed. Margaret went on to suggest the farmers of California should send new lists of subscribers from their neighborhoods: "With ready cash, to enable the improvement of the columns of the Farmer in every respect."

She wrote of the enjoyment the *Farmer's Weekly* visit had brought to her hearth stone, signing off with a fashionably Dickensian flourish: "May heaven bless and prosper your labors in the future and much more abundantly and may you enjoy a "Merry Christmas" and a "Happy New Year" all the many years to come."

The California Farmer and Journal of Useful Sciences was the first magazine to be founded on the west coast. It was directed at literate, middle-class readers and published from 1854 to 2013, at which point it merged with *Western Farm Press*.

Founding publisher, British-born nurseryman and merchant, Col. James LaFayette Warren, came to California from Massachusetts in 1849. The magazine's lengthy name was changed to *Pacific Rural Press* and again to *Southern Pacific Rural Press*. Later, at a circulation of a half a million, it returned to its roots as *The California Farmer.*

Alas, technology has infiltrated the contemporary holiday tableau to such an extent that winter's evenings spent together are now shared with a collective swath of hundreds if not thousands of social media "friends" within our phones. It's hard to imagine Margaret's satisfaction with a singular news source.

During dinner with girlfriends on a rainy winter's evening a few days before this outing, we'd talked about our childhood memories of playing board games and working on puzzles during enforced hours of indoor time. We all agreed that technology has all-but ruined the fun of family games. Our conversation made me curious about the candle and lantern lit fireside evenings of old Fog Valley before electricity.

Winter is the most tempting time to be glued to a screen. Let's take a tip from Fog Valley's old-fashioned entertainment roster and unplug for a few hours here and there. What did people do before television, internet and social media scrolling? They played blind man's bluff, Simon says, blind shadow tag, spinning tops and jackstraws.

Remember playing hide-and-go-seek, hand shadows, dominos, marbles, charades, balls and jacks, checkers, cat's cradle, tic-tac-toe, card games galore?

As I drove this quiet country road, I fondly remembered playing word memory games with my family on winter holiday nights, gathered around a roaring fire in my grandparents front room in England. I imagine the old farmhouse I'd stopped to ponder, was scene of many a candlelit parlor game over the past century and a half. Internet is patchy in places so perhaps our rural counterparts have preserved the art of conversation around the dinner table better than most.

It is all the more important these days that we capture the magic of the holidays for our children and our children's children, or they'll never know such simple joy and real connectivity.

Historic barn, west Petaluma

HUTCHINGS'

CALIFORNIA MAGAZINE.

VOL. I.   JANUARY, 1857.   NO. VII.

A CHRISTMAS CAROL FOR CALIFORNIA.

BY DR. DOT-IT-DOWN.

Hail, Christmas! Hail, of olden time!
Usher in Thee, ev'ning chime,
From ev'ry town, and ev'ry steeple,
From ev'ry country, creed and people.
Hail! thou bless'd day of the year;
Welcome, welcome all thy cheer.
Hail Christmas! time of mirth and glee,
Frolic, fun and jollity.

Chapter 5

*oh Christmas tree —
a Victorian holiday tableau*

Shortly after Christmas, I followed through on visiting a neighbor's Fog Valley home built in the 1860s that had, until that point in time, remained in the same family as its original owners. Much of the home's formal Victorian-era furnishings populated the parlor and dining room. A beautifully decorated Christmas tree took pride of place in the same spot as more than 150 predecessors from all of those Decembers past. Holly bushes lined the quintessentially English-style gravel driveway.

British writer and social critic Charles Dickens' depiction of: "The brightness of roaring fires in kitchens, parlors and all sorts of rooms" certainly was standard fare of the more affluent members of a Victorian Fog Valley town and country community.

Heritage homes are well preserved in Petaluma today. Holiday lighted parlor tours reveal the splendor of many of these lovely, old houses. Costumed docents do their best to evoke the spirit of Dickensian-like figures presiding over these lavishly decorated parlors — a Victorian holiday tableau to transport us back in time.

Hardscrabble settlers might not have had the means of their more enterprising neighbors of bankers and businessmen and increasing numbers of pioneering widows. Yet some sort of sentiment employed in the keeping of winter holiday festivities gradually infiltrated most households.

As with the grafted grapevine, smuggled in by Italian, French, Swiss, German and other immigrants (Buena Vista was the first winery established in Sonoma County, in 1857), the illuminated European Christmas tree took hold of the farthest corners of the Western World, not least in frontier land. Even the most humble of households managed an evergreen version of their own.

These first Fog Valley Christmas trees were foraged from native evergreen growth in the area. The first American Christmas tree market popped up in New York in 1851 with trees from the Catskills Mountains cut and brought in by the wagonload, though the concept of farming the profitable Christmas tree didn't fully take hold until 1901.

A crop of some 25,000 Norway spruce planted for commercial purpose in rural New Jersey set the pace for a multi-million dollar business in the States alone.

Today, almost thirty five million Christmas trees are sold across the country each year. Of those, 90 percent are farm grown. Several Christmas tree farms flourish in Fog Valley, today.

The multi-generational Mungle and Larsen family's reinvented Fog Valley chicken ranch, Little Hills Christmas Tree Farm, draws thousands of people from all over the San Francisco Bay Area, to Chapman Lane, off Western Avenue, in Petaluma today.

Fragrant fir trees are farmed on the rustic western edge of town, a picture-perfect location for families to cut down their evergreen of choice, sip on cocoa and pay a visit to Santa in the old barn.

Two of my sons have worked winter holiday jobs as lumberjacks at Little Hills Christmas Tree Farm. Sturdy work gloves, boots and waterproofs permeate the aroma of fresh fir at the end of each winter's workday. I'm happy for my sons to have experienced the exhilaration of working outside with other energetic young people, sharing the magic of Fog Valley in winter with families from outside of the area.

Though their hands were callused from a season of bracing labor, these tired and contented worker boys (and Fog Valley ambassadors) walked home in the dark evenings filled with the festive spirit of the region.

Penned in the east, period classic *The Night Before Christmas* as it came to be known conjures the simplicity of the season prior to electricity and modern conveniences. This was the penmanship of Clement Clark Moore (1779 — 1863), celebrated scribe and professor of oriental and Greek literature at the General Theological Seminary in New York.

Clement had written his one and only poem for his children — originally titled *A Visit From St. Nicholas* with the specific intention of reading to six of his (nine) beloved offspring at their home in Manhattan on Christmas Eve, 1822.

It took another 24 years (the Winter of 1846), for Charles Dickens' roaring fireside favorite — *A Christmas Carol* to further influence the English-speaking world and its idea of what a Victorian Christmas should be. This tome arrived in perfect timing for shaping the newly built parlors of Fog Valley.

Charles Dickens may have invented Christmas as we know it in the Western World — but Clement Clarke Moore's poem was every bit as poignant in the farthest flung corners of the American western frontier.

Evocative texts of *The Night Before Christmas* and *A Christmas Carol* depict a quintessential Fog Valley holiday season that varied in food and specific custom according to the culture of each household.

Thousands of miles from fashionable London parlors, founding families of Fog Valley, civilized citizens of New York and all who'd settled in between would wait until 1870 for American President Ulysses Grant to get around to declaring Christmas a legal holiday in the United States.

Puritanical Americans were not keen on keeping Christmas — its ancient roots established in ribald Roman as well as Pagan rites. By the mid 1800s, however, the wave of incoming European immigrants settling the country was united in its mostly common core of a Christian mid-winter celebration.

Another of its earliest popularizations as a holiday immortalized in literature and common lore in the two volume 1868 novel *Little Women* written over a three month period by trailblazing 35-year-old New England Transcendentalist Louisa May Alcott.

"Jo was the first to wake in the gray dawn of a Christmas morning. No stockings hung by the fireplace and for a moment, she felt as disappointed as she did long ago, when her little sock fell down because it was so full of goodies."

Louisa May not only introduced a distinctly American Christmas to U.S. literature of the day, she brought to life the first of the country's literary juvenile heroines. Jo March loved Christmas. Her character marked a turning point from the country's dour, puritanical past. Louisa May deftly channeled Jo to bring this message to the masses.

Missouri-born newspaperman and West Coast transplant, author Samuel Langhorne Clemens, better known by his pen name as Mark Twain visited and lectured in Petaluma in 1866.

This literary giant, a passionate cat lover whose feline, "Lazy" reportedly lounged "around his neck like a stole" penned a later-published Christmas morning letter of his own in 1875. The letter, from "The Palace of St. Nicholas, In The Moon," was address to his three-year-old daughter Susie.

This handwritten missive captures the Victorian-era spirit of kindness and compassion. Mark Twain had a fun-loving tendency to take on the familial role of a most benevolent Santa Claus.

Hailed as the country's "Lincoln of Literature," his missive from the moon demonstrates the message of philanthropy that ran through international Victorian literary works.

Samuel Clemens had traveled to the American West with his brother, later publishing *Roughing It* — a volume of notes and essays from their adventures, in 1876.

The writer had fallen in love with the state, tried his hand as a miner and coined his pen name whilst writing for the San Francisco-based weekly literary journal, *The Californian*.

"It was a splendid population," he wrote of California. "For all the slow, sleepy, sluggish-brained sloths stayed at home — you never find that sort of people among pioneers — you cannot build pioneers out of that sort of material. It was that population that gave California a name for getting up astounding enterprises and rushing them through with a magnificent dash and daring and a recklessness of cost or consequence, which she bears until this day — and when she projects a new surprise, the grave world smiles as usual and says, "Well that is California all over."

The idea of a winter celebration in which Santa played a leading role enthralled.

Immigrant children from the Netherlands had popularized the gift-giving legend of St. Nicholas, fourth-century bishop of the Turkish town Myra, throughout the New World colonies as "Sinterklaas."

"Father Christmas" to British American newcomers, Père Noël to the French, the religious figure of St. Nicholas duly morphed into Santa Claus as one and the same.

As early as 1809, author, historian and diplomat Washington Irving's *Knickerbocker's History of New York* featured a pipe-smoking old man flying his wagon over rooftops, delivering presents to good boys and girls.

It's not surprising that North America's fur-clad, non-denominational "Santa" would usurp the shaggy, scarier old gift-bringer of medieval Europe, taming the image of the fairy-tale character of old to suit a New World melting pot.

It was during the Civil War years when political cartoonist Thomas Nast visually stripped Santa of his ancient garb, bedecking his new, chubby, grandfatherly version in the familiar red and white fur-trimmed suit that we recognize so instantly today.

In flew Santa, complete with sleigh and reindeer, delivering gifts to soldiers in the *Harper's Weekly's* 1863 "Santa Claus in Camp." In this heady time of print, the cartoon went viral.

Children's books and women's magazines did their part in popularizing traditional holiday customs and menus of the era — evoking a Victorian parlor portrait of Christmas as a joyous, family celebration.

America's first popular women's magazine, *Godey's Lady's Book*, brimmed with paper decoration templates for trees from hilltops and woods. Popular cutouts featured a cavalcade of fairies, stars, hearts and cornucopias for thrifty decorators. Children helped decorate trees by stringing fruits, berries and popcorn. Nuts were gilded and silvered. Real candles clipped to fresh fir.

Winter months marked the leanest of times in the fledgling communities of town and country, the cuisine of which was influenced by season and place. Household and hotel menus are indicative of the sorts of wildfowl, seafood and other indigenous foods of the region. Poultry, eggs and other dairy were in no short supply. Coffee, beans, sugar, flour and rice featured amongst the few staples that were brought into Fog Valley from outside.

Practical and thrifty housekeepers bedecked Christmas dinner tables with an array of mirrors, ferns and evergreens. A sideboard or second table served to hold a range of garnishes.

According to *Buckeye Cookery and Practical Housekeeping* of 1880, a popular "American" Christmas dinner of the day consisted of an assortment of: "Clam soup, baked fish, Hollandaise sauce, roast turkey with oyster dressing and celery or oyster sauce, roast duck with onion sauce, broiled quail, cranberry sauce, chicken pie, plum and crab-apple jelly, sweet potatoes, baked squash, turnips, cabbage, carrots and corn."

Non-English speaking settlers from Europe and the Orient had their own delicious holiday repertoire, of which we will explore in more detail in subsequent chapters and in vintage regional recipes at the back of this book.

"And I do come home at Christmas. We all do, or we all should. We all come home, or ought to come home, for a short holiday — the longer the better... As to going a-visiting, where can we not go, if we will, where have we not been, when we would, starting our fancy from our Christmas tree!" — Christmas issue of *Household Words*, 1850.

Fort Ross today

Chapter 6

the Russians are coming

There is an old tradition in Russia, in which everyone at the holiday table has drunk enough and said enough when someone starts singing the sort of song that encourages everyone to join in — a rowdy cacophony of uncoordinated voices. I think of this when I'm out and about in Fog Valley's neighboring Russian River area or on the rare occasion I make it all the way up the coast to the lonesome spot on the Pacific edge that is Fort Ross, a Russian stronghold long before the rest of us arrived.

The Russians were a long way from home. Revelry, especially in wintertime, was undoubtedly a sanity saver.

It was the Russians, not the Spanish who were the first non-natives to settle the northern California coast for an extended period of time. First on the scene though had been Elizabethan explorer Sir Francis Drake and crew of his galleon, *The Golden Hind,* who'd made port 65 miles south of what would be the Russian settlement, for five weeks in the summer of 1579.

The Russian fortress, some 17.8 winding miles to the north of Bodega Bay warranted me an essential foray into Fog Valley's neighboring territory.

Intrepid Russians ushered in a period of massive change in California. Their settlements in Alaska had clung to life in the most brutal conditions, posing an enormous challenge to sustain.

The number one issue was maintaining settlement stocks of food and supplies in such a bitter climate for much of the year. A dwindling sea otter catch in Alaskan waters in the early 1800s launched a ripple effect in exploratory searches south on the Pacific coast.

It was the increasing presence of roaming Russian fur hunters in the North Pacific that first motivated Spain to occupy land north of Mexico, as far back as 1769. Neither the Russians nor the Spanish formally earmarked the north coast of California as permanent settlement territory prior to the more intense exploratory searches by the Russians in the early 1880s.

Trade relations were established in what was then known as Spanish Colonial Alta California, with Monterey as its capital and the San Francisco Bay its northern boundary.

The Spanish began to take considerably more notice of Russian movement in wide-open Alta California, keeping a close eye on whether these fledgling settlements were likely to encroach further inland and up and down the coast.

Russian nobleman and statesman Nikolay Rezanov masterminded his country's colonization of Alaska and, subsequently, California. And after initial ventures into Spanish California, Nikolay presented two ideas to his fellow countrymen — a plan to develop permanent trade relations and to establish a trading base in the region.

Moving south from Alaska on a ship named *Kodiak*, a longstanding employee of one of Niksolay's most trusted and ambitious merchant friends landed in Bodega Bay on January 8th, 1804.

Ivan Kuskov and his party of around 200 Alaskan natives and Russians explored the promising region for months before settling

Coastal route from Fort Ross south

on a site. It would take until 1811 for Ivan and his crew to start construction of a colony on what they'd deemed the most suitable site — a seasonal Kashaya Indian village known as "Meteni."

Heading north on Highway One, I set out to revisit this partially restored haven of historical significance with the book's conceptual editor, Fog Valley frequent cohort and road trip enthusiast, Elaine Silver. It did seem to us a sensible choice of location to construct a sturdy fort, given its peaceful plateau, a rare topographical site in a craggy coastal region. Almost 4,000 acres of flat land protected from the outside world — the Pacific Ocean acting as a moat on one side, rugged coastal mountain range the other.

There was no such thing as a direct and convenient coastal road this far up into coastal Sonoma County — not until the 1880s. Access at the time of the fort's construction was by Indian trail, boat or ship and later, by wagon-width horse trail cross-country.

Fort Ross is State Historic Landmark Number Five and, since its inception in 1909, one of the oldest parks in the California State Park system. A eucalyptus grove at the fort shares the earth and air with magnificent, wind-bent Monterey pine and cypress trees. Though considered "invaders" eucalyptus form a leading role in the landscape of Fog Valley and its neighboring north.

The forest at Fort Ross is a windswept haven to 47 native California bird species and favored not only by the occasional winter tourist and historian, but by spectacular wintering monarch butterfly congregations. It didn't take us long, as we made our way through the park to spot which lone eucalyptus tree is reportedly the largest of its species in the whole of California. A massive elephantine trunk and towering reach pose a natural lure for those with a penchant for nature's mighty arbors.

Elaine was recovering from a recent leg injury that she characteristically hadn't mentioned in our long drive up the coast. I noticed her hobbling slightly on the hike down to the fort from the roadside. "It's nothing to worry about," she said. "I wouldn't have missed this, but I'll have to sit down every once in a while."

We and several other bewildered visitors had followed hand written instructions penned on a posted sheet of paper pinned on the park's locked gate. "Feel free to explore the grounds," it said, though the fort and visitors center was, we read, otherwise inexplicably closed for a few days.

It wasn't a holiday and I had dutifully checked the park's website before heading out on our roughly 100-mile round trip, a lesson once again that coastal attractions are unpredictable and, whenever possible, wise to call ahead before making such a trek.

Salt spray and wind, thankfully wasn't a problem that particular day and after a grumble or two on the irony of an impenetrable fortress, I pottered, Elaine hobbled onwards along the meandering pathway through the forest toward the historic structure itself.

According to historic accounts, the original village was bought from the Indians for a mere: "three blankets, three pairs of breeches, two axes, three hoes and some beads."

Between 1812 and 1841, the industrious Russians built their first settlement — originally named Ross Colony (after its imperial Russia), then Ross Settlement and later Ross Fortress, for the purpose of commercial sea mammal hunting, farming and raising stock to supply their Alaskan settlements.

"The first to arrive were met by a small group of California natives, who looked on in astonishment in the cool of an overcast day in March 1812 as a large sailing ship anchored itself in a little cove beneath their bluff-top settlement. For the next few days the natives continued to watch as some 25 Russians and 80 Alaskans came ashore, set up a temporary camp and began building houses and a sturdy wooden stockade — the colony and fortification of Ross" — California State Parks Association's *History of Fort Ross.*

We stood a while in front of the sturdy, shuttered fort and pondered an unspoiled scene. Elaine was particularly struck by the ocean's peacefulness in comparison to the crashing surf of Bodega Bay to the south. The fort is an impressive, if not bewildering structure to come by when traveling the north coast. It's likely that not all that many people are well versed in the historical connection of early Russians in California.

By 1828, we discovered, the settlement housed 80 native Alaskans (Aleuts), 60 Russians and 80 Kashaya Indians. The fort itself was made of sturdy coastal redwood, fully armed and manned against any unforeseen invasion. Natives worked as day laborers and domestics, paid with food and clothing. Many Russians and Alaskans married Kashaya, Miwok and Southern Pomo women, all in the employ of The Russian American Company.

It is widely recorded that Russian settlers and their cooperative workers enjoyed a cordial relationship, yet study of Pomo and other tribal accounts paint a different picture in which villages were burned and plundered, kidnap and abuse was every bit as rife as in Spanish secularization.

The first windmill west of Mississippi was built at the fort in 1814, a second followed, in 1841. The windmills ground grain into flour for baking bread for this and Alaskan settlements and powered the stamping of tan bark for the hide tanning industry.

Ships and boats docked in and out of the coastal settlement on a frequent basis. The Farallon Islands, 30 foggy and windswept miles to the west of San Francisco served as primary fishing base for the settlement through 1830.

Sometimes referred to today as "The Galapagos Islands of Central California" and for centuries prior, as "Islands of the Dead" — Native Americans were unable to reach the chimney like mounds in their fragile tule reed boats, so rough are the waters. The Russians were the first to navigate safely in search of such a wealth of wildlife.

Those sent to the remote Farallon Islands processed bundles of seal and otter pelts, sea lion skin and sinew, bird meat, eggs and feathers. They lived for weeks in crude earthen huts on the island's rocky slopes, salting and drying sea lion meat and blubber for oil lamps and food.

The islands, first protected by President Theodore Roosevelt in 1909, were fully incorporated into the newly designated National Wildlife Refuge Program, in 1969. Today, only researchers from Point Reyes National Seashore are allowed to set foot on the islands.

Back at the fort, hunters and fishermen expertly tracked sea mammals and birds, salmon, perch and sea bass, they harvested shellfish, herded, logged and farmed. Artisans crafted furniture, barrels, plows, boats and ships.

The Russians brought with them Eastern Orthodox Christianity, a complex, layered religion steeped in philosophy, mysticism, and ideology. A chapel, built in dedication to St. Nicholas — his first representation on the North Coast, remains intact inside the fortress itself.

Most lived outside of the fort, only officials of the Russian American Company and their visitors lived inside. We looked for a village complex of houses and gardens northwest to the stockade walls, but it is long gone. In its place, we stopped to peruse remnants of last season's vegetable garden planted by visiting school groups.

What would it have been like to spend Christmas at the fort, I wondered? Christmas Eve traditionally marked the last meatless meal of the fasting period of advent for Russians —the Holy Supper, known as "Sochevnik." Surely this tradition would have been honored, despite the isolated geography of transplanted celebrants.

Sochevnik is derived from "Sochivo," also known as "Kutya" is an ancient food ritual that consists of boiled wheat, sweetened with honey. Imagine a 12-course, Christmas Eve supper served by custom after the first star was spotted in the night sky, in remembrance of the Star of Bethlehem.

I also like the idea of the Russian's upholding another old custom and spreading hay on floors and tables to represent the holy manger. This was also believed to insure good luck for crops for horse feed for the coming year.

Russians of the day covered their dining tables with white cloth, symbolic of the Baby Jesus' swaddling clothes. A tall, white candle, placed in the center of the table represented guiding light. "Pagach," a round loaf of Lenten bread was duly placed on the dining table alongside the symbolic candle.

Christmas Day at Fort Ross, might very well have featured the sorts of traditional Russian rowdy festivities of gun and rifle practice, followed by a feast of freshly slaughtered meat and a festive procession around the stockade exterior.

By 1820, the California coastal sea otter catch started to seriously decline. Coastal fog, gophers and poor farming techniques made for poor wheat harvests. The grass inevitably grew greener elsewhere. Between 1833 and 1841, the Russians moved inland to three ranches — the largest of which was east of Bodega Bay in the Upper Salmon Creek Valley of what would come to be named "The Russian River," scenic and splendid Fog Valley's next-door neighbor.

Stock raising of cattle the Russians had bought from the Spanish proved considerably more profitable than the growing of crops. Dense redwood forests surrounding the Russian settlement were ripe for the plundering with seemingly unlimited raw materials for timber, housing, barns, shipbuilding, barrels and beams. Commercial exchange was rife, despite an ineffective Spanish rule of no foreign-trade.

Today, according to the World Wildlife Organization, only four percent northern California's original virgin redwood forests remain. A visit to redwood territory never fails to inspire me both with awe and sadness at the speed in which the boom development of the mid-1800s decimated the vast majority of these sacred groves.

I think of the diversity of animals these forests once harbored. Long gone are the bears and wolves of old, yet Pacific salamanders, red-bellied newts and tailed frogs, bright yellow banana slugs and other invertebrates, millipedes and freshwater mussels survive under close protection.

Mexico and its rebel forces fought and won independence from Spain in August 1821, opening the floodgates for trade, a boon to the Russians who still had full control over the port at Bodega Bay. They had made an indelible imprint on the region. It was visiting Russian scientists who had been the first to record the state's cultural and natural history. Colonists introduced many Old World innovations to California, including all-wood housing, glass windows and stoves.

By 1839, however, the Russian American Company had completely abandoned its colony, site of northern California's first windmills and shipbuilding. Mexican government land grants that encouraged more new settlers into the region had been specifically designed to seriously impact Russian monopoly on the territory.

British traders were the first to turn down an offer from the Russians to buy Fort Ross (not its land, which was at that time owned by Mexico). The French also declined a stake. It was newly minted Mexican citizen, Captain Johann Augustus Sutter (formerly of the Swiss Guard) who ultimately saved the fort from ruin in 1841.

Swiss immigrant, Captain Sutter came to California with a trapping party and settled in Sacramento. Landing in the right place at precisely the right time, the savvy explorer's prime legacy of association came to be with the founding of Sutter's Mill, starting point of the Gold Rush.

Johann swiftly filed for papers as a Mexican citizen in order to qualify for a land grant. His strategy certainly paid off when he received title to thousands of acres of land in 1840.

One year after the enterprising newly minted Mexican citizen took control of the fort, 100 of the last remaining Russian colonists sailed their final Russian ship from Bodega Bay to New Archangel (now Sitka) in Alaska. After 30 years, the Russians were gone. They took with them the largest collection of nineteenth-century Pomo baskets in the world. These beautiful baskets reside in the Great Museum of Anthropology and Ethnography in St. Petersburg, Russia.

Today, Reef Campground provides a nearby base for overnight visitors to Fort Ross, providing secluded cove access to miles of coastal hikes, tide-pooling, picnicking, whale watching, fishing and diving. I'm surprised by the amount of people who enjoy coastal camping in the colder months, I'm not that hardy, but my sons are.

Yet even the best prepared aren't accommodated for camping here at this particular time of year —day use area and campground opens from April 1st to October 30th only. And even then, it's a take-your-chance sort of facility that operates on a first-come, first served basis.

Timber Cove Inn on the other hand clings to a cliff overlooking the Pacific Ocean a two-minute drive north of the fort. This landmark northern coastal inn with its warming fireplaces and spectacular views, framed with redwood and stone and designed in the style of architect Frank Lloyd Wright, in the late 1960s is open year round, despite dwindling traffic in winter.

Three decades is a mere blip in geological time and yet the Russian legacy lives on at Fort Ross albeit in splendid isolation, today.

Elaine's new pair of leather soled boots echoed in the stillness and solitude of the day as she hobbled along in the glorious, winter sunshine. We slowly made our way back to my car via concrete pathway and through the closed off parking lot by way of a secondary route. A canopied pathway cut through the eastern edge of spindly Monterey pine and cypress trees. "They're otherworldly," my companion declared. "This must have been heaven on earth for the Russians." Drought conditions had dried the bottom of creek bedding that was otherwise bursting its banks with bracken and greenery of five-finger ferns, sword and wood ferns.

If we'd waited for spring, we would most likely have been welcomed by a wonderland of northern California natives — sweetly named woodland forget-me-nots, Indian paintbrush, thimbleberry, western sweet coltsfoot, silk tassel bush, slim Soloman's seal (starry false lily of the valley).

Instead we contented to keep our eyes peeled for jewels of the sky, Kestrel Gull, Pelican, Great Egret, the agile and powerful raptor, Golden Eagle, Osprey, Red Tailed Hawk, a Great Blue Heron.

Much to her delight, the sharp-eyed, foot-weary native New Yorker spotted a Golden Eagle diving for its prey as we traversed a one-track, old Fort Ross Road, cross country, heading back to Fog Valley through a veritable tunnel of mighty redwoods and sweeping vistas. We took the Russian River route home, avoiding the alternative of a surprisingly busy coastal road.

Our day out along the coast in search of Russians remained dry and sunny, roads in this neck of the woods are often impassable during the season's heavy rainfall, but there was no apparent sign of precipitation as we ventured back into the wild.

We talked of "Black Bart" and other Gold Rush bandits who reputedly hid out in these parts after a notorious stagecoach hold-up. Stashed treasure, it is said, remains hidden in these hills. Lore has it that Wells Fargo & Company's eccentric nemesis, Black Bart never fired a single shot during his 28 robberies between 1875 to 1883.

A local cycling club aptly describes this majestic back road route as offering intrepid travelers "an embarrassment of riches" — Black Bart's haul not withstanding.

We'd lunched on fresh crab and focaccia sandwiches that morning in a stop off at the coastal hamlet of Jenner. Cafe Aquatica was teeming with coastal tourists and their dogs, keen to perch outdoors at packed picnic tables by the mouth of the Russian River as it feeds into the Pacific. Seals and wildlife teem with every bit as much enthusiasm at this stunning site.

It struck me, as we dropped back down, into the isolated hamlet of Cazadero (Spanish for hunting place — population around 300), northern terminus of the North Pacific Coast Railroad, that this unincorporated community, six miles from the main route through the Russian River, is the embodiment of the end of the line for so much of Fog Valley's storied past.

Its narrow gauge rail was laid in the 1870s primarily for the purpose of transporting Redwood logs to San Francisco. This long gone artery of commerce and industry provided a vital thread of connectivity through lonesome and isolated coastal backwoods, a lifeline for settlers who depended on its energy for getting their goods to market.

My sensible navigator came to the conclusion that what we both needed by then was a cup of tea. It was late afternoon and she suggested a little place called Raymond's Bakery, another remote outpost nestled amongst the Redwoods on Austin Creek, a short ways out of Cazadero, one of the wettest places in California.

Should you find yourself on the road in this neck of the woods in the wetter months, be prepared in the knowledge that Cazadero holds a regional record for rainfall levels. There's not all that much for the ardent winter visitor to explore in a rainstorm other than the refuge of its bakery, one general store, two old churches, side by side and a large, old redwood garage that restores classic old movie-quality

Jeeps. If you're driving a Jeep and you're having trouble, then you're in luck I suppose, but don't get stuck in a winter storm, or you might be there a while.

An award winning, far-flung bakery is a labor of love for its owner and his wife. They transformed an abandoned old restaurant and four tired, old cottages several years ago. For the wandering New Yorker and me, our teatime taking was, unfortunately not timed too well.

Lucky for us, baker Raymond was outside sweeping the porch of the bakery, dust particles illuminating in the fading late afternoon light in the Redwoods. The bakery, he said, was closed. "But let me bring you some treats."

Off he scurried, returning a minute later with a napkin carefully wrapped around one the day's remaining brownies and an organic almond tart. As a stranger in those parts, I was thoroughly won over by a hard working baker's gesture of genuine kindness and generosity.

According to an interesting article on the Russian River resort area in *Sunset Magazine's* August 2015 issue, the tiny resort town of Cazadero was first known as Ingrams.

The Bohemian (men's) Club, based, historically in San Francisco, provides the richest and most powerful American male a summer time escape. Bohemian Grove takes place the same time each year in a super-private 2,700-acre forest hideaway housed deep in the redwoods of the Russian River's Monte Rio.

Old guard founded the Bohemian Club's first grove in 1872. Exclusive members of the country's gentlemen elite infamously camped under the redwood canopy and stars of Muir Woods. By 1893, the three-weekend event made remote Monte Rio its permanent summer encampment. Some fifteen hundred invite-only members gather for seventeen days each July.

"For all the Redwoods and swaying pines and wild grassy smells, you couldn't say the appeal of the Russian River is that of a pristine, northern California wilderness," wrote Chris Colin in *Sunset Magazine.*

"The charm, rather, is that of a faded resort town. If you can dial into that frequency — if you love the ghosts of vanished railroads, the seedy whiff of dwindling grandeur — you're home."

Intrepid Spanish had not been far behind the Russians in infiltration of pristine northern California. Mission San Rafael de Archangel, built in 1817 and Mission San Francisco Solano — Sonoma in 1823 ushered in an entirely new era of how the Spanish thought life in the region should be.

A week or so after visiting Fort Ross I was out and about on assignment for an article on a food and wine pairing experience, this time in Healdsburg, a fifty minute drive inland along the Russian River from the coast and about the same distance from Petaluma, to the north.

Wild boar wasn't on the menu for the pairing, but its abundance in the hills of the more remote parts of the region was a main topic of conversation.

My husband Timo likes to cook a mean wild boar ragu (featured at the back of this book) around Christmastime, thanks to the hunting prowess of our middle son Luc's best buddy, Declan Villa, whose family, on his dad's side, has been hunting the region since his Italian immigrant great-grandparents settled in the North Bay in the early 1900s.

Timo calls for a one-pound shoulder or leg of wild boar, which he, in due time, slices into small chunks. The first time that Declan delivered this haul, I was home alone. The back of his truck held what appeared to my non-trained though imaginative eye, a human-size carcass, wrapped in a white covering.

Declan is well versed in educating me and my family by showing us the ropes of the more rustic arts of "northern California country living" and his instructions in handing over a portion of it, were direct and simple: "Hang this piece somewhere dry and cool for a couple of days."

If you mix in hunting circles, it will come as no surprise to hear that wild boar in central and coastal California outnumbers the combined population in most all other states. I, for one, had no idea.

I did my research and according to the California Department of Fish and Game: "Pigs (Sus scrofa) are not native to North America and were non-existent in California before the early 1700s. Spanish and Russian explorers and subsequent settlers introduced domestic swine to California and allowed them to forage freely, especially in the fall, to take advantage of fallen acorns."

This practice, not surprisingly, led to a large volume of pigs running "feral." Since then, an occasional domestic pig has escaped and joined the wild population in its wanderlust.

The wild boar invasion is not unlike that of the wild turkey and the non-native deer in Point Reyes, only on a broader scale than the deer problem. According to the Department of Fish and Game, it was a Monterey County landowner who introduced the European wild boar, a wild subspecies of Sus scrofa, into California in the 1920s. "European wild stock from this introduction bred with the established feral pig population, resulting in a wild boar/feral domestic pig hybrid."

California's drought might have lessened the present population of wild boar slightly, but more than 30,000 are typically taken during each winter hunting season.

Woodland, chaparral, riparian, marsh and open grassland are home to the wild boar, a species that prefers dense oak forest in its northern California surrounds. Experienced hunters are required to carry a license before embarking on an expedition to hunt down a ferocious, super-sized boar (adults males weigh over 200 pounds), so that counts me out for a first-hand account.

Some hunt with bow and arrow, others with rifles. Meat from younger boars is considered the most delectable.

Wild pigs must be gutted, skinned and cooled as soon as possible after being killed to prevent rapid spoilage. I wouldn't advise joining in on a wild boar hunt if you're the slightest bit squeamish and/or not in peak physical condition, yourself. This is serious stuff for the uninitiated.

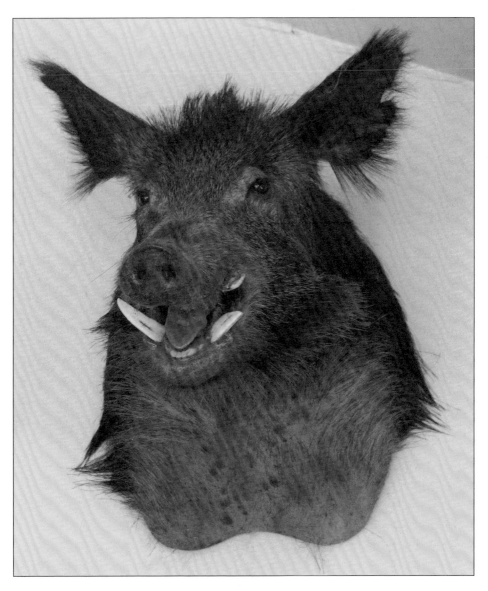

Sonoma County wild boar trophy

Bust of General Mariano Vallejo (1807 – 1890)
at the Old Adobe, Petaluma, CA

Chapter 7

the Mexican era

Declan's mother, Susan, suggested she and I pay a winter's morning
visit to Petaluma's odd-duck of a National Historic Landmark, located
along the venerable Sonoma County historical trail.

The stately Old Adobe sits in splendid isolation much of the time.
Drivers passing by on Adobe Road, a busy, rural connector route, pay
it scant attention, despite its visibility from the road. Locals rarely
speak of it, except, on occasion of an annual sheep shearing, a spring
time Living History Day and a fall Fandango that bring the place life
for a few days each year.

Tourists to the area seem to draw a bit of a blank when it comes
to this significant historic attraction. I wondered is there some karmic
influence from its origins as a glorified workhouse? Is this what
prevents The Old Adobe from being fully embraced as an historic
landmark? This important place certainly is deserving of considerably
more use, attention and restoration.

Susan had kindly arranged for me to meet with Sonoma County-based archeologist William Roop. The three of us arrived there bright and early, a little ahead of the park ranger who opened security gates to an otherwise deserted parking lot. Wind whistled its shrill winter welcome through trees along the Petaluma Creek. Bill described how this particular spot (now a parking lot) was once home to an extremely industrious Indian village.

Mexican General Mariano G. Vallejo had chosen prime land to the east of the Petaluma River for his ambitious Rancho Petaluma, a sprawling adobe (mud and straw brick) hacienda and original 44,000-acre ranchero. The fact that it had its own on-site labor force was as big a bonus for the 27-year-old commandant of the Presidio at San Francisco as was its on-site water supply, moderate climate and rich soil.

It was 1834 and a land grant by Governor Jose Figueroa had been devised to reward Mariano and encourage his leadership in deterring Russian encroachment by settling unclaimed lands north of San Francisco. Along with the generous land grant, Mariano Vallejo became "Military Commandant and Director for Colonization for the Northern Frontier."

When Mariano first saw Fog Valley in 1833 he waxed lyrical over its beauty: "I have made a visit to Paradise — the fairest land in all the world. Nothing in all California is comparable, everything is readymade for civilization — soil, climate, abundant water, a great harbor, opportunity for commerce with the world and for landscape, for variety, a land of pure enchantment."

Up to two thousand native people from villages along the Petaluma River as well as Pomo Indians from Sonoma were commandeered to labor at the Adobe, its harsh conditions profoundly less than enchanting for them as for Mariano.

Though the southwest section of the Adobe contained a family living area, local lore claims Mariano's Adobe (designed by his brother,

Salvador) as a more of an elaborate estate for his mistress as well as a cattle ranch and mass money-making factory enterprise.

The General resided for the most part, in full Victorian-Gothic-home domesticity and comfort with his wife and children, a few miles to the east, in the town of Sonoma. The location of his military headquarters had been moved there from San Francisco.

Wine Country visitors flock to the mission in the town of Sonoma (we'll visit the 21st and last of the Spanish missions founded in California from San Diego to Sonoma, in the next chapter). The General's Barracks and his family home are now equally popular on the tour. Comparatively, those who venture over to the ghostly and structurally imperiled Old Adobe are few and far between.

In 2007, journalist and author Beth Winegarner wrote a book that I stumbled upon by chance in the basement of Copperfield's Bookstore in Petaluma. Beth wrote in *Sacred Sonoma* that she'd detected a palpable air of unrest in and around the adobe during an overnight school trip that she'd participated in.

This hands-on-interpretive environmental living program for children in fourth grade has been offered to schools in the area since the 1970s.

A 1997 report in the *Sonoma County Independent* by journalist David Templeton eerily mirrored the pervading negative energy at the historic Adobe that Beth had written about. The newspaper went so far as to name the Petaluma Adobe as its most haunted site in Sonoma County. This claim was based on research by the writer who had consulted a respected medium in the region to accompany him on a visit to various spooky sites.

According to the journalist's "spirit" guide, the lonesome fields and hills around the Adobe teem with unhappy souls who choose to roam outdoors so as to avoid a return to the interior. My visit had been an early morning one and with no preconceived ideas, I too had sensed it to be rather a sad place.

I had initially been keen to hear what Christmas had been like in the Adobe. William, the archeologist we'd arranged to meet at the Adobe, wasted little time in bursting my bubble in telling me there had been no recorded findings of Christian ceremony, with no chapel on site. The ranger who had opened the gates for us was by now hard at work vacuuming rooms on the lonely upper floor of the building. She was reluctant to engage in conjecture, a little ticked off, perhaps, that we hadn't made provisions to be asking these sorts of questions, ahead of time.

"Anyone with any interest in Christian services would have traveled 14 miles from the Adobe to the mission in Sonoma," she said, hastening a return to a more pressing task of tackling the property's ever-present dust.

William reinforced the notion that there simply was: "Nothing warm and fuzzy about winter in the Adobe."

Conditions were intense for the Indians laboring in the hide and tallow trade that helped make Mariano Vallejo one of the richest and most powerful men in Alta California. A kitchen and manufacturing rooms contained a hive of activity in the processing of lard, dried meats, blankets, carpets, shoes, saddles and bridles — trades that had been learned at the mission. Horses, sheep and cattle were tended to outdoors, as well as crops of wheat, barley, corn, beans, peas, lentils and other vegetables.

Mexican and Miwok vaqueros (horse mounted livestock herders) rounded up Longhorn cattle that had been introduced by the Spanish. Longhorn hides were referred to as "California banknotes" and used as money in trade for other items and as tax to the Mexican government.

Hides were cured 25 at a time in salty ocean water. This part of the curing process cleaned and softened them in readiness for being transferred to large vats with extra salt added to the seawater. After 48-hours in the vats, hides were pickled or preserved and stretched out on the ground to dry in the sun.

Workers rendered (melted) animal fat (suet) in huge iron kettles heated over low fires within the Adobe. After it was cooked and before it solidified into the solid, white substance that is called tallow, they poured it into airtight bags made from hide.

The largest market for tallow, then, was South America, although candles were in big demand at the California missions, especially in winter. Hundreds of candles were made and used in the missions at the Adobe, each day. Tallow would also be commonly used as a fuel, a base for soaps and as a treatment for leather.

After harvest season, November was a particularly hard month of work at the Adobe as hides and tallow were prepared during the colder months in part for the handling of the strong smelling product's extreme heat requirements and also for winter trade.

As Christmas drew near, rancheros such as Mariano and his family relaxed their schedule, if not that of their workers, decking themselves out in their finest clothes to gather and feast with their nearest countrymen within the region. The general was renown for hosting elaborate hunting parties.

Meanwhile, merchant ships departing from California sailed, heavily laden, around the southern tip of South America to return to the eastern seaboard, selling tallow at various ports en-route.

Construction of the Adobe began in 1836, steadily developing for a decade, until the Mexican territory of California, overthrown by the United States of America, ended an era of prosperity for the general in 1846. The Adobe, initially designed as a quadrangle two-story building, was never fully completed.

All of the lumber used in its building was redwood and except for some that was processed by a Captain Stephen Smith's Bodega Bay early sawmill, mostly hand hewn. Walls were partly plastered and whitewashed. An original roof was thatched, though replaced by hand split shingles in the 1840s.

The general first leased his ranch to a group of French colonists, but, plagued with debt and legal issues, he sold the Adobe and 1,600 acres, to a man named William H. Whiteside, of Petaluma, for $25,000 in 1857. It subsequently sold again less than three years later and slipped into gradual ruin after suffering considerable earthquake damage.

According to reports by the State Parks Association, Mariano returned to visit the ranch as a 72-year-old man. It is written that he told one of his sons: "I compare that old relic with myself and the comparison is an exact one; ruins and dilapidation. What a difference between then and now. Then youth, strength and riches, now age, weakness and poverty."

The site was an early contender in its having been considered as a possible location for the University of California. Leaders of two early institutions, the private College of California, in Oakland and a new state land-grant institution, the Agricultural, Mining and Mechanical Arts College, decided to join the two schools in 1868. Ten faculty members and 40 students made up the new university when it opened. By 1873, it was 200-student-strong when it moved not to Petaluma but to a new campus in Berkeley.

Had the University of California settled on the Petaluma Adobe, Fog Valley would have taken on an entirely different identity from the still comparatively sleepy, small, Victorian river city and farming community of today.

The Sonoma/Petaluma State Historic Parks Association, founded in 1982, supports the Historic Parks in Sonoma and Petaluma. This organization, fortunately, is one that is committed to saving Petaluma Adobe State Historic Park. A comprehensive business plan to operate and maintain the park has been under development for some time and it is encouraging to note that creative fundraising efforts for the future are in the cards. I hope that this important landmark has the makings of a new, more positive future in store. While we can't sweep history under the rug there are many ways to honor those who struggled and wander its storied past.

There are two highly worthwhile stops for food lovers who do venture out to the Adobe. Angelo Ibleto is an institution in himself and his Meat Market, nearby on Adobe Road, does indeed stop passersby in their tracks. It might be something to do with the pungent aroma of a busy smokehouse — spices, brine, roasting smoke, or it might be Angelo's legendary personality, but most likely, a combination of both.

The Italian native set up his smokehouse and jerky factory three decades ago, producing hundreds of thousands of pounds of old-school sausages, smoked ham, hogs, bacon, salami and deli items enjoyed throughout the region over the years.

Angelo is in his eighties, but you'll find him behind the counter most days, more often than not in deep conversation with a regular crowd of Italian Americans and Fog Valley aficionados. A fire in the smokehouse in 2014 made Bay Area television news. Lucky for Angelo and for his legions of loyal customers, the smokehouse was repairable and no one was hurt.

Green String sustainable farm at the far end of Adobe Road traveling towards Sonoma is must-stop any time of year and especially for the holiday produce shopper. Not only does its shelving, indoor and out fill to overflow with farm fresh goodness, depending upon what's in season, inside under rustic eaves, you'll find all sorts of wonderful jams and sauces, cheese, breads, meats, nuts and olive oil to adorn the most discerning locavore's holiday table.

Mission San Francisco Solano bell, Sonoma, CA

Chapter 8

Mission San Francisco de Solano, Sonoma

A short thirty-minute drive on Stage Gulch Road (CA State Route 116) from the Adobe to Sonoma transported me to the heart of regional Spanish and Mexican culture. My chosen, most direct route cuts through scenic, vineyard-lined mountains over into Fog Valley's small, neighboring city of Sonoma.

This small and charming city of a little under 11,000 people has an international reputation as heritage hometown of wine country, built to General Mariano Vallejo's Mexican-Colonial era design of the early 1880s.

Food, wine, and western history lovers flock to visit its well-preserved nineteenth-century and adobe architecture, restaurants, shops, tasting rooms and places of cultural interest.

Locals such as myself enjoy having the city of Sonoma and its extensive selection of winery grounds and tasting rooms a mere half-hour visit away. Summer is splendid for picnics on the central plaza, outdoor dining at dozens of world class eateries in and around town, wandering through vineyards and gardens, but wintertime is best for tapping into the past, pottering around at leisure and avoiding the crowds.

Although I've visited Sonoma's Mission many times over the years, this visit was designed specifically for a wintertime perspective into the impact of Christianity on the region's indigenous people.

I found a spot to park downtown in a free lot behind the general's historic barracks. It was past my lunchtime. The morning had been overcast and threatening rain, but now the sun was out. I stopped in at one of my favorite haunts — the plaza's historic Swiss Hotel, to indulged myself in a small glass of sauvignon blanc (Benziger, North Coast, 2013 — not bad), and a plate of calamari with spicy marinara and lemon aioli.

The "Swiss" as it is referred to by the characters who take their lunch or dinner at the hotel, several times a week, was built as a family home between 1836 and 1840 by the general's brother, Don Salvador Vallejo.

It served as a stagecoach stop in the 1870s and was converted into a hotel in 1892, serving railroad employees and passengers. A dark and traditional, wood-paneled bar has remained the same through four generations of ownership. I stepped inside and perused its walls for a photographic recap of regional history.

There are all sorts of fancy restaurants around the central plaza in Sonoma. To say that visitors are spoiled for choice is an understatement. I returned to the Swiss Hotel not because its food is the best in town, but for its friendly service, its jovial buzz in the bar, dining room and outdoor patios and most of all, a taste of Sonoma's rich heritage.

Sunshine in winter is a wonderful tonic. I took a seat at a small bistro table with a cheery red-and-white checkered tablecloth out front, overlooking the subtly decorated plaza. Several other solo diners were seated on tables nearby, everyone amicably soaking in the sun and enjoying people watching in peace and quiet — except for one woman who talked non-stop and in detail to her lunch date about recent acquisitions for her personal wine cellar. I couldn't make my mind up why her banter was so distracting, the fact that she talked at a broadcast volume or my concern that her elderly date was about to snooze off at the tail end of their shared bottle, in sheer boredom.

There are wine snobs and then there are wannabe wine snobs. This woman, I feared, fell into the second category. It's a price you pay in wine country. Most who know their stuff tend not to flaunt it unnecessarily in public. I tried my best not to catch her eye to fuel her performance, enjoyed my calamari and my wine, paid up and made a swift departure in the opposite direction.

If the Old Adobe in Petaluma was devoid of winter celebration, neighboring Sonoma Mission rang in the Christmas season, as it does on a special Christmas at the Mission day in December each year, in devout Catholic tradition.

Mission San Francisco de Solano – Sonoma, operated in a short life span of just 11 years. In his annual report for 1832, the end of the mission's most successful year, Father Fortuny recorded 127 baptisms, 34 marriages and 70 deaths.

The self-supporting 21st and final mission and its land was in Father Fortuny's words, in possession of some 996 "neophytes" (unbaptized Indians considered novices in the Catholic faith), 6,000 sheep and goats, 900 horses, 13 mules, 50 pigs and 3,500 head of cattle, 800 Spanish bushels of wheat, 1,025 bushels of barley, plus beans, garbanzos, peas and corn.

Twenty-one missions were built a day's ride apart on the "Camino Real" (King's Highway), a major artery in California's highway system from San Diego to Sonoma, today.

It was the intention of the Spanish that once all the natives had been converted to Catholicism and taught European farming methods, each of these missions would become independently operated parish churches after 10 years. This plan was never realized.

The missions were, in actual fact, built on the backs of each region's first people, many of whom were baptized only to run around the back of its main building and have their Catholic rites reversed by waiting medicine men and women.

If you visit the mission and historic barracks in Sonoma, tread reverently as you cross the road on First Street East by its adobe church. It is said that hundreds of haunted spirits float about town — they are the ghosts of the native people wiped out by brutality and disease and buried under the street by the mission and barracks they helped build.

A series of three plaques by the outside wall of the chapel and erected by the State Parks Association in 1999, at least bears testament to loss with an imprint of the (Spanish given) names of those who died. I paused to pay my respects and read through the Christian names of so many Coast Miwok Patwin, Wappo and Pomo tribal men, women and children who died there.

I paid a bargain $3 admission and wandered the mission's interior and courtyard. Main buildings built around a large, square enclosure and 27 rooms in the priest's quarters were in a state of disrepair by the time the 1906 San Francisco earthquake wiped them out. Reconstruction work began in 1915, so what we see today is not actually the original, built with blood, sweat, tears, adobe bricks made of mud and hay, plaster made from the lime of seashells, tiles of clay and boards of redwood.

Orchards, gardens, vineyards, grain fields, a gristmill and housing for soldiers and Indian families were located outside of the quadrangle. Beyond the main structure sat a jail, infirmary and cemetery.

Pomo/Miwok lawyer and Executive Director of the California Indian Museum and Cultural Center in Sonoma County, Nicole Lim, gave a talk I'd attended at the Petaluma Historical Library and Museum prior to my revisit to the mission. I had this in mind as I stood in silence, alone in the beautiful mission chapel.

Nicole had talked passionately and in-depth of the importance of rewriting a woefully inaccurate history of her people in the region over the past century and a half.

She'd described the Bay Area as home to the largest native population center north of Mexico prior to enslavement for the provision of labor and goods for Spanish Presidios, that were constructed to protect from a hostile native or pirate invasion, neither of which were much of a threat in 1776.

New Spain had fortified The Royal Fortress of St. Francis, now a part of the Golden Gate National Recreation Area located at the northern tip of the San Francisco Peninsula (a former U.S. military base) in its foothold on Alta California.

It was the beginning of the end for the peaceful indigenous people of northern California, who, according to Nicole, had an average lifespan in the mission era that followed, of a mere 10 years. "Diseases ran rabid — syphilis, smallpox, measles, diphtheria, influenza. They lost their teeth and they were chronically underfed."

If they, or their parents attempted escape, they were flogged, starved, physically and mentally abused.

Almost all children under the age of 10 died during the California Mission era of 1769 to 1833. This brutal reality is barely mentioned in the teaching of California history — an immense, unspeakable tragedy that is continually swept under the proverbial rugs of time.

The years in-between the Mexican/American War (1846 to 1848) and the Gold Rush, were, in Nicole's words "the most violent." In fact: "Most of the Indians who were left, didn't make it past this point."

Mexican government secularized Fog Valley's Mission San Rafael de Arcángel and Mission San Francisco Solano (Sonoma) in 1834.

Everything of value was stripped out of all of the missions built along the California trail. Spanish landholders depended on surviving Indians for labor. "What we don't read about," said Nicole "are the Indians who worked the gold mines. They were considered completely disposable. One hundred at a time were sent into a mine. With no food and no water, two or three would survive."

In 1851, land treaties were negotiated between the U.S. government, the Coast Miwok and native tribal people across the country. Most were never ratified and were put under an injunction of secrecy for twenty years. The majority of these land treaties represented territory considered far too immensely valuable to hand over. Sutter's Mill, site of California's first, epic gold strike, a prime example.

Adding insult to injury, huge environmental issues followed the Gold Rush, mercury polluted rivers, streams, watersheds and flood plains. Grasslands were decimated, wildlife, forests and natural habitats forever changed.

The University of California Berkeley and Los Angeles as well as San Francisco State University's Native American Studies departments brought about a first public consciousness to conditions on surviving tribal reservations in the late 1960s and early 70s.

Though the general public still turned a blind-eye to the atrocities of the past, policy changes began, finally to figure-in some degree of support for the economy, education, self-sufficiency and culture of Indians.

Casino gaming has become a controversial factor in the subject of Indian sovereignty. Ironically, people flock from outside of the area to Fog Valley's Graton Rancheria Casino and during the holidays in particular. Nicole recognizes the issues of tribal communities depending upon gaming monies. She spoke of the need for tribes to diversify and to place more emphasis on educating their young people.

"There is a renaissance in California Indian culture," she said. "It is time for tenacity after generations having been driven underground."

I thought of my lone experience at Kule Loklo. It is time to fully acknowledge and pay our respects to what happened to the Coast Miwok and all Native Americans and to encourage and support a return to the land.

. . .

I paused in the chapel for a deeper sense of what had happened there in the past. Franciscan priests at the mission had been keen to teach Coast Miwok and neighboring tribal "converts" how to play the flute, violin, bass viol, trumpet and metal triangle and to sing a plain chant or Gregorian Christ's Mass in Latin.

Spanish in the region celebrated Christmas by singing "Villancicos," carols dating back to the Renaissance and Baroque periods and it was important to them to have everyone on board with their customs and traditions.

Traditionally, Villancicos were sung in most religious ceremonies, though would gradually come to be most associated with Christmas.

Mariano Vallejo built the mission chapel in the military style in 1840 after an original church structure had burned down. Restored along with the rest of the mission buildings in the early 1900s, I was glad for its typical California mission decorative style with appropriate Native American nature and religion-themed frescoes very much at the forefront. A blue strip running through the design with a central gold thread to represents the river of life.

Back in the Spanish and Mexican days, rehearsals for dramatic enactments of the church play known as Los Pastores, La Pastorela and El Diablo en la Pastorela took place each night during advent until Christmas Eve. The play derived from fifteenth-century Spanish mystery plays. It was performed as dusk fell on December 24th — "La Noche Buena."

I pictured candles and bonfires being lit. Attendants rang the mission bells calling all to "La Misa Del Gallo" (the mass of the rooster) in which an image of baby Jesus was held for attendants to kiss. Guitars twanged, it's said and worshippers cleared room for six costumed women, three men and a boy to walk in, holding festive banners.

Women represented shepherdesses and the men: Lucifer the devil, Ermitano the clownish hermit and Bartolo, a lazy vagabond. The Angel Gabriel was portrayed as per custom by a young boy.

After the play ended and the devil defeated in his efforts to detour shepherdesses on their journey to the manger, a bustling crowd would greet one another at the mission door with protestations of "Feliz Noche Buena" (Happy Christmas Eve).

Joyful and atmospheric (at least to the Spanish), Los Pastores continued over the Christmas period. Presentations were not only in the missions — they took place in regional chapels, patios, plazas, anywhere with an audience and potential impact in the Christian conversion of the Coast Miwok and neighboring tribes.

Next door to the barracks, the 1851 wood framed Toscano Hotel sits as a time-warp in itself, half a block along from the mission. This historic building exemplifies the flavor of early Fog Valley, after the Mexican era.

Though the site was first used as a warehouse for the general's wine and later, built out as a store and lending library, its long tenure as a Wild West lodging house is captured as a moment in time.

I stopped by for a fresh look at the former Eureka Hotel (serving Gold Rush traffic) that Settimo Cuicci an Italian (Tuscan) immigrant and his partner, L. Quartaroli rented and renamed as a working man's hotel, in 1886.

Residents of the Toscano Hotel were Italian immigrants hired to quarry basalt from the hills behind the hotel. Basalt blocks paved the streets of San Francisco and are admired today on many fine old buildings in and around Sonoma. In 1902, Settimo added on a kitchen and dining room annex and raised what had been a one-story building to provide additional rooms.

It is a dark and shadowy place, complete with authentic wallpaper, bar furnishings, saloon tables set with Victorian era china, a pianoforte, even a game of cards in progress.

The hotel closed in 1955. Fortunately, The Sonoma League for Historic Preservation restored it to its days as the Toscano. It is open for free docent led tours on Saturday, Sunday and Monday afternoons from 1 pm to 4 pm.

Seven days a week a State Parks ranger unlocks the front door to the hotel and every passerby is able to take a good look at the ground floor saloon through cast iron metal bars. Sound effects from the once bustling bar startle those not expecting to hear an echo of the past. I was alone as I peeked through the bars, that day. I quickly looked away from a large, bronze mirror above the bar. In my mind's eye, if I looked a moment longer, I thought I might catch a glimpse of an early twentieth-century face looking back at me. If I'd dared to stay that dark and stormy night past midnight, I'd not have been at all surprised to have heard whispers in Italian along the hallways, a footfall on creaky wooden floorboards.

Mission San Francisco de Solano, Sonoma

Point Reyes lighthouse

Chapter 9

to the lighthouse

Artist Nicky Ovitt's beautiful cover illustration captures the essence of coastal Fog Valley. Flip to the back cover and look for the lighthouse, tucked behind a hill. This seafarer's beacon — historical landmark in itself is one of the most compelling icons of the most remote outpost of the northern California coastline.

A PBS report on legendary U.S. lighthouses considered Point Reyes: "Not exactly in a desirable location. It is located in the foggiest point in the Pacific Ocean and possibly all of America."

Point Reyes (Punta De Los Reyes) is in fact, the nation's windiest headland, a narrow finger of land curving seaward for 10 long miles. It is a place that is cloaked with fog for three quarters of the year — a recorded average of no less than 2,700 murky hours in an average 12-month period.

Prior to 1865 the only access to Point Reyes was by sea or by horseback over private and narrow craggy wagon cart roads from the small inland hamlet of Olema. In winter and especially during the rainy season, it was all but impossible to make a safe journey all the way out to the peninsula.

I'd bid my goodbyes to Kule Loklo in Bear Valley mid-afternoon on the day that I'd planned to reach the lighthouse by dusk. Still operational, nineteenth-century dairy farming culture is all that has altered the ancient landscape of an 18.7-mile journey from Bear Valley Road, to the lighthouse, heading west on Sir Francis Drake Boulevard.

The Marin Journal, as far back as 1902, reported on the sorry state of what had, at the time, been a vital stage line. "The Olema stage was an old-time mud wagon swung on thoroughbraces — thick leather straps hanging over irons extending upwards from the axeltrees. The wagon was covered in canvas and seated 12 passengers besides the driver. A platform on the rear end attached by chains and covered by leather was the depository for trunks and freight. In the wintertime, when roads were bad, six horses were often needed." Railroad reached the area in 1875.

That wintry afternoon, I passed no more than a couple of cars traveling in both directions.

Fog aside, the wind currents on the peninsula that deter visitors on a blustery day have confused sailors for centuries. The Pacific Ocean was long since deemed too deep for mariners to utilize lead lines to determine depth or positions.

It was here, for five weeks in the summer of 1579, that Elizabethan naval commander, explorer and privateer Sir Francis Drake succeeded in navigating his ship *The Golden Hind* into safe harbor, claiming Nova Albion for England. Historical records tell us even this bold and enterprising man who circumnavigated the world considered a supremely foggy reception to be austere. It came as a pleasant surprise to find inland conditions so much more hospitable.

Sir Francis was fortunate. The first historic maritime disaster in California took place close to his storied landing place (known today as Drake's Beach), some 16 years later.

Mighty Spanish Manila galleon, *San Agustín* wrecked and sank along this rocky, hostile shore in the year of 1595. Miraculously, 70 crewmembers made it through treacherous waters and safely onto shore. It was a prime example of the great treasure ships of the world, one of an extensive fleet of prolific Spanish cargo ships to set sail from Manila to Mexico over a 200-year history of robust trade.

Silver from Mexico and Peru was, at the time, in big demand in China and, in return, cargo loads of Oriental silk and spice and other luxury goods for an affluent European market.

The wreck itself has yet to be excavated, though architects have traced a multitude of objects from the *San Agustín*, washed up onto shore to land into the hands of the Coast Miwok.

To this day, the ghostly Spanish ship lies deep beneath the waters deemed Drake's Bay Historic and Archeological District. It was designated a National Historic Landmark by the U.S. Department of Interior in 2012.

Cattle were first introduced to the peninsula during the Mission and Mexican ranchero eras. According to the California Milk Advisory Board: "This initial herd of 200 longhorn Spanish range cattle grew to nearly 74,000 by the year 1800."

Most of the cattle belonged to the missions, raised for beef, leather and tallow. "Additionally, the laws of 1795 awarded each soldier two milk cows."

Missionaries, who taught the native people the word of their Christian God, also taught them to make the region's first dairy product, "Queso Del País," a soft, creamy cheese made with surplus fresh milk.

The cool, moist climate was ideal for fledgling dairy farming. Grass stayed greener, for longer on the peninsula.

According to the National Park Service: "Record yields of butter and cheese emerged from the dairy farms at Point Reyes throughout the late nineteenth-century. Herds of Devons, Jerseys, Guernseys and later on, Holstein cows, numbering from 100 to 250 per ranch, catapulted the Point Reyes enterprise as one of the largest operations in the early years of the state."

As I drove, I conjured the park service's vision of this windswept, fog-enshrouded landscape before cattle. "Imagine the Coast Miwok co-existing with tule elk, grizzly bear mountain lion, whales, dolphins, countless birds and their innumerable prey species. Then imagine the beginnings of these formerly remote ranches as you drive by en-route to the lighthouse."

Though Spanish cattle populated the peninsula through late 1850s, early land sales sold for a bargain price of a few dollars an acre. Immigrants following their respective ranching cultures eyed a region where cooler days made for happy cows. Ideal territory for dairy farming became the main supply source for butter and other dairy products.

During a five year period ending in 1857, the San Francisco law firm of Shafter, Shafter, Park and Heydenfeldt obtained title to more than 50,000 acres of land at Point Reyes, encompassing the coastal plain and most of Inverness Ridge.

Unlike the small dairy operations that had initially taken hold in the area, a group of enterprising lawyers from San Francisco seized an opportunity to market large amounts of butter and cheese to the city's thronging mass. By 1880 dairy produce was duly branded under a distinctive and superior Point Reyes star-shaped stamp.

Look for this star-shaped stamp on packs of creamy organic butter from Straus Family Creamery, if you're shopping in the region today. The previously sleepy, isolated outpost was, by then, in perfect tune with escalating demand for fast-paced delivery of dairy products to the foot of Market Street, some 30 indirect and difficult miles away in San Francisco.

Depending on fog and wind conditions, it would take anything between seven or eight hours to three days for a schooner to navigate the choppy waters from Tomales and Point Reyes, around the perilous coast and into San Francisco Bay.

"The pioneer dairymen of Point Reyes proved to be the foundation of California's dairy industry," wrote west Marin author and historian Dewey Livingston in a 1993 Historic Resource Study.

One such pioneer family was Clara and Rensselaer Steele and cousins, Isaac, Edgar and George, who traveled from Ohio to farm the area. Clara hired a Coast Miwok man to rope some of the wild Spanish cattle that grazed around her rustic new home, in 1857.

She milked the cows that she'd corralled and, using a recipe from her English grandmother, made the region's first Cheddar cheese. This was a big hit in San Francisco, prompting the Steeles to start a commercial dairy making high quality butter and cheese. Looking to expand, the Steeles explored more of the Point Reyes area, surveying it with their business partner, a man named Colonel Lewis, who declared it the "cow heaven" that it is to this day.

The family's 6,000-acre dairy farm prospered in the rolling grasslands and moderate climate, kept cool by near constant fog. Within four years of launching their business, the Steeles managed 600 cows without a single mechanical milking machine.

They hand produced some 640 pounds of cheese and 75 pounds of butter each day. Prior to the introduction of steam separators, fresh cream was separated from buttermilk by being allowed to rise naturally in shallow placed on the creamery shelf. A horse on a treadmill powered the industrial butter churn.

In return for cheese and butter, cash account records reveal all sorts of comforts of city life brought back by returning steamers, holiday treats such as smoked salmon, sarsaparilla, brandy, clothing, a Steinway piano, as well as life (and death) necessities such as coffin trimmings.

The San Francisco partners who had taken ownership of a large portion of the land had done so as the result of a lawsuit. They soon signed new leases with established dairy farming families.

It was in 1866, when the partner's land (with the exception of Tomales Point, sold to an old pal from their native Vermont named

Solomon Pierce) would be divided into the tenant dairy enterprise of 33 ranches that distinguishes the properties today.

Three years later, dairies were further partitioned into six tracts, a collection of coastal plain and ridgeline ranches. Letters of the alphabet were used to name individual ranches with "A" ranch closest to the headlands. Several letters were left unused.

I found it intriguing to pass by these well-preserved alphabetical ranch parcels, most still intact, frozen it seemed, in time except for a modern truck or two.

After a good, solitary 20 minutes or so, I pulled over to catch a glimpse, in my mind's eye, of Pierce Ranch Road schoolteacher Helen Smith, walking into one of the ranch creameries to scoop a small cup of cream from the cooling pans to pour over her breakfast pancakes.

Helen's tenure was around 1916. What a brave soul to take on the elements in the call of her vocation to educate the few farm kids out on the peninsula. It had been Portuguese farmer Joseph Vera Mendoza who had financed the schoolhouse that would be of great a benefit to his immigrant wife Zena, as to their offspring.

Zena, who turned out to be a formidable pioneer ranch owner in the area herself, had learned to read and write in English alongside her children.

Fourteen gates separated Inverness and the peninsula point in the area's early farming days. Though wandering around Fog Valley on self-assigned explorations such as this was long and lonesome work, I fathomed the hardships of transportation in an age before many of the public roads in the region, must have been relentless by comparison.

I had my car, working windscreen wipers and the vehicle's reasonably good (if noisy) heating system. If I'd been around prior to the 1937 completion of the Golden Gate Bridge across the San Francisco Bay, I'd have had my work cut out to visit the peninsula Point Reyes at all.

It takes at the very least an hour to drive out to Peninsula Point from the city limits of Petaluma. During my meandering around here on my rainy day research trips for Fog Valley Winter, my youngest son, Dominic (then 16), was a Winter Wildlife Docent volunteer for Point Reyes National Seashore, weekends in January, February and March.

Dom was one of the youngest docents to train and take to the remote west for the winter whale watching/elephant seal-breeding season.

I hoped to catch a glimpse of my adventurous son in action in his bright red docent tabard over layers of windproof outerwear. It was getting late into the day and I feared I'd miss him. Still, driving over cattle grids and giving way to the occasional stray bovine is not to be undertaken at any great speed. I took my time and hoped for the best in tracking him down at one of the several locations from Drake's Beach to Peninsula Point, where docents were typically posted.

Dom and a handful of students from Petaluma High School were making their wintry weekend pilgrimages as far out west as geographically possible at what we all hoped would be the tail end of California's historic four-year drought.

Wilderness areas such as this actually consume less than two-and-a-half percent of U.S. land. The chance to work in the wilderness an hour from his own back yard had struck outdoorsman Dom as too good an opportunity to pass up, despite a heavy study load at school. I was proud of him.

He and his fellow intrepid young stewards of the land were rotated around the seashore, positioned either at the lighthouse for educating observation deck visitors on gray whale migration, down by the protected elephant seal breeding grounds, an historic lifeboat shed, or over at Drake's Beach — another favored spot for these supersized, oceangoing, earless, carnivorous seals to be seen.

These earless, true seals, I learned, are part of a family of 19 groups of marine mammals (including the walrus) that are known as Pinnipeds. They differ from other marine mammals such as whales, dolphins and porpoises in that they spend part of their life out of water. Pinnipeds mate, give birth, moult and rest on land or ice.

Dire lack of precipitation had made for balmy winter visits to the peninsula in spring and fall, but the chronic lack of rain had proved an enormous stress on the natural environment. Too many tule elk and uncountable other species of the natural world have perished on land and within the ocean itself.

Rains returned in early 2016 and, as happens after the ground has hardened for so long, pathways to and around the coast become a more perilous a place with extreme storms wreaking potential havoc in flashfloods and landslides.

If you go, pick a clear day for a winter visit to the peninsula. Park in the lot at Drake's Beach and hike a trail to where the former Drake's Head Ranch once stood, a bluff that is high enough to take in sweeping views of the peninsula, Limantour Spit and Estero close by. Look for spectacular Limantour Beach, Arch Rock, Wildcat Beach and Double Point to the south and Chimney Rock to the north.

One of the most astonishing sights when traversing the peninsula is that of the region's legendary tule elk. It never ceases to stop me in my tracks and enthrall and this time was no exception.

Endemic to California, over half a million tule elk roamed coastal prairie land from Santa Barbara to Sonoma County and through the Central Valley before 1800.

It was the early Californios, including huntsman General Mariano Vallejo who decimated the elk population by hunting elk for tallow and hides during the Spanish and Mexican eras.

Lavish hunts hosted by Mariano and his insatiable men wiped out as many as 50 at a time. Tule elk were only further decimated by habitat loss and cattle grazing, bringing them dangerously close to extinction.

In his 2015 *North Bay Bohemian* article: "Wild Meets Wild — Do Elk Have a Place in Point Reyes?" journalist James Wright wrote of elk bulls as being: "Tangled up in a controversy that has dairy and cattle ranchers, environmentalists and the national park service asking far reaching questions about the future of the seashore."

According to the report, elk, when caught in cattle ranch fence wire, are able to survive only if they last long enough to drop their antlers or be darted down by the park's ecologist to have the wire removed.

Hike, cycle or drive, depending on season, in Point Reyes National Seashore and you might very well see no other human for hours. A chance of sighting a herd of tule elk is much more likely.

Thought to have been extinct by 1874, a rancher in the Central Valley fortuitously spared a few that he'd found dwindling around drained marshlands. Some 22 herds (equating to 4,000) tule elk have descended from those few and are free to roam public and private land in California today.

Tule elk today have no natural predator since wolves long since made their way up to Oregon, mountain lions prefer the easier prey of deer and coyotes pretty much leave them alone.

Herds that we see when visiting the Point Reyes area today have emerged from 10 individual elk placed in segregated conservation at Tomales Point in 1978.

Twenty years later, the park service decided it was time to move a portion of the fast-growing herd to the region's Limantour wilderness area. Two enterprising females reportedly made a break for it some time ago, making their way to where the grass was greener in the pastoral zone across Drake's Bay.

After heading home for the rut that October, they returned to their newfound haven of grassy hospitality with calves in tow.

Five to six thousand beef and dairy animals rule the roost at Point Reyes, but the tule elk population is giving the bovine ranchers a run for their money. And while visitors and environmentalists thrill at the sight of up to 100 male elks, prime bulls gathered with their massive antlers complete with downward curling tips, ranchers are understandably loathe to share dwindling resources, especially in drought conditions, with wild herds.

Elk not only eat the green grass earmarked in the pastoral zone for cows, they positively eradicate it. Calcium, phosphate and other vital minerals are depleted from the earth beneath, heightening discussion of a need for a reinforced elk-proof-fence.

Today's ranching families are not keen on allowing the rampant tule elk to roam free on pristine pastures of multi-generational heritage dairy land. Yet dairy farming itself on this pastoral zone, in the mind of many, remains, itself, a privilege, not a right.

Continuous operation is allowed only as long as Point Reyes National Seashore keeps agreeing to it.

I lost count of how many hand painted signs dotting fence lines through Fog Valley that day, a literal grass-roots campaign calling for a truce between the dairy industry and the region's wild herds.

Tule elk and black tailed deer are the only two species of wild ungulates native to the California Coastal Ecosystem. The National Parks Service decision to rid the region of non-native fallow deer and axis deer has been another major subject of controversy in the past few years.

It was a man named Millard Ottinger, a coastal-based surgeon and owner of 5,000 acres on the peninsula, who had inadvertently set the wheels in motion for a calamitously disruptive fallow deer invasion of Point Reyes back in the 1940s.

A keen hunter, Millard paid his young neighbor, Ambrose Gondola, to drive a pick-up truck to San Francisco Zoo to collect a surplus of 23 deer for release onto the gun-toting surgeon's ranch.

Ambrose likely had little inkling how pivotal his role in transporting a two-dozen deer haul into Point Reyes would be. Shortly before he passed in 2014, he recorded this historic experience with West Marin's *The Story Shed*.

The first generation Italian-American, a native to west Marin, recorded on tape how he had been pulled over by police not just once, but twice, on his return journey from San Francisco.

Ambrose's deer-laden truck was not what the lawmen were looking for. If only they had known. Whatever it was that had been stolen in a burglary that occurred that same day, it would likely have had far less of a long-time impact on a region than the cargo he'd been charged with.

Fallow deer, the most common species in the world, are natives of the Mediterranean and Asia Minor. Non-native deer rampage through riparian and woodland habitat in their particularly quiet way.

They are considered threatening to endangered species of the region, including the California red-legged frog, Coho and Chinook salmon and steelhead trout that Ambrose recalled catching in abundance as a child.

A 2008 plan to rid the park of fallow deer subsequently resulted in professional wildlife sharpshooters having wiped out over half of an estimated 1,100 deer. Reports have reverberated far and wide of large family groups of deer shot from helicopters. Those that weren't killed instantly, were found dying in meadows and on beaches.

Shocked hikers, animal rights activists and outraged citizens from around the region, were horrified at the slaughter. They called for more humane treatment, successfully replacing sharpshooting with trapping, relocation and fertility control.

Those that remain, mostly along the southern edge of the park are sterilized females. The park hopes to see the last of the non-native deer in the area by 2021.

Early landowners on the peninsula had been reluctant to sell off any of their highly prized acreage to a government that had selected the headlands as a site for one of the original West Coast lighthouses.

Who could blame them? I pulled over again to take a better look at this stunning, sweeping relic of ancient coastal wilderness.

It took 17 long years for the Federal Government to seal a deal for a partial donation of land for a lighthouse "in the interest of humanity."

During a time of high sea traffic, at least 14 shipwrecks were recorded along the coast. The lighthouse was built, finally, in 1870. It was located at the tip of the headlands as opposed to the top, where it would surely have been shrouded in near perpetual fog.

The lighthouse lens and mechanism, preserved for visitors to peruse today, were constructed in France, in 1867.

I parked and walked the rickety road, unpeopled at that late hour, down to the headlands. I thought of the ox-drawn carts hauling the massive mechanism, glass prisms and dense housing of the lighthouse machinery that was shipped via steamer around the tip of South America, into San Francisco and on to Drake's landing. Rocks blasted by dynamite leveled the building surface sufficient for the magnificent mechanism's resting point at the perilous tip.

I didn't find Dom that day. I didn't find anyone. I was a little too late for the winter wildlife-watching crew and crowd. What I did find pause to consider, however, was a little, white painted wooden desk built into the lighthouse, emptied of its storied past.

A partial reproduction of its keeper's log serves as a reminder of the early individuals whose job it was to climb an original set of 638 steep steps down to the freezing tower and foghorn house from the warmth of a keeper's dwelling.

Today's staircase of a modified 300 steps is less than half as physically demanding but, in my experience and on this particular visit, plenty steep enough to insure a set of sore calf muscles the next day.

As I climbed, I considered, for company sake, a man named John Bull — the first lighthouse keeper (through 1875) and by all accounts, a robust individual who'd set the bar rather high.

Unfortunately, the second keeper was reportedly not nearly so together, neither were his two assistants, both of whom, according to

Lighthouses and Lifeboats of the Redwood Coast, refused to go on duty until after sundown.

By 1876, just one year after John Bull had moved on as keeper, his successor and two hapless assistants, were fired.

Incessant, noisy fog signals, wind, battering rain and ever-present fog certainly took an understandable toll on lighthouse keepers and their families.

In 1885, eloquent keeper E. G. Chamberlain articulately recorded: "Solitude, where are the charms that sages have seen in thy face? Better dwell in the midst of alarms than reign in this horrible place. So city, friendship and love, divinely bestowed upon man, O' had I the wings of a dove, how I would taste you again."

A yet-later keeper, in his final log notation upon transfer, penned of his destitute post: "Returning to USA."

In January 1889, another keeper's log entry recorded the unfortunate news that: "The second assistant went crazy and was handed over to the constable in Olema."

It is hard to imagine a more austere holiday season than those spent by keepers and their families at Point Reyes lighthouse in the late 1800s.

There was little improvement to report in the following decades spent out on the edge of the world. In 1926, the superintendent of lighthouses wrote that Point Reyes was positioned in the most undesirable location in his district, noting keepers going about their business in a "zombie-like" state, stunned by the whir of the wind and the oppressive clamor of the fog signal.

It is interesting to note that the last keeper at Point Reyes Lighthouse, one Gustav Zetterquist was a formidable fellow who defied all odds and stuck it out at Point Reyes with his family for more than two decades, from 1930 to 1951 when the U.S. Coast Guard took over the station.

The Lighthouse Board had seemingly grown wise, encouraging the employment of keepers with wives and children. Families, it proved, provided unpaid, yet constant, consistent help and vital companionship.

We know from lighthouse journals and logbooks that lighthouses along the coast were run in (human) part on constant pots of hot coffee on the keepers stove. Day and night, coffee and hot soup proved the mainstay of winter warmers. Whatever the weather, a keeper had to do his job, he had to work in even the worst of bone-chilling conditions, in fact, especially so. Nightshifts in winter were long and arduous, outside and inside of a damp tower. A bowl of soup and a cup of coffee were lifesavers.

My winter visit brought to mind the importance of basic home comforts. A pot of coffee and a bowl of soup would have been some small comfort if I'd been faced with overnighting alone, due to inclement weather, at the lighthouse.

In her vivid accounts: *Guardians of the Lights: Stories of U.S. Lighthouse Keepers,* author Elinor DeWire noted that days spent outside in the salty air tending to lighthouse duties, worked up the heartiest of appetites.

"So did duties like rescuing, which usually meant launching the station boat and rowing out into wild seas to an overturned boat or a full-scale shipwreck. Lighthouse keepers were sure to get soaked in the process and the sodden castaways they saved were brought into the warmth of their quarters for dry clothes and a hot meal."

Elinor suggested maintaining a pot of soup on the stove as a sensible practice all around. "At times, lighthouse keepers ran out of provisions and had to improvise."

Running out of food so far out west is an easy to imagine scenario, especially during extended stormy weather at Point Reyes. Supply wagons and boats struggled in making deliveries in such conditions.

According to Elinor: "The potato and onion bin could be emptied, the canned items used up and the fishing poor or impossible in stormy seas."

Keepers and their families frequently made do with biscuits and beans, foraged greens and whatever else they were able to cobble together with winter stores of flour and dry beans.

At Point Reyes, I reasonably assumed there was a steady supply of milk, cheese, butter and cream from neighboring dairy farms. Keepers or their wives kept hens for meat and eggs.

I looked out over the choppy sea and conjured the steaming image of a popular lighthouse soup of clam or oyster chowder with potatoes and onion and canned or dried corn.

When the U.S. Coast Guard took over in the 1950s, an automatic light was installed. The National Park Service was subsequently tasked with the preservation of the lighthouse when it became steward of the 71,000 acre National Seashore in 1962. The lighthouse that I had to myself that late afternoon, was finally retired, after more than a century in service, in 1975.

I returned to Drake's Beach and to the lighthouse the following weekend, this time in the company of intrepid adventurer and friend, fellow Brit, Gail. We were back in search of the lesser-spotted Dominic on his Winter Wildlife docent duties.

His station that day was fortuitously, our first stop at Drake's Beach. There'd been little winter whale-watching traffic that particular Saturday, due to an overdue though ultimately underwhelming winter storm alert. We took our chances on the elements as proverbial mad dogs and Englishwomen such as she and I are want to do.

To our good fortune and better timing than the previous week, we'd arrived just as Dom and his fellow docents were wrapping up their duties for the day. Drake's Beach has a terrific visitors center, a shop and a large, public parking lot.

Though buses generally run from the Drake's Beach lot on a regular basis during weekends from January through March, transporting whale watchers and nature lovers around the peninsula to prevent traffic build up, it's a wise idea to check ahead if the weather is bad.

Drake's Beach is the easiest to reach and most convenient spot to see the magnificent elephant seals in their natural habitat during the winter months. The peninsula is rife with thousands of bird species, harbor seals and sea lions, too. We looked for osprey, for white and brown pelicans, Peregrine falcons, too.

According to the National Park Service: "After being absent for more than 150 years, elephant seals returned to the sandy beaches on the rocky Point Reyes Headlands in the early 1970s. In 1981, the first breeding pair was discovered near Chimney Rock. Since then, researchers have found that the colony is growing at a dramatic annual average rate of 16 percent."

Severe storms of 1992, 1994 and 1998 wiped out huge amounts of pups. Storms and high tides of the El Niño winter of 1998 washed away an estimated 85% of that year's 350 young pups that had yet to learn to swim. Thankfully, though, the Point Reyes elephant seal population, one of only eleven breeding sites in the world, has risen to between 1,500 and 2,000 today.

Growing up to 16 feet long and weighing up to two and a half tons, adult male elephant seals spend most of their lives at sea, coming ashore to molt, mate and for the females to give birth.

Dom explained to Gail and I how huge elephant seal bulls engage in violent battles to establish dominance, with alpha bulls taking most of the glory in the mating game. Smaller females arrive and form "harems" on the beach reserve, giving birth to pups conceived the previous year.

Pups are nursed for up to 28 days. It is a natural phenomenon and astonishing to see, up close and in person. It's essential for the park to have docents such as Dom and his friends in place in this remote, though accessible location, throughout the season, both to protect the colony and also to insure that eco-tourism does not run dangerously (for all) amok.

"Don't get too close," he warned. "An elephant seal can outpace and crush anyone who poses a threat."

We left him to finish up his duties for the day and drove on to the lighthouse. To our utter astonishment and delight, a migrating grey whale passed close enough to shore for us to spot her tell-tail spout and emerging form. There have been winter days when I've stood for hours in the hopes of scanning a passing whale at one of a handful of popular Fog Valley coastal spotting locations. This immediate gratification was reward for my return visit, a thrill and a reminder of nature's random force.

So late was the afternoon hour, the sky grew navy blue to match the sea. We drove home through the shortest of showers to a shared pot of tea and oven-warmed scones.

Fishing boats docked at Bodega Bay
courtesy, the Sonoma County Library

cool climate crab fishing —
coastal seafood express

Fishing as an industry was one of the first and continues to be one of the most influential commercial enterprises in coastal Fog Valley.

Salmon, sturgeon, perch, pike, chub, drake, suckers, hardheads and narrow tail fish were caught in vast amounts to satisfy the seemingly bottomless market demand of the Gold Rush years.

Today, Fog Valley's 17-mile stretch of Sonoma Coast State Park is best known for its Dungeness crab fishing.

I was keen to learn about the history of the fishing industry. My friend Mike Marino is a boat builder and so I asked him to meet me at the Spud Point Marina in Bodega Bay and walk me through the basics of regional fishing boats.

Mike's a native New Yorker who moved to Fog Valley about five years ago, never to look back. Natural harbors occur along the seascape of his east coast upbringing, every handful of miles. In stark contrast,

Bodega Bay is the only natural harbor for almost 60 rugged coastal miles. When I think of New Yorkers I think of men and women in business suits, closing deals and dashing around the big city in taxi cabs. This is stereotyping to the extreme and I ought to be far less amazed by my friend Mike's incredible talent as a fine craftsman in the building of beautiful, artisan wood boats.

We'd picked a late afternoon in January, in between storms to take a look at the different sorts of boats employed in the fishing business, be it commercial or sport. As it happened, Spud Point Marina was fully berthed due to an unresolved natural catastrophe in the annual crab fishing season.

Commercial crab season generally opens in November on the Sonoma Coast when conditions are ideally, prime. Stormy weather, dock pricing disputes and crab reproductive cycles (every five to seven years) are apt to stall the season, much to the disappointment of fisherman and customers alike.

Large populations of Dungeness crab occur along the coast of Bodega Bay. Many consider a Fog Valley holiday not a celebration without fresh Dungeness crab, though the 2015/2016 season certainly put this to test.

Fishermen, friends and neighbors, chefs and holiday visitors experienced almost an entire season without their beloved Dungeness crab haul due to a naturally occurring toxin known as domoic acid, caused by the rise of the tiny pseudo-nitzschia plant.

This nasty little toxic bloom infiltrated crabs at levels that are potentially fatal when eaten or at the least, cause mild to serious sickness after consumption.

The California Department of Fish and Wildlife was forced to call a temporary halt to the season and restrictions were lifted for sport fishermen in February 2016.

Some 2,000 San Francisco Bay Area fishing fleets were forced to await a government declaration to call the season so that insurance might prevent more mariners from losing their homes and livelihood.

A Crab Industry Relief Plan was finally announced to waive fees and rents for three months for the berthing, storage and leasing for commercial crab fishing owners and receivers, devastated by the drastically shortened season.

Mike and I talked about four years of drought having led to unusually warm water temperatures along the coastline. Although the Department of Fish and Wildlife was reluctant to formally link coastal warming to this particular toxic bloom, the fishing industry was vocal as to its hopes that a cooler, nutrient rich ocean upswell with the on-set of an El Niño winter pattern would rid the region's Dungeness crab of this nasty invasion. The commercial season finally opened at the end of March 2016.

Crab lovers throughout Fog Valley had been looking for alternative seafood sources for their favorite dishes over the holiday season and few people I'd talked to had resorted to purchasing Washington State crab, largely on principle of local solidarity with the fishing industry. The holidays came and went and desire for crab, if anything, would only intensify for seasons to come.

Storm clouds overhead threatened but held back. Neither Mike nor I were up for a drenching. "I don't particularly like being out at sea," he confided. "I just always knew, as a small boy, that I wanted to build wooden boats."

I'm intrigued by his passion and knowledge for wooden watercraft. Mike first took summer classes in boat building at the Woodenboat School in Brooklin, Maine as a teenager. After he graduated high school, he traveled to the east coast of England for boat building school in Lowestoft, Suffolk, about 100 miles from the small town where I was born and raised. Mike went on to live and worked on boats in France for quite a few years in his 20s.

As a newbie to fresh crab when I'd arrived on Fog Valley shores in my 20s, I was surprised to find these delicious crustaceans far less of a luxury and more of a mainstay in coastal California, having been harvested in seasonal abundance for centuries by the resourceful Coast Miwok with spears and traps, boiled or cooked over a fire in sand.

Mike is of Italian heritage. We talked about early development of Fog Valley's commercial fishing industry. Enterprising Italian immigrants in San Francisco, fishing for smelt, sole, flounder, sardines and anchovies, first migrated up the coast in 1848.

"Initially, crabs were probably taken incidentally with other fish in nets," suggested Walter A. Dahlstrom in a vintage *History of Dungeness Crab Fisheries in California* report for the California Department of Fish and Game.

By 1860, crab was heavily marketed in San Francisco. During these early years, I learned how Italian fishermen employed the hoopnet or ringnet for crabbing. This type of rudimentary net was made of two reinforced and netted hoops on an iron rod with a cap of woven wire lashed to enclose the bait.

Floats of cedar, cork or copper were attached to mark the location of the nets. A series of 20 nets were thrown overboard one at a time as boats ran slowly against the tide.

Fishing boats went out early in the morning hours and were hard at work by sunrise. According to Walter's report: "Nets were hauled at intervals of a half hour or more until the early afternoon when the boats returned to unload their catch."

Mike explained how boats with small gasoline engines gradually took the place of sailboats in the early 1900s and crabs were caught year-round, with few restrictions.

Historical reports indicate a haul of some 93,000 crab in northern California in 1888, mostly by Italian fishermen. New laws in 1887 were calling for fisheries to license boats, fishermen and dealers.

A subsequent law was passed a decade on, given the increase in fishing along the coast, protecting Pacific crab by: "Prohibiting the possession and sale of female Dungeness crab."

Sonoma Coast
Dungeness crab

By 1914, open season was switched from August 14 to November 16, prolonging the closed season when male crabs molt. This allowed shells to harden and meat to fill out.

"Look for the boats with the two long poles," said Mike, pointing to a row of docked boats. "Between the 1920s and 1960s, the most popular pot fishing boat in Bodega Bay was the double ended Monterey clipper, complete with clipper bow, wide flare forward and a broadly pointed stern, generally built between 26 to 32 feet long."

By the 1970s, the Monterey clipper used for trawling and pot fishing had made way for other styles of fishing boats in the San Francisco Bay Area, but prior to that time, these classic boats were found throughout the bay, its tributaries and rivers and northern California coastal regions in general. It remains the fishing boat most associated with the region.

"They were mostly manned by two Italian family members," said Mike, "a father and son, or two brothers typically. The fishing industry was such that these two people could fish for salmon, tuna, sardines, crab and other fish and make a living for an entire family."

Most of these trusted old fishing boats were built in San Francisco. "They're similar to the felucca, a lateen (triangular) sailed traditional fishing boat of the Mediterranean," said Mike. "The origin of this style of fishing boat is, in turn, traced back to sailboats of many years ago."

The Monterey clipper was (and some still are) used as both a trolling boat and a pot fishing boat. I learned that dedicated trolling boats differ from pot fishing boats in that they are designed for faster species of fish that chase a lure. Long-poled trollers tow several baited hooks through the water to catch salmon, tuna and other fish.

Commercial fishing ramped up in the region in 1947. In a good season, traps are set in a straight line around 200 to 300 feet apart, as many as 50 to 100 at a time. Traps are fished from day one to day 10 depending upon weather, ocean condition and time of year.

Since the 1950s, dealers keep surplus crabs alive in crab crates or boxes that are floated in the water to receiving stations. Live tanks aboard vessels are common, too.

Since the Coast Miwok, those who live in the coastal reach of Fog Valley have long since caught sufficient crab in winter without the use of a boat. Drop a baited snare box off the old pier at Dillon Beach and you might be lucky enough to catch as many as 10 a day.

Be sure to have a California sports fishing license before embarking on a crab fishing expedition. Commercial fishermen drop 300 to 500 pots in order for a business to be viable these days.

We talked about how, in the past, it was commonplace to buy crab straight off the boats at Spud Point, but not today. Liability insurance and theft became the game changer.

Coastal Fog Valley is the most sustainable crab fishery in the world. The fishing boats we looked at sail from the Port of Bodega out past rocky shallow waters to the open ocean to drop spots where they lower their baited crab pots. At the start of a good season fishermen hope to haul in as many as 25 crabs at a time.

Mike's certainly not the first east coast mariner to settle the area and I'm sure he won't be the last. Fog Valley's first family of fishing emerged from a robust cultural pairing of Coast Miwok with English lineage of a Massachusetts-born sea captain named Stephen Smith. This pioneering fellow was first owner of coastal Spanish Land Grant Rancho Bodega.

Stephen subsequently fathered William Smith — patriarch of Bodega Bay's fishing industry.

William was born around 1844 to the captain's mistress, a young Miwok woman named Tsupu. Although William did not read or write, he was widely respected throughout the region for his enterprising ways in fishing and farming.

By the 1930s, William and his wife Rosalie produced five girls and six boys. They ran the largest fleet in Bodega Bay and their commercial fishing wharf was the first in Sonoma County.

The Smith family was the first native family to incorporate a business in the State of California. Though the fishery closed in the 1960s, members of the family are still active in tribal affairs of the region today.

I learned that only male crabs are taken from the Sonoma Coast, captured in environmentally friendly crab pots with escape rings for the smallest of crab. Fortunate females are returned to the water.

Opposite the marina, I'd expected to see crowds gathered for the last haul of the day, served over the counter at retired firefighter Tony Anello and his wife Carol's popular Spud Point Crab Company. The couple has owned and operated their no-frills, fresh seafood shack since 2004. For a few years it was a best-kept secret in Fog Valley. In more recent years, the place is mobbed from dawn til dusk. It serves as a morning meeting place for fishermen who gather for tri-tip sandwiches and coffee. Tourists clamor for crab and clam chowder.

It was almost dark and Tony (a long time fisherman himself, as are many firefighters) and Carol had shut shop for the day. Crab season's failure to launch had widespread impact in Fog Valley, though there is no doubt in my mind that the crowds will be back.

When shopping for crab during open season, it's wise to educate ourselves in what to look for. Keep in mind that crabs are identified by grades — "cripples" are small, with missing claws and legs; "select" are mixed in size; "premium" are the biggest and most desirable.

Commercial crabs are required to have hard shells measuring a minimum of six and a quarter inches across. If caught for sport, shells of five and three quarter inches across suffice.

Never eat a cooked crab that has loose legs and claws, is spongy or has a cracked shell. It was probably dead before it was caught. Barnacles are also a big no. I've learned to look for healthy crab with legs and claws tight against the body.

In peak season in a good year, reputable fishmongers in Fog Valley such as the fish department in independently owned G&G Market sell around 30,000 pounds of Dungeness crab each week.

One of my favorite Fog Valley traditions and initiations into the culture of my adopted community is the customary "crab feed" fundraiser. After I first settled in the Pacific west coast the concept of a crab supper was utterly foreign and decadent to me. Crab had been a luxury for me as an English girl from the sticks. It took a while for me to get to grips with crab!

Most years, I have dozens of local feasts to pick from in the winter months, usually after New Year — eating crab and socializing for a good cause is a sport in itself.

Crab feeds that I've enjoyed over the years raise money for non-profits and organizations in the area with family-style bowls of fresh crab for cracking at row tables, salad, fresh bread, lots of butter, chilled brews, good wines and bibs.

Mike has worked on several of the wooden fishing boats in harbor at Spud Point. "Wooden boats, if properly cared for, tend to last longer than boats made from other materials," he shared. Although Mike must on occasion, take on woodwork in other forms, I saw that his eyes went misty when he talked about building a boat from scratch. "It's really all I ever want to do," he said.

Salmon, oft described as one of nature's miracles, has been another core centerpiece of protein on Fog Valley tables since the region's pioneers recognized its tastiness and nutritional value.

Smoked, poached, cured or grilled this red-fleshed, densely flavored fish is far more healthy and rich in omega-3 fatty acids in its wild form than its farmed sibling.

So delicious and abundant was this wonderful wild salmon when the region's first settlers arrived, they deemed it an endless source of natural sustenance for the taking. Mining and logging would destroy river habitat to such a dire extent, that tragically, today, the state of California now has less than 10 percent of its historic salmon in the wild.

Scientists are right now developing innovative technologies to combat the threat of an extinction vortex of wild salmon, specifically focused on Fog Valley and its neighboring region.

Salmon are anadromous fish meaning that they travel upriver to spawn. After hatching in freshwater, they migrate downstream to the ocean to mature in nutrient-rich saltwater. In time, they return to freshwater to spawn and to complete the life cycle. Miraculously, they return to their birthplace by following chemical cues in the water. Salmon are unstoppable until they find the cleanest gravel areas in which to lay their eggs. Both male and female die after they spawn, the females leaving behind as many as 7,500 eggs that take two to three months to hatch.

Coast Miwok legend and ceremonies surrounded the life cycle of the salmon that were so vital to their health and survival. The first Italian immigrant families who migrated out to coastal Fog Valley caught an abundance of salmon and steelhead trout in the creeks running into the ocean. After the heavy rains of late winter, fish flowed into the Pacific in massive numbers. Children chased salmon with sticks. Families lit fires on the beach and cooked fresh fish to eat with loaves of fresh bread.

European settlers were quick to trap and fish for their families as soon as the rains had come, though in the 1860s, commercial salmon season was deemed later, in spring, when the most dense numbers of fish swam to the river's mouth — typically May through August.

California's Commissioners of Fisheries first recognized the significance of the species, declaring in 1870: "Salmon is the most important visitor to our rivers. It has appropriately been called the 'King of Fish'. The richness of its flesh, its large size, the certainty of its annual return from the ocean, the rapidity with which, under favorable conditions, it is multiplied, all render it an important article of human food."

In the century and a half since commercial salmon fishing took hold, not only mining and logging, but flooding, over-harvesting, urbanization, industrial development, pollution, dams, water diversions and reduced flow have contributed to what scientists today describe as "the perfect storm" in the drastic decline in salmon populations.

Low waters and high temperatures of the recent drought served to compound issues. Restoration efforts have never been more critical if we are to restore California wild salmon to healthy populations.

State regulators in 2015 requested around 650 landowners along Sonoma County's four main salmon spawning streams to reduce water diversions to protect an imperiled coho salmon species that has barely hung on after coming close to extinction in the 1990s.

Though The Sonoma County Water Agency and the Department of Fish and Game are working hard to restore salmon and steelhead spawning areas and passage on the Russian River, re-grading, repairing canopy and planting native trees and shrubs along the riverbanks, leading scientists have implemented latest genetic techniques to reverse the work of hatcheries, in place since the late 1880s.

Man-made salmon spawning hatcheries may well have done as much harm as good in producing a less hardy species and the proliferation of inbreeding of salmon that could accelerate the process of decline.

Geneticist Dr. John Carlos Garza, who runs the molecular ecology and genetic analysis team for the National Oceanic and Atmospheric Administration, leads a team of scientists at the Russian River and at University of California Santa Cruz, studying the DNA fingerprinting of individual fish from several regions including Sonoma County's Russian River after they return to the hatchery.

A front page report by Matt Richtel in the January 17th, 2016 issue of *The New York Times* outlined the basics of the geneticist's elaborate breeding program, a complex matrix that matchmakes unrelated male and female coho salmon.

This new "salmon mating service," as jokingly described by the scientific team, has high hopes of enabling coho salmon in the region to once again fend for themselves in the wild.

According to *The New York Times:* "When the fish return to the hatchery, scientists there separate them into individual tubes, clip their fins, then Fed-Ex the tissue samples to Dr. Garza and his team. They then analyze each salmon's DNA and match breeding pairs that have no genetic relationship to each other."

Scientists are now seeing that past trends for breeding "the biggest, best and most productive" of a species is not proving beneficial in the long run. This about-turn instead, mimics nature more closely in that species are able to survive the predators, disease and the myriad challenges of nature.

It makes sense to me, though I'm certainly no expert. Not everyone agrees with the doctor and his team. In fact, within the University of California system, according to the *New York Times* report, some scientists are skeptical that this new technological fix will create its own problems. Time and Mother Nature will ultimately decide if we're to see wild salmon return to historic populations in the region, or anywhere in the state, for that matter. At least we have the technology to try.

On a local level, installation of low-flow household appliances and the removal of lawns have contributed, region-wide, to sparing sufficient fresh reservoir waters to be released into these endangered rivers.

Tomales Bay oysters on the half shell at Tony's Seafood Restaurant

a visit to oysterville

Oyster-rich "Hangtown Fry" is said to be the first real dish of California cuisine. Fried breaded oysters, eggs and fried bacon when cooked like an omelet was a one-skillet meal for miners with big appetites in the camps of the late 1880s. The iconic former Pine Cone Diner in Point Reyes Station was renowned for its "Hangtown Fry," as is the Fremont Diner in Sonoma, where I've enjoyed this classic fried oyster dish served instead with scrambled eggs, arugula and potatoes with a lemony-remoulade and bacon bits. Delicious.

Live oysters were transported to the Sierra foothills from the Bay Area in barrels of seawater. Hangtown Fry, at its peak of popularity, would have cost a hungry diner a small fortune. In those days, a $6 a plate price tag would have been equivalent to around $96 today. Hangtown, in the Sierra foothills of Placerville, was a supply base for mining towns. It earned its name from three unfortunate desperados having been hung on the same day.

Mountain Democrat reporter Doug Noble wrote a particularly interesting account of the origins and reputation of the decadent dish:

"In 1849, just a short time after Old Dry Diggins had been renamed Hangtown in honor of the recent hanging of three desperados from the large oak tree on Main Street, a prospector rushed into the saloon of the El Dorado Hotel announcing that right there in town, along the banks of Hangtown Creek, he had struck it rich and had every reason to celebrate."

Untying his leather poke (purse) from his belt, the prospector reportedly tossed it on to the bar where it landed heavily, spilling its shining contents of nuggets and gold dust.

He was a rich man and intent on celebrating his good luck. Turning to the bartender he loudly demanded: "I want you to cook me up the finest and most expensive meal in the house."

The bartender, according to the *Mountain Democrat* report, called to the cook and relayed the prospector's order. The cook stopped what he was doing and came out of the kitchen. Looking the prospector in the eye he told him that the most expensive things on the menu were bacon, eggs and oysters.

Eggs were carefully packed to travel the rough roads from Fog Valley. Bacon made way by ship around the horn from the east and the fresh oysters were brought up each day on ice from the cold waters of the San Francisco Bay.

Local lore has it that the prospector replied: "Scramble me up a whole mess of eggs and oysters, throw in some bacon and serve 'em up. I'm starving. I've been living on nothing much more than canned beans since I got to California and at last I can afford a real meal." The cook did just as he asked. According to Doug's story in the *Mountain Democrat*, the cook whipped up a full plate of the mixture. And thus, Hangtown Fry was invented.

My compass was once again set west with a mission in mind for cruising near-coastal "Oysterville." This delicious stretch of waterside roadway is a slither of Highway One that runs along the edge of Tomales Bay to the north and south of the small, historic diary farming community of Marshall.

Tomales Bay is a 15-mile-long, one-mile-wide, narrow inlet of the Pacific Ocean, separating Point Reyes Peninsula from the mainland of Marin County. Tomales Bay itself is neither state park nor designated wilderness area.

The magnetic pull of Tomales Bay for oyster lovers is nothing new. Steady streams of weekday visitors and many more on weekends vie for bayside parking and picnic table seating to taste oysters at the source.

To drop down from a hill-climbing, cross-country drive directly into Marshall itself, I opted for a mind-clearing ramble along one of the least-traveled, most isolated back roads in the region.

In the best of conditions, the Petaluma/Marshall Road adds an extra half an hour on to any coastal jaunt, given its constancy of steep curves, compelling twists and turns amidst soaring hills of pristine dairy land.

In winter this is a particularly suspect route. Sizeable potholes are wont to appear with any slight amount of rainfall, making for a quasi-off-road experience for the unsuspecting. Large chunks of sodden asphalt might wash off the very edge of this wild and unruly road, rolling downhill into the embrace of brambles and brush.

It is a route not for the fainthearted. I speak with experience with a warning to embark in this direction with at least a half tank full of gas. You won't find a single gas station for miles. Eager back road explorers pottering along on a wing and a prayer are in for a surprise when running low on fuel. I found this to be true at a cost to my nerves, a few years ago — having wrongly assumed that I'd find a gas pump in Marshall. After freewheeling downhill onto Highway One, finally, with fingers crossed and humble as pie, I made it another 15 minutes on to Point Reyes Station for a fleecing — a premium-priced fill-up at the only gas station in miles.

If you have ever traveled it in full, you'll know what Highway One runs 500 miles from Dana Point in Orange County to Leggett, north of Fort Bragg. In many of the more rural parts, including Fog Valley's portion gas stations are as much as 100 miles apart.

I hadn't given this useful information the time of day until several years ago, setting out to collect my son, Luc, from camp at Walker Creek, the one and only destination point on Marshall/Petaluma Road that warrants a signpost. Visions of my then 10-year-old, stranded with his backpack and sleeping bag, last of that summer's week campers waiting patiently for a wayward guardian, propelled me onwards, riding as I was, on that energizing current of parental anxiety. That he has since traversed Europe by rail twice before his 21st birthday helps me to put things into perspective.

The gas tank was just full enough, I'd naively assumed to drive there and back. I was completely unprepared for the long and rambling rural ride into what felt to me like total wilderness. It was my first time on the Marshall/Petaluma Road and I'll never forget the experience. Watching the gas marker and willing it to somehow conserve its last drop of fuel. I had foolishly assumed that there would be a pump and gas in Marshall to get us back home, so I made the call to pass the camp, coast downhill and crawl onwards for a few miles.

Panic-stricken by my bad choice, with no cell phone service, I was forced on another 10 long miles out of my way through gas-strapped Marshall and on to Point Reyes Station. By the time I made it back to Walker Creek, a small group of the more stalwart campers were, to my massive relief, still enthusiastically belting out the last of the farewell circle songs. Luc didn't bat an eyelid at my being at least an hour late. My relief was palpable. I learned my fuel check lesson well. Luc's younger brother Dom, undoubtedly picked up some bonus choice vocabulary en-route.

The mysterious Marshall/Petaluma Road is not a route that you're likely to stumble upon, unless by taking Western Avenue out of Petaluma you happen to hang a left on Chileno Valley Road and persevere onwards to Wilson Hill Road across San Antonio Creek for the sheer fun of it.

Instead of looping onto Hicks Valley Road, forge ahead further into the deepening countryside until you meet up with Marshall/Petaluma Road. Pass by the Stubbs family's scenic, off-the-grid vineyard down below to your right and, after a little while, follow signs for super-remote 1,700 acre Walker Creek Ranch, a former Miwok village and later dairy ranch, owned and operated today by the Marin County Office of Education.

Walker Creek Ranch is home to a bucolic outdoor school, dorms, conference center, two barns, a four-acre pond for nature study and swimming, an amphitheater, large, organic garden and sports fields. The secluded property that I'd so foolishly misjudged the distance of is, in itself, twice the size of San Francisco's Golden Gate Park. The fact that you don't see a lot from the road was part of the appeal of a rather more unconventional incarnation of the sprawling property, back in the 1960s to 80s.

Long after the Coast Miwok had moved on from the property (a huge grinding stone for grinding acorn mush is visible at its entrance), an extended, almost forgotten episode in these otherwise, rustic ranchlands housed the Synanon Commune — an infamous alternative lifestyle community/wealthy, authoritarian cult, that started out as a drug and alcohol rehabilitation program.

Though this particular time-period came later than the main historical focus of Fog Valley Winter, Synanon is too fascinating as a side-story to exclude. The cult, founded by a man named Charles E. "Chuck" Dederich, Sr. in 1958 in Santa Monica, CA first came to my attention in conversation with a former child resident several years ago.

Up to 2,000 members lived at the Walker Creek outpost in the Synanon heyday. Kids' heads were shaved — boys and girls. Members dressed and ate according to rules laid down by the founder and were forbidden from interacting on the outside. If anyone wanted to leave, they packed their bags and got out as fast as they could, generally in the middle of the night.

The New York Times reported on accounts of violence and the insistence by Mr. Dederich on forced birth control and: "the divorce of more than 230 of its married couples who were to switch to other partners led to investigations and unfavorable newspaper publicity."

I'd heard how the former child resident lived boarding-school style, separated from parents who were living in other locations of the commune, somewhere else in the United States.

The New York Times report attested that "community members came from all walks of life, many were recovering alcoholics and drug addicts, some were teachers and caregivers, all were assigned specific jobs within the community."

During its tenure on site, it was Synanon that built the residences, meeting rooms, a sewage system and a water treatment/distribution system still in use today. A tax case would eventually shut Synanon down, but not before many of its former members battled to expose the group for civil liability in brainwashing.

My son Luc, like thousands of other Bay Area children each year, enjoyed the best of outdoor education on this rural property. Most parents, teachers and students have little knowledge of the more bizarre episode in the outpost's past, preferring to skip that period to focus on its earlier settlements. Coast Miwok bowls, arrowheads and other native artifacts discovered on the site are displayed in the ranch museum.

Moving on, the drop down to the Bay at Marshall is well worth the twists and turns of the journey.

Welcome to Oysterville! I was on my way to Hog Island Oyster's home base in Marshall. Though the renowned company, founded by three biologists in 1983, has its own fancy oyster bars in the Ferry Building in San Francisco and the Oxbow Market in Napa, die-hard aficionados travel the winding road out west for a taste of some of the best bivalves in the business, at source, newly harvested and freshly shucked.

Hog Island Oysters keep good company. Neighboring Tomales Bay Oyster Company and its Marshall Store and nearby Tony's Seafood Restaurant continue to put (unofficial) Oysterville on the map as the region's gourmet waterside ghetto.

It was too early in the day for a pit-stop at Tony's Seafood Restaurant. Locals' night on a Friday is a lot of fun and is a good time to pull up a chair and partake in a glass of crisp Sonoma coastal chardonnay and a platter of dollar oysters fresh from the bay.

If you take a window seat for a prime sunset view over the still waters, watch for the last of the day's fishing boats to meander back into dock. Keep company with a crowd of coastal ranchers, artists and aging musicians sporting cowboy hats, wranglers and boots and "native" tribal gear — rock and roll t-shirts and Birkenstock sandals worn with chunky, hand knitted socks.

Fishermen John and Anton Konatich, grandsons of the original Tony's run the show today. It's an institution in these parts, in operation since 1948. Anton (Tony) Konatich was an immigrant fisherman from Croatia. His original outlet for selling local catches of salmon, crab, herring and perch is mostly unchanged.

The craze for oysters attracts city folk by the hundreds, particularly on weekends, packing every outlet and eaterie in sight. It's best to visit during the week, though take note, as is typical out west, Hog Island Oysters may well be the only one open on a Monday and Tuesday.

I'd made an appointment at Hog Island online to take a tour. There's always something new and exciting to learn when we step behind the scenes in food and farming environments and food and farm tours in the region take this concept to a new level.

Parking is an issue in the area, given the sheer lack of concrete real estate — the narrowness of the road through Marshall and along Tomales Bay.

The folks at 160-watery-acre Hog Island Oysters introduced a valet parking system to prevent backup and accidents. It felt decadent to be handing over my keys for a potter around an oyster farm, but I could see the point and so conceded.

"Frances — hello! Welcome!" I recognized the face but, still a little flustered from the indulgence of valet parking, the morning's tour leader took a moment to register. Dr. Gary Fleener is a man not easily forgotten.

I'd met Gary as a fellow guest my friend Suzanne's collaborative dinner parties. For those who read my first book, *Fog Valley Crush*, you'll recognize Gary from the hunter/gatherer dinner featured at the start of the book. This intrepid former biology professor and food geologist made a mean homemade wild turkey sausage that proved particularly popular amongst readers. I appreciated the degree of effort and expertise involved in hunting, plucking, preparing, grinding, seasoning such spectacularly earthy fare and so did many others.

Gary popped up a second time as a leading light in a later foraged feast featured in the book's final chapter. Another of my friend Suzanne's super-collaborative dinners, this one was designed to preserve fall season's fullest flavors in a trademark flamboyant style. Gary's interpretation of our dinner directive: "Plucked from the wild, or harvested in the backyard" emerged as perfection in poached seafood cioppino served over polenta.

I hadn't seen Gary for at least a year. In fact, I'd never met him outside of our mutual friend and Fog Valley feast instigator Suzanne's kitchen. Was this serendipity or what? I couldn't have been more delighted. With Gary as my guide on a tour through Hog Island's watery kingdom, I knew I'd be in for a treat.

Though utterly at home in the wilds of northern California, Gary is a native Midwesterner. I found that we had something in common other than a shared penchant for accepting extreme and elaborate group cooking invitations. Despite his lifelong love of the natural world, Gary had never eaten an oyster before his first visit to Hog Island in 2010.

I told him that the first time I consumed an oyster was as a wide-eyed exchange student in a small fishing village in southwest France. I was 15-years-old and a five-day winter foray to the rustic coast wasn't exactly what I'd had in mind. Billed as a two-week exchange trip to Paris, it was rather a cultural awaking of all things wild, oceanic and untamed — especially the cuisine.

"I fell in love with this beautiful estuary," Gary explained. "As a biologist I was keen to understand precisely how an oyster comes to be."

He was hooked. After visiting on a regular basis, Gary talked Hog Island Oyster partners Gary Finger and John Sawyer to add him to the tiny roster of trusted tour guides.

There are many misconceptions surrounding the history of oysters in the San Francisco Bay area and its neighboring waters. Native oysters in the region were tiny bivalves (Ostreola Conchaphila) re-branded and marketed at the start of the Gold Rush as Olympia oysters and described by writer Mark Twain as "poor, little insipid things."

Olympia oysters, similar to mollusks native to France and England, are about as big as a man's thumb and consequently, extremely hard to shuck. We know from shell mounds that Native Americans foraged for these tiny oysters for thousands of years. The native oyster flourished in the cold, salty and clear waters of the San Francisco Bay and coastline areas.

By the early 1850s, commercial fishermen had completely overharvested the native oyster beds and smothered them into obscurity. A temporary solution sought to reintroduce Olympia oysters from Washington State, some 750 miles to the north.

A traveled man, Mark Twain, like most of his peers, had a predilection for the much larger, fleshier Atlantic oysters, first transported via rail to farmed beds in the San Francisco Bay in 1869 in barrels of cold water.

Winter of 1862 had brought record rainfall to northern California, washing mining debris, dirt, mud, sand and rock down the rivers and into the bays, dramatically changing the ecosystem and creating conditions that had made oyster farming increasingly difficult.

With demand on the rise, oyster farming expanded to the north of San Francisco in Tomales Bay, in 1875. Experimental beds were laid by the United States Fish Commission in the clean waters of the inner tidal zones after large-scale oyster farming in the San Francisco Bay was shut down due to pollution and oxygenation.

Hog Island's neighboring Tomales Bay Oyster Company is the oldest continuing operational oyster farming operation in California. It first operated as Pacific Coast Oyster Company, with underwater acreage in 1907. Two years later, the Morgan Oyster Company built more oyster beds in the area. Both companies changed hands several times before a merger combined operations.

Manager Oscar Johannson took the reins in 1926, eventually taking ownership and cultivating tidelands through the late 1980s. The Pacific Oyster, a variety introduced from Japan, in 1928 would soon become the West Coast standard.

Former vintner Todd Friend and his family purchased Tomales Bay Oyster Company from its longtime steward and subsequent owner, Dave Alden, in 2009. Todd and his daughter Heidi and son Shannon also own and operate the nearby Marshall Store, a charming, little dockside shanty on the shores of Tomales Bay and as great a place as any to pull up an outdoor bar stool and enjoy an oyster feast or bowl of clam chowder.

Though neighboring Hog Island, established in 1983 might be considered the jewel in the crown of the stars of Oysterville — a state-of-the-art sustainable "grow out" oyster farm producing four of the five oysters to be found in the northern hemisphere, locals have a soft spot for the grounded reputation of Tomales Bay Oyster Company.

Hog Island's most popular mollusk — the Pacific varietal — is marketed as the Hog Island Sweetwater.

Gary stepped forward for a closer look at the waters where the magic happens after the introduction of oyster seed grown to order. Hog Island is considered a medium sized oyster farm, producing up to eight or nine million oysters a year. It has its own hatchery in Humboldt Bay.

He explained how a company called Pacific Coast Hatcheries partners with Hog Island to nurture single oyster spats onto fragments of shell, grown to the size of a chunk of granola.

At this stage of an oyster's 18-month maturation process, seed is placed into mesh cylinders named Stanways and floated in the bay for a gentle tidal roll. Nutrient rich algae develop the oyster's tough shell.

"There are three things to consider," said Gary. "Greatness of place satisfies growth. Without it, the bivalve won't put down its real estate. An oyster needs nutrition. It is the brackish conditions of the bay that allows the oyster to thrive."

Pollution-free Tomales Bay is fed by the currents of dominant weather patterns swirling along the wild Pacific's west coast as well as the fresh water rivers and streams that flow in.

Beyond the waterway, a backdrop of Point Reyes National Seashore sets the stage for this prime location. "It's very clean and completely protected," said Gary. "Big north Pacific swells drive cold water from deep in the ocean, maintaining nutrient rich water that is something really special." The oyster wants to eat plankton and there is plenty of it here.

I learned that the oyster spawns once a year in response to warming waters. "The average female releases 10 million to 100 million eggs," said Gary. Males release their sperm into the bay, fertilizing billions of eggs in the coastal environment. "Ninety-nine point nine percent will not make it to maturity," said Gary, hence the need to culture a brood stock of young oysters in a hatchery before introducing them to the elements.

These little seedlings are grown to the size of little jelly sacks that are able to catch microscopic bits of food. "Baby oysters receive a primordial message cue to grow a tiny foot, which it knows it must secure onto something," explained Gary. Once the little foot has made its choice on crushed shells in the bottom of the hatchery tanks, it has its real estate for life and it begins to build its shell.

Juveniles are introduced to the "merrior" (a watery terroir) in groups of two thousand positioned as the bay tide comes in and out in gentle waves. Rocked and bathed in these nutrient-rich waters they start to toughen and grow.

Gary pointed out an oyster "shepherd" at work, wading into the bay for the day's harvesting. "All of our feed costs are covered by the bay," he said. Large sacks of freshly harvested oysters are hung on racks and funneled along an open-air conveyer belt and sorting cylinder. "Every single oyster is sorted by hand."

We walked over to large water tanks of newly bagged oysters. Here, Bay water is filtered in and cooled to encourage the fresh haul to slow down metabolism and shut down systems for 24 hours in preparation for transportation to the company's bustling oyster bars and a handful of select restaurants — long-time supporters.

A single oyster, I learned, is capable of filtering up to 30 gallons of water a day. Filtering helps to remove nitrogen and pollution and creates an environment for fish to flourish. Water tanks purge the system of the oyster, ridding it of any residual sediment to insure it as nutritious, hydrated, fresh and plump.

Coldwater oysters are farmed year round. Gary had a few minutes to spare before his next tour. We took a seat at the bar in an invitingly rustic outdoor barbecue area overlooking the water.

Winter is the ideal time to plan a visit. Groups of oyster lovers were grilling their purchases under mid-day sunshine, sipping wines cooled in ice buckets at the foot of wooden trestle tables. I wished I'd brought a few friends along for the ride and pledged that next time I'd plan for an afternoon. I said my goodbyes to Gary and lined up for a haul of a dozen oysters to take home for supper.

Armed with two oven gloves and a makeshift shucker, Timo chilled a coastal Chardonnay, flamed up the backyard grill and together we toasted my day's adventuring.

Much has been written in the media and online on the sorry saga of the government-enforced closure of the region's most controversial oyster operation, Drake's Bay Oyster Company — located a little under 20 miles to the south west of Marshall, in the heart of Point Reyes National Seashore's protected Drake's Estero.

The significance of Drake's Bay Oyster Company's battle story in the region is unprecedented in its debate for the case of eating local and supporting small family owned farms versus protecting the only designated wilderness area on the west coast to include marine waters.

Back in the 1920s, Estero oyster beds were laid in the fashion introduced over on Tomales Bay by a man named Larry Jensen (we'll hear more about him later).

In 1957, Larry sold Drake's Bay Oyster Company to an oyster worker in the area called Charlie Johnson. The Johnson family ran it as The Johnson Oyster Company for 27 years during which the Drakes Bay Estero became a part of the National Seashore encompassment.

In 1976, Point Reyes Wilderness Act legislators heard arguments on both sides for allowing this long-standing pre-existing use for oyster farming to continue within the wilderness zone.

In line with agricultural leases in the park, land was leased back to the Johnsons by the government for 40 years. With a cannery on-site, Charlie and his family went on to farm 50 percent of oysters grown in the state of California.

Twelve years prior to the end of the lease, in 2004, a Point Reyes peninsula farming family purchased the precarious oyster company from the Johnsons in a particularly optimistic move.

The Lunny family believed that the government would see fit to extend operations, renamed Drake's Bay Oyster Company.

To the lament of the family, its workers and thousands of sustainable food supporters throughout the region, the park service changed its mind with regards to the potential of a 2005 extension, citing charges of environmental harm to the wilderness environment.

Tens of thousands of shorebirds and waterfowl live in Drake's Estero, plus 20 percent of the mainland breeding population of harbor seals in California. According to the scientists who were studying the waters, this longtime operation was outdated in its use of environmentally undesirable materials in its oyster beds. Could this have been fixed? Most probably yes. But the fact remained, it had been the park service's plan since the 1970s to retire oyster farming in this specific wilderness area. And environmental groups supported its removal.

A bitter nine-year battle ensued with "Save Our Drake's Bay Oyster Company" hand-painted signs posted by the score on fence posts in a 100-mile radius.

Oyster enthusiasts and supporters of sustainable farming praised Drake's Bay as a classic example of high quality food production in harmony with the environment and yet after immense legal wrangling, the National Park Service ultimately persisted in the removal of the oyster farm's on-shore operations in 2014. Historic buildings are under demolition, oyster racks have been dismantled and removed and several families who lived and worked on the property are moving on (with relocation assistance).

Drake's Estero was named after Elizabethan explorer, Sir Francis Drake and his visit to the area in the 1500s. This waterway was home to oyster farming for over a century. The Lunny family had been farming and ranching in and around Drakes Estero for three generations.

"We fought long and hard all the way to the U.S. Supreme Court," Kevin, Joe and Bob Lunny posted in an impassioned statement after their regional battle went national and the Supreme Court refused to hear their case. "Along the way, we stood up for family farms, for sustainable food and for scientific integrity in government," they said. They had no alternative but to settle a drawn out Federal lawsuit that had ignited oyster aficionados and long time customers against the National Park.

"At the end of the day, although we lost this battle," said the Lunnys "it was important for us to be a voice for justice for family farms."

Old Railway station sign at Tomales History Museum

The lost community of Hamlet prior to destruction.
photographer Kathryn LeMieux
courtesy, the Tomales History Museum

Chapter 12

Hamlet, Tomales, Dillon Beach, Valley Ford and Freestone

On my way back to Petaluma after my adventure in Oysterville, I opted for an extended loop of heading north along Tomales Bay-side through the town of Tomales where the highway eventually joins up with Valley Ford Road. That way I'd avoid the twists and turns of scenic Marshall Road I'd driven earlier that day.

For a while, I'd been intrigued by the idea of the vanished settlement of Hamlet — a recreation spot and flag stop on the North Pacific Railroad and a shipping point for dairy, poultry and fish.

"It (Hamlet) boasted a mercantile, a dairy, a fish cannery and one of the earliest and longest lived oyster beds in the region," wrote historian Dewey Livingston in 1989 in a detailed report for the National Park Service.

Hamlet was located precisely 13.5 miles north of Point Reyes Station and three miles south of Tomales, overlooking the bay, directly across from the National Seashore wilderness area. Its sardine cannery was abandoned at the end of World War I.

Dewey painted a picture in words of a peculiar little place that was "many faceted" and with its own unique and captivating history: "At Hamlet lived Coast Miwok Indians, Marin County pioneers, families, respected businessmen and women, artists and craftspeople and it had its own share of eccentric characters."

The land was a part of sprawling 156,000-acre Rancho Nicasio Spanish Land Grant, initially intended to preserve native grounds for the Coast Miwok. Sadly, this honorable plan was contested in the 1850s and the land was in part gifted to aristocratic state senator, acting lieutenant governor, U.S. marshal and district court judge, Pablo De La Guerra.

Later, in 1870, John Hamlet, a dairyman from Tennessee bought the land he named after himself from a fellow Tennessee farmer for $9,000 in gold coin, after it had already changed hands several times.

Its namesake sold it on to Canadian potato farmer Warren Dutton, three years later. This enterprising young Canadian appeared on the scene in Tomales in 1852. Warren partnered with the town of Tomales' founder — John Keys and their short-lived business relationship would dissolve into a long-standing rivalry that split the town of Tomales in half.

It was Warren who developed the rail stop and early facilities at Hamlet, selling it, lock, stock and barrel for $12,000 to popular dairy rancher, miner and merchant, Abraham Huff, in 1877. Coastal directors described Abraham as a: "Hearty and whole-souled gentleman, who stands as the best type of the self-made American."

Although one George Russell of Petaluma bought Hamlet from Abraham in 1904, he failed to fulfill payments for the princely purchase sum at the time, of $20,000. History leaves us little clues as to why, after it foreclosed, Abraham re-sold in 1905 to a Dane named Hans Larsen Jensen, for the bargain price of $10.

The 1906 San Francisco earthquake caused considerable damage to the area. The depot pitched into the bay and was destroyed, a landslide consumed the railroad tracks, taking the south county road along with it. A wharf was broken up.

Dewey's report stated that Hans Jensen was born in Denmark in 1859. He'd been drawn to California for the dairy industry in the 1880s, having first leased a ranch nearer to Tomales.

Hans and his Danish wife, Annine Marie Johnson raised three children, two boys and a girl. The youngest boy, Henry, was the one to stay on in Hamlet after childhood.

The Jensens were old-fashioned and hardworking and their home in Hamlet was well respected as a clean and hospitable house, boasting goose down beds. Outside, white fences were re-painted each year.

I looked for homes of the era as I made my way along the bay. Geographical surveyor William H. Brewer's journal *Up And Down California* depicted no such luck in suitable lodgings in the area back in 1860 to 1864. "At Tomales there are several houses, but the only one where we could get "accommodations" was a very low Irish grogery, kept by a "lady" — he wrote. "The place was filled with Irish potato diggers, all as lively as the poorest whiskey could make them… The 'rooms' of the house were far from private, the beds not highly inviting and the customers twice as many as the accommodations. Drunkeness, singing, fighting and the usual noise of Irish sprees were kept up through the night."

To the north of the Jensen's home in Hamlet, sat a small, old cabin that had likely housed original railroad crews. Mayor of the city of Healdsburg, O. H. "Slim" Price (1946 – 1954) owned this rather notorious little party cabin for 30 years.

In due course, the Jensen's son Henry and his wife, Gertie had a son of their own, another Henry, to make things somewhat confusing. It was the younger Henry who built a new house on the bay across from his parents, still living and farming the original Jensen homestead and dairy lands at that time.

In the 1930s, the Jensens decided to replant some of the area's early experimental oyster beds and rebuilt an oyster house that had burned down by the old Morgan oyster farm site. The family started serving beer and wine to people passing through on a newly improved highway.

The railroad, built in 1874, to open up the wild coastal reach was dismantled after the advent of the combustion engine and the motorcar, in 1930. Still, the construction of the modern highway, followed by the opening of the Golden Gate Bridge in 1937 brought an influx of tourist traffic seeking fresh food and libations.

The enterprising family rented rowboats to visitors and tenants for duck hunting, spearing angelfish and collecting abalone.

Documented Miwok villages: Echa-kolum (south of Marshall); Sakloki (opposite Tomales Point); Shotommo-wi (near the mouth of the Estero de San Antonio) and Utumia (closer to the town of Tomales) were for thousands of years, home to many of the last of the Coast Miwok.

Henry and his native Coast Miwok wife Virginia purchased 40 acres of tideland property from his dad in the 1950s. They cut down a grove of eucalyptus trees and barns to expand the parking lot for their oyster enterprise and to house a bar and restaurant. It had been half a century since the family had first settled in Hamlet.

Customers flocked from all over the Bay Area, staying the day to steam oysters on seaweed and coals. Jensen's Oyster Beds and Restaurant grew in reputation and popularity, except for a closure for the duration of World War II presumably due to the sudden cease of "Pacific" oyster starters from Japan.

Virginia raised children, took care of cabin rentals, planted, harvested, shucked, canned and delivered oysters while her husband brought in vital income (and extra food for the family) as a fisherman.

Henry moored his 52-foot boat close by Nick's Cove, an historic seafood restaurant and cottages that remains a big attraction in the area today. When he wasn't fishing, he raised cattle and sheep.

Tomales Bay, Miwok for west, is in fact, a submerged section of the notorious San Andreas Fault. It forms the eastern boundary of the National Seashore and is, today, protected by the California Bays and Estuaries Policy. This deceptively calm looking waterway proves perilous in unpredictable conditions.

Henry drowned in the mouth of Tomales Bay in November 1971. His pregnant widow, soon to be a mother-of-five ran the roadside restaurant herself. It continued to be a big hit with visitors from far and wide and a much-loved institution in Fog Valley for many years. A devastating storm that destroyed most of the oyster beds in 1982, proved, in Virginia's words, her: "Last tally-ho."

"Back in the '50s and probably the early part of the '60s, we used to wholesale oysters out, delivering them to Nick's Cove, Tony's Seafood, Tides Wharf...I was in the oyster business from the time I got up until the time I went to bed opening oysters. In those days everybody wanted their oyster opened...you couldn't con a person into buying an oyster in the shell to kill yourself with...every one was opened,"

It all became too much for Virginia. Hamlet was sold to the National Parks in 1987. The tiny ramshackle village was demolished in 2003 and the Jensens along with tenant artists, writers, musicians and fishermen who'd lived there for decades, dispersed to nearby Tomales and beyond.

It used to be that to find a ghostly marker of the old settlement by wandering Tomales Bay's wooded edge for miles, you'd not find a single physical marker of the Jensen's legacy. Someone, I was glad to see, has had the sentimentality or wherewithal for history to hang a small hand painted sign, a nod to the past.

"Only locals know about Hamlet's long illustrious history as the center of the Bay's fishing, oystering and shipping culture," wrote

SF Gate's Judith Coborn. "But if you pull off Shoreline Highway across from a tiny farmhouse with the tongue-in-cheek sign "Hamlet Acres" out front, you'll spot a footpath worn in the weeds down to the coastline. There, it'll be up to you to conjure up some history in the rotting wharf and collapsing oyster sheds before neglect banishes it forever."

Onwards I journeyed into the small community of Tomales. A man named John Keys founded the town of Tomales in 1850 after sailing in from Bodega Bay on a long, narrow, now completely silted-over estuary in his 15-ton schooner *Spray* squatting on what was land grant territory and, with the help of local, Alexander Noble, planted the region's first potato crop fed to Gold Rush miners.

In its heyday, this isolated, though prosperous young town consisted of two churches, a grammar school, hotels, stores, blacksmith shops and livery stables. Though the loss of the railroad crippled the fledgling economy of the once-bustling town surrounding communities, one silver lining for preservationists is that the character and architecture of the town is largely unchanged.

Tomales today is a picturesque and popular stopping-off point for motorcyclists and road biking groups — leather and spandex-clad weekend warriors who gather on benches and chairs outside of tiny but welcoming hole-in-the-wall that is another top-spot of mine to stop off at, Tomales Bakery.

An old general store and historic 1877 William Tell Roadhouse are each a stone's throw from the bakery — poised at the crossroads to everywhere else and serving as many oysters and burgers as pints of beer.

The bakery is one of the best in the region, but don't make the mistake of missing out on the morning's fresh goods. This is a first-come, first-served kind of place, cinnamon twists, chocolate raspberry croissants, Danish fruit pockets and raspberry lemon bars fly off the counter and into the hands of a steady stream of early bird ranchers, fishermen, locals, bikers and tourists alike.

After 11am, coastal residents and visitors hope for the last of the morning's warm pizzette, raisin focaccia, quiche and soup of the day. On many an occasion, my rumbling tummy has met with a handwritten "sold out — see you tomorrow sign" on the bakery door. This day I was lucky, I made it into the bakery in the nick of time for a cup of tea and something sweet to see me on my way.

When I conjure in my mind's eye a Fog Valley character such as Irish-born George Dillon (1826 - 1906), I'm reminded of the classic American Heritage Dictionary definition of pioneer — "one who ventures into unknown or unclaimed territory to settle."

Intrepid George arrived in the United States in 1848, crossing the Great Plains in 1856 with his wife Mathilda. The couple settled on the western edge of Tomales in 1868, where they grew many of the potatoes I read about in William H. Brewer's journal *Up And Down California.*

The geographical surveyor had described Tomales at that time as being a place where: "Irishmen abound." He found this to be a decidedly cool region of low, rounded hills, near the mouth of Tomales Bay, near the sea. "It is subject to intense winds, so it is nearly treeless. It is the greatest place in the state for potatoes, both as regards quantity and quality. The number raised here is enormous."

After an uncomfortable overnight in a lively establishment in which William had walked in on the culmination of an Irishman's three day celebration of a substantial potato digging contract, he was clearly pleased to be back in the great outdoors on the long narrow arm of the sea that runs up into the hills, surrounded by what he described as "Picturesque California scenery. The bay is pretty and the number of waterfowl surpassed belief — gulls, ducks, pelicans etc., in myriads."

*Father Salvin
and
George Dillon*

*courtesy,
the Tomales
History Museum*

Two decades after George Dillon had established himself in the potato industry, the by-then affluent settler built an 11-room hotel and dining room out at the beach, mostly for he and his friends to enjoy the abundant spoils of fishing, crabbing and wildfowling noted by William Brewer.

In 1903, when George sold a section of prime beachfront he stipulated that it must always bear his name. A stagecoach ran from the beach to the train station in Tomales after the second owner took over. The former hotel looks like it could do with a lick of paint today. It still exists as a store and cafe serving beachgoers and a small community of 280 people, though it is somewhat weather-beaten and not exactly a tourist attraction in itself.

Still, Dillon Beach, the only private beach in northern California ($8 parking), remains my favorite shore-walking destination as it is for many of my fellow Fog Valley's inland residents as well as hoards of coastal-craving folk from the Central Valley and Sierra foothills.

Some 420 public beaches lie along almost 10,000 acres of the California state park designated coastline. Rare spots of privately owned historic beaches, including Dillon, are not as off-limits as we might imagine.

The public has the right to access the wet sand of the beach by walking along the coast, swimming, or boating into these areas. The state of California owns the tide and all submerged land seaward of the mean high tide land.

A ten-minute drive north on Highway One from Tomales to Valley Ford, in my mind, delivered me into a quintessential Fog Valley Wild West town, population 150 and one that is fully deserving its own pit-stop each time I pass through.

Gold Rush days are evident in its architecture, but the history of Valley Ford is much deeper entrenched.

"Here the old Spanish and Indian trail leading from the interior ranchos to Tomales Bay and the coast, crossed the Estero, hence the name which was given to the farm adjoining and subsequently the town," wrote Robert A. Thompson in a richly detailed *1887 Historical and Descriptive Sketch of Sonoma County, California.*

"It was the custom among the Indians in the back country to take two or three journeys each year to the coast for the purpose of feasting on shell-fish and gathering shells for the manufacture of Indian money... After 1857 they ceased their annual pilgrimages. Often previous to that time their bands might be seen filing along the way... from "El Capitán," who usually rode a lean, half-tamed mustang, to the old crones with high baskets hung to their backs by a band across their foreheads, loading with a promiscuous assortment of rags, old blankets, attole (gruel), pinole (a cooling, nutritious drink), papooses, cooking utensils, etc."

It was after many hardships in San Francisco in the Gold Rush era that two brothers from New York, carpenter/farmers Stephen and James Fowler chanced on what was then known as Big Valley, or the Valley of the Estero Americano — an unfenced wilderness. "Not a furrow had been plowed and a wealth of grass clothed the hills."

This former Indian trail would become a well traveled stagecoach route as more families joined the Fowlers in newly named Valley Ford in setting up ranch homes, a grist mill, lumber yard, blacksmith shops, two hotels, a bank, church and school.

In the summer of 1876 the North Pacific Railroad Company extended their road through the town and built a depot. Valley Ford residents were able to reach San Francisco within four hours. Previously, goods and produce had to be hauled by wagonload some 18 miles to and from Petaluma, the county's market town with its (first) potato warehouses and grain mills.

"Valley Ford had its own grain mail in the mid-nineteenth-century. Sanford & Stone received a portable grist-mill from the east and in the winter of 1852 and 1853 the first grain raised in the neighborhood was ground," said my Fog Valley farmer friend Deborah Walton during a visit to her lovely Canvas Ranch. Deborah, whom I featured in *Fog Valley Crush* is a chief instigator in a modern American revival of heritage grain farming.

The mill was small and the flour was coarse and unbolted, but they were kept busy by the settlers, who waited their turn at the mill.

Deborah grows 20 varieties of heirloom shell beans on her 28-acre Two Rock Valley family farm, alongside a variety of fruits and vegetables. She was the first to introduce Tuscan ancient grain farro to the region.

If tending her flock of Olde English Babydoll Southdown sheep and an idyllic menagerie of cashmere goats, Ameraucana chickens,

Maremma livestock guardian dogs, cats and barn owls isn't enough for this enterprising, sustainable farmer, Deborah is one of the founders of fast growing non-profit organization, the North Coast Heritage Grain Alliance.

I talked to Deborah about the importance of enhancing desirability of choosing whole grain options for our breads and products and supporting small-scale growers. She explained how vital early grains were in ancient and not-so ancient society for people to be able to settle.

Early grain growers in Fog Valley had found conditions ideal for growing in the region — and grain was what fueled the economy, especially during the Civil War when all grain utilized in the San Francisco Bay Area was locally grown.

The fact that heritage grains were so utterly pushed aside in the twentieth-century in favor of mass market grains of wheat developed and grown for disease resistance and volume, made for a long time, small scale farming of wheat, barley, corn, rye and buckwheat, peas, beans and potatoes, a thing of the past.

Studies continue to indicate that small-scale, locally grown non-hybridized wheat with an actual origin has lower levels of gluten than those found in mass-grown wheat.

With increasing numbers of people suffering wheat allergies, heritage grain growers rule the roost at farmers markets up and down the north coast of California. Their super nutritious breads and grain products are extraordinarily tasty, rich and nutty. "We know that modern wheat is making people sick," said Deborah. More and more people are turning to the old ways when it comes to grains, for a healthier lifestyle.

According to Deborah, The Petaluma Gold Rush bean has a thrilling history — introduced by a Peruvian whaler who jumped ship at the start of the Gold Rush and smuggled to Petaluma. This flat, kidney-shaped bean is tan in color with specks and stripes of maroon.

Deborah is one of the few farmers in the region to grow and sell this creamy, meaty and full flavored bean that she grows on vigorous vines reaching up to 10 feet tall. Her husband Tim routinely sells out of this high-demand bean at farmer's markets throughout the Bay Area. Deborah shared her Petaluma Gold Rush Bean Soup recipe at the back of this book, incorporating heritage farro, an ancient grain from Tuscany that she has pioneered in the region.

Similarly, an historic regional potato known as "Bodega Red" is back in big demand at farmers markets today, grown and sold by sustainable small-scale farmers in the area. The Bodega Red was a Peruvian varietal favored by John Keys and Alexander Noble in their coastal potato crops that eventually reached as far south as Valley Ford.

Narrow gauge steam North Pacific Coast Railroad extended 93 miles of track from a pier at Sausalito to Duncan Mills and Cazadero in the Russian River. I can't help but think of what life in the region would be like today if this vital lifeline threading the more remote coastal community's farming and logging industries had remained operational.

After the last of the rail service ceased running the population boom in Fog Valley's western reach was literally frozen in time.

I wouldn't have minded a rail option to get me to a book signing for *Fog Valley Crush* at the former Wool Mill and Mercantile in Valley Ford one stormy Friday night, a week before Christmas.

"Are you still coming?" messaged Ariana Strozzi, pioneer in guided equine education, the Wool Mill's founder, that afternoon. It had rained cats and dogs (and possibly, sheep) all day and the night before. The road approaching Valley Ford was flooded in its most notorious parts.

Locals know the back road routes like the back of their hands and though not advisable, it is possible to traverse the west country in severe storm conditions, given the right sort of sturdy vehicle and alternative route awareness.

I took notes and we set off, Timo in the driver's seat of the extreme mom mobile that we have finally let go of since — a battered but sturdy old Suburban that had seen us through the raising of three sons, soccer tournaments, camping, mountain trips, a teen band.

This particular evening I'd been invited to participate in a holiday book signing, cheese, wine and herbal tea tasting a couple of weeks after the launching of *Fog Valley Crush*. My friend and editor Elaine came along for the ride.

"We can make it," Timo informed, despite my ardent protestations, as he deftly bypassed Ariana's suggested alternative turn a few miles east of Valley Ford, from Petaluma, off Bodega Highway.

Much to my consternation, we plunged forward, slowly, into the deeply flooded road. A young girl in a compact car passed us, seemingly unflustered, water half way up her car's doors. A line of ranch hands were patiently awaiting their turn, rusty trucks ready to take on the elements. Though I was sure that we'd be stuck, my stubborn chauffeur drove us through and into adventures ahead.

Ariana's Wool Mill, a former store and art gallery in the center of Valley Ford (opposite the Valley Ford Hotel and next to the General Store), launched in 2013 and processed wool grown in the surrounding area. I've heard tell from farmers in Fog Valley that prior to the mill's existence, it wasn't unusual to see sheep wool dumped into ditches during shearing season.

Fiber artists in Fog Valley have been super keen to reduce their carbon footprint while supporting the local economy. And besides, the custom wool produced here provides alternative bedding, home and outerwear options, custom fabrics and wool felting that appeals to a public looking for healthy, authentic, quality goods.

Educational tours and workshops including natural dye applications, spinning, weaving, knitting and felting pulled in crowds of appreciative people, some of whom were simply looking for environmental bedding options, and drawn in by the Mill and

Mercantile's magical hum and charm. (Valley Ford Wool Mill since moved all operations as well as its store to Point Arena, Mendocino County, in February 2016).

No one other than a handful of local folk was likely to make it to the signing on such a night. I knew this, but didn't want to let Ariana and her team down. Besides, I enjoy Valley Ford and the prospect of a late Friday night supper at a less crowded Oyster Rockerfella's, the warm and welcoming restaurant in the Valley Ford Hotel, was to be our reward for making the trek.

Ariana, marketing director Kathleen, Mark, the master brewer of Tea and Trumpets, Timo, Elaine and myself made merry over a glass of wine, followed by tea and talk about the wonders of Fog Valley's modern artisan world. One woman popped in for something else from the mercantile shelves on her way home along flooded roads, sat with us a while and left with a book.

A little while into the evening, much to my surprise and delight, in walked four of my stalwart pals from Petaluma, who'd also driven through the most heavily flooded parts. Michael's electric car was new and he, being the intrepid sort to say the least, thought he'd test its measure.

His fellow travelers, Bill, Jane and Lesley thought this not the wisest move, but luckily, the fearless four, as we an hour before, somehow avoided being stranded. It was big smiles all around as this merry bunch of arrivals made our little party complete.

After touring the mill, we reconvened over the road, lured by the glowing lights of the Victorian era hotel, its old, authentic bar serving food from an only slightly more formal restaurant kitchen. If no one was getting into Valley Ford, no one was getting out and that night's food (five kinds of fresh oysters) and drinks (served in mason jars) was especially abundant and delicious.

We made it back from Valley Ford in the pitch dark, Timo and Michael caravanning a maze of back roads, not because they'd finally thought better of it, but because, by then, Bodega Highway's most flooded parts were officially closed off.

If we'd been forced to stay the night at this lovely little hotel, we'd have made a beeline over into neighboring Freestone the following morning. Freestone is a Fog Valley destination for some of the best-baked goods to fortuitously stumble upon anywhere in the world.

Several little Victorian-storefronts work together to put 27-house Freestone on the map, though it is baker Jed Wallach's Wild Flour Bread Bakery that draws the country crowds. Bakery staff work at a large brick oven in the wee hours with a view of fields and barns and cows for company — at least until swarms of bakery devotees begin their early morning pilgrimage from all around the county, Friday, Saturday, Sunday and Monday. The bakery is closed Tuesday, Wednesday, and Thursday and Christmas Day.

If you pass by at night, you'll spot the glow of the 550-degree oven. By four in the morning, wood turns to ash and flavorful hard crust breads, sticky buns, cheese fougasse, goat cheese flat bread and scones emerge to greet the day.

Freestone is a small, unincorporated historic community, a little under five miles from Valley Ford, positioned between Bodega, Sebastopol and the logging town of Occidental.

For a town that is a little under half a mile long and boasts a population of less than 50, this former stop on the former North Pacific Railroad has a lot of pull in attracting attention of west county tourism and locals alike.

Its unique Osmosis Day Spa is the only day spa in the country offering a peculiar, yet pleasant cedar enzyme bath experience — a Japanese rejuvenating heat treatment that I've enjoyed a couple of times over the years.

Mushrooms of Fog Valley
courtesy, Dominic Rivetti

Chapter 13

mushroom foraging

In late fall, early winter, sometime after Thanksgiving and the season's first heavy rains, Fog Valley's early settlers, especially those from Eastern Europe, but also the French and Italians, proved adept at seeking out edible mushrooms to supplement and enhance their seasonal diet.

Seasonal storms lead to an explosion of mushrooms along the coastal bioregion's forest floors. Mushroom foragers passed their wisdom from generation to generation to safely identify which ones were safe and delicious to eat, which ones to avoid and which ones were deadly if ingested.

Although the Coast Miwok had been using hallucinogenic varieties of mushrooms in curative ceremonies for centuries, pioneer families didn't have a lot of time for any sort of escapism of the existential type. Instead they were looking to augment their meal table with nutritious and tasty mushrooms such as chantarelles, porcini and, if they were lucky, crown jewel of mushrooms, the elusive truffle.

Truffles grow in California in the most secluded of spots, generally around 3 1/2 inches beneath ground near oak, beech, chestnut and hazelnut tree roots. The fact that they are best sniffed out by trained dogs or pigs make the pursuit of the elusive truffle all the more challenging for today's professional and educated mushroom foragers. Immigrant newcomers trusted their well-honed instincts initially in figuring out new hunting grounds.

Some of the most popular mushrooms increasingly foraged in Fog Valley to this day include delightfully named: pungent, orange hued candy caps; coral mushrooms; poor man's slippery jack and most commonly — black trumpets and hedgehog mushrooms.

Resourceful immigrant settlers had keen eyes when it came to foraging not only mushrooms, but also mustard greens, miner's lettuce, sea beans (pickleweed), quail eggs, seaweed, nettles, fennel, wild strawberries and blackberries.

These natural treasures are even more highly sought after today by the most prestigious restaurants in wine country. Two of my favorites, Sir and Star in Olema, and Chez Panisse in Berkeley, champion featuring foraged items high on their lauded menus, employing professional foragers who are licensed with the Department of Agriculture to harvest from the wild (and know what they are doing).

It is illegal today to forage mushrooms from most state, regional and town parks in California as well as from private property (without permission).

Mushroom foraging is allowed, by exception, in Salt Point State Park, a 6,000-acre expanse of rough, rocky Sonoma County coastline, 27 miles north of Bodega Bay, past Jenner and Fort Ross. There are 20 miles of hiking trails and six miles of coastline in this far flung park, considered the most abundant in the area for wild fungi hunting after first rains.

Members of The Sonoma County Mycological Society, a non-profit organization offer well organized meets several times throughout the rainy season with certified foragers emphasizing the hunting and foraging of and eating of wild mushrooms as a dangerous and potentially deadly activity if undertaken without proper knowledge.

Rather than join the increasing throngs of city folk crawling up the rain-slicked coast for an organized wintry meet, I accepted an enticing invitation for a drizzly hike on the dense forest floor of a sprawling private property a little ways over the Fog Valley border.

Rich aromas of composting grasses, leaves, pine needles, berries — layers of organic woodland life met us full-on as we bounced out of my friends Susan and Richard Villa's truck onto spongy, crimson-colored topsoils amongst the towering redwoods, pine trees and magnificent native madrones (Strawberry tree, named by Spanish explorers after a similar Mediterranean variety).

Hunter/foragers don't give away the location of their hunting grounds. Suffice to say, I was grateful for the generosity of my friends' time and their enthusiasm in taking me into their private wonderland of mushroom nirvana at the peak of the rainy season growth cycle. We met with Richard's long-time family friend, one of the property's owners, out and about on his rounds on an all terrain vehicle. We chatted about the history of the land and its popularity amongst Italian heritage friends and family for mushroom hunting over the decades.

This stunning, secluded woodland was drenched with moisture from the Pacific and the morning's gentle rainfall called for layers of clothing and rain gear. I found it hard to imagine the heat of a 100-degree day come August or September.

The ecosystem was at work, thanks to the welcome return of the rains after such a long drought. Mushrooms are revered for their powerful source of nutrients and for being hearty and filling, yet commonly mistaken as being a part of the earth's vegetable family. My foraging companions talked, as we tiptoed over leaf litter and mossy ground, of three separate food kingdoms — plants/botany, animals/zoology and fungi/mycology, in which mushrooms belong. Here, we were in a timeless zone — the heart of the matter.

Italian/American mycophiles (mushroom devotees) are not the only living beings to forage the forest for its gifts today. We found skunk, wild turkey and boar prints under ruffled detritus of leaves surrounding the large hardwood trees where the "gambones" or "big legs" mushrooms with their giant stems were most likely to be found.

"Someone's been here before us," said Richard, an experienced outdoorsman since childhood. Richard's dad, Al, a first generation Italian American raised on the borders of Fog Valley, hunted with the same multi-generational family friends, on their properties throughout the region.

Richard's uncle is the family's patriarch of mushrooming. I'd talked to him at the Villa's house at Christmas about his penchant for the large mushrooms he finds under the madrones, pines and live oaks on the property I'd been invited to explore.

These particular mushrooms, with their distinctive dark brown caps and meaty, swollen stems are likely members of the seven-species California porcini mushroom family and taste best, I'm told, when dried and added to soups, sauces and stews after several months.

We were as careful as could be to not disturb the woodland's billions of spores waking from their winter sleep, taking pictures of our finds instead of adding any potentially toxic varieties into an inspection bucket.

After an hour or so we stumbled on some plastic piping, discarded in a clearing, incongruous in such a place of secluded natural beauty. Richard explained how important it is to avoid stumbling into an outdoor "guerilla grow" — an illegal field of marijuana manned by trespassing, armed campers, during the optimum growing months of late summer into fall.

The problem has become so prolific in the coastal western counties, particularly those of the renowned Emerald Triangle:

Humboldt, Mendocino and Trinity Counties and neighboring Lake and Butte Counties, land owners monitor their hundreds of acres with tree cameras and frequent patrols.

Until the federal government regulates the nationwide growth and sale of cannabis, landowners and valuable water resources will continue to fall prey to increasing pockets of water-guzzling grows. It is a monumental problem in the region, likened to the Gold-Rush in its attraction of fortune seekers.

This time around, though, an international army of guerilla growers has infiltrated the region. Many of those on the ground in the thick of the forest canopy for months at a time were forced into the forest by blackmailing and murderous drug cartels.

All the more reason for me not to go wandering off-road and deep into private or national park property without an authorized guide. A downside to paradise. I didn't have to be told twice.

The friendly, ATV-riding owner of this particular property told me how he'd spotted a herd of 40 wild boar the previous weekend. "I'd ridden by a young boar standing by a tree," he said. "I stopped to take a look at him and around the corner came his momma and the rest of them."

Richard said if I saw one while we were out and about in the woods that morning, most likely I'd be alright. "Unless you take it by surprise or hurt it, chances are it'll take off in the other direction," he said. Another note-to-self — solo hiking for me in wild boar territory is off the bucket list.

And unless I am absolutely certain of a mushroom's identification, it is perfectly clear to me how vital is to follow Sonoma County Mycological Society's sage advice when foraging: "If in doubt, throw it out."

I wonder how settlers in the area figured this out for themselves, given that many of the mushrooms they encountered are native to the region. Trial and error must have been a tricky thing.

The mycological society has a slew of recommended West Coast mushroom field guidebooks on its website — sonomacountymycologicalsociety.com. Don't go out without one.

Mushrooms are fruiting bodies of fungi that live as a network called mycelia, made up of tiny branching threads in vast, ancient swaths beneath the ground. Fruiting bodies grow back year after year, hence winter hunting expeditions being assured of some reasonable success after wet weather.

Commercial foraging field trips and cooking classes have boomed in recent years, a cause for concern amongst environmentalists.

While we move towards an increased focus on fresh, seasonal food, depletion of natural resources is a real threat given how many more people live in Fog Valley today. In the late 1880s, peak period of mushroom foraging, there was, fortunately, more than enough to go around.

Whatever we source from the wild, it is wise to consider the philosophy of the region's first people and take only what we might reasonably need.

As interest grew in the nutritional value of mushrooms, entire American cookbooks devoted to fungi began to appear. One of the first was amateur cook and naturalist Kate Sargeant's *One Hundred Mushroom Receipts*, published in 1899.

As Tori Avey of *The History Kitchen* points out, Kate's work featured the sorts of tongue-twisting recipes that would be perfectly in tune today in J. K. Rowling's *Harry Potter* books — "Coprinus Comatus Soup (Shaggy Mane)," "Lepiota Procera Stew" and "Baked Tricholoma Personatum."

In her 1899 introduction, Kate recorded: "The general opinion in this country regarding mushrooms has been, that with one or two exceptions, all forms of fungus growth are either poisonous or unwholesome, but it is very gratifying to observe the change that is rapidly taking place in the public mind. Soon public opinion will acknowledge that it is an established fact that the great majority of the larger funguses, especially those that grow in fields and other public places, is not only wholesome but highly nutritious."

Despite the fact that expertise in identification is all that keeps us from eating a mushroom and death, humans have been munching on mushrooms longer than they've been eating meat.

Kate acknowledged the mushroom as "the meatiest" of natural foods and that the butcher's bill would decrease if mushrooms replaced a few meat entrees. This was progressive indeed for the day. The mushroom's nutritional values are commonly found in meat, beans and grains. Mushrooms are, quite simply, a superfood.

Many of the earliest mushroom recipes in California involved cream sauce and toast. Other recipes were more involved. In her 1911 book *Studies of American Fungi*, prolific cookbook writer and domestic pioneer, Sarah Tyson Rorer suggested a dinner theater of baking mushrooms under a glass bell. The bell was lifted at table so that the eater "may get the full aroma and flavor from the mushrooms."

Chinese herbalists have long since utilized the mushroom under careful scrutiny as an anti-diabetic, anti-hepatic and for skin regeneration and weight loss. Scientists in Japan have recently discovered that many mushrooms, especially the Shiitake more than double in size after a thunder or lightening storm.

I find it fascinating to read that mushrooms, protectors of the environment are being used in bioremediation around the world today to absorb and digest dangerous substances, industrial waste and pesticides.

To fully appreciate the wonder of the landscape and food chain of the foraging settler, I returned to the pages of the journal of William H. Brewer. In his 1860s account *Up and Down California* he captured the wild beauty of the place in his striking prose. "There are turkey buzzards, also a large vulture...owls are very plenty and the cries of several kinds are often heard the same night.

Hawks of various sizes and types are very tame, live on the various squirrels and gophers. I see a great variety of birds with beautiful plumage, from hummingbirds up.

It is in reptile and insect life that this country stands preeminent. There are snakes of many species...several species of large lizards. Salamanders and chameleons are dodging around every log. But insects are the most numerous. Ticks and bugs get on us whenever we go in the woods."

A lot of country homes in Fog Valley were (and some still are) little more than crude wooden shacks. Many of these early shelters are still visible, clinging on despite their abandoned existence, most often than not, next door to newer farmhouses built to replace them in the 1950s.

If you or I were to pry open a door to one of these shacks on a late December's evening, we would likely walk into a time warp of peeling wallpaper and curling floorboards, ghostly echoes of families gathered around the fireplace at Christmas time. These homes were constructed with whatever materials were available before paved roads and sanitation were standard. Still, they were home to several generations of family and represented all that was simple and good and comforting, especially in winter.

Gold Rush chronicler Alfred Doten, a friend of Mark Twain, wrote of a particularly appealing country "Christmas Spree" of his day. It featured: "A glorious game supper of fried deer tongue, liver, quail and hares, washing down with barrels of cognac and accompanied by violin, flute, banjo, clarinet and accordion music."

I imagine mushroom hunters of post Gold-Rush Fog Valley being especially pleased with a fine haul of fungi to add to such rustic repertoire.

Turkey buzzards and vultures are part of the same landscape
and foodchain that has changed little since foraging settlers arrived

Speakeasy exit in Volpi's back bar, Petaluma, CA

Chapter 14

the old home brew

Prohibition era (1920 to 1933) attempted to enforce its constitutional ban on the sale, production, importation and transportation of any and all alcoholic beverages in Fog Valley.

It would, however, prove extremely difficult for law enforcement to contain and manage implementation of the Volstead Act in such a tight-knit, innovative and conveniently remote coastal region.

Winter in this coastal realm was a bootlegger's most opportune season. Thick fog and rainstorm conditions in December, January, February and March made for splendid conditions for keeping a maze of country back roads impassable by law enforcement.

Every home had a fireplace blazing through the winter, a ruse for smoke from illegal stills throughout the countryside realm.

"The bootleg years on Point Reyes were rowdy and romantic," wrote historian Jack Mason in 1970 in his evocative book *Point Reyes, The Solemn Land.*

"Fortunes were made but few reputations tarnished, for Point Reyes winked at the Volstead Act."

According to Jack's and other's research, back when many of the bootleggers were still alive, the majority of action took place out on the ocean and on the beaches of Tomales Bay, in the pinewoods, along Inverness Ridge, on Sand Point, at Marshall and Millerton Point and on private wharves.

Just as some of the most remote forest terrain in Fog Valley and Mendocino County to the north are peppered with hidden marijuana grow operations today, barns and garages were swiftly converted into booze storage sheds during Prohibition. "Trucks fled down local roads at midnight leaving teams of baffled agents far behind," wrote Jack.

Perks were appealing and a state capital based liquor mafia paid well. Transporting rum and other booze from coast to state capital was the risky part. The rules were simple and played out mostly at night. "Every road out of the area could be used by the player (to decoy the federals) and was."

I took a drive out to the coast one late January afternoon, retracing these notorious players' possible routes, imagining myself, heart pumping in the moment of chasing a shipment cleverly diverted to bootleggers who were traveling in droves.

It was said that the Feds, who were posted in pairs and lived in a cottage in Point Reyes Station, considered nocturnal high tides in Tomales Bay to be far too dangerous, thus establishing the most common night time drop spot onto an awaiting, white sandy beach.

I stood alone on the rocks overlooking the wild Pacific Ocean at dusk to fully grasp this action-packed history of the area. It took the nerve of a highly skilled navigator to risk running the third wave in high tide to bring in the bootlegged bounty into the 50-foot mouth of wild and unforgiving Tomales Bay.

Horses and wagons were tucked away in secluded spots for transporting caseloads of rum and scotch that would later be unloaded

William Tell House, Tomales, CA

into the back of trucks or fishing boats headed for a places such as Chicken Ranch or Millerton Point.

The Feds carried an arsenal of pistols and long rifles. A white bulldog and a fleet of handcuffs were not much of a deterrent to deft bootleggers, adept at hijacking and murder.

Bottles of cheap home brew and smuggled Canadian whiskey were deftly stashed under floorboards of bars such as the historic William Tell, a traditional roadhouse bar and restaurant that still packs in the patrons in downtown Tomales, today.

"As soon as the agents left, up came the floorboards and it was "what'll you have?" all over again," according to Jack. "What you had was usually straight alcohol colored and flavored with Kitchen Bouquet (a browning and seasoning sauce from the 1880s, composed of caramel with vegetable flavorings)."

The community of Hamlet was particularly active during prohibition. According to the "Old Timer of Tomales" columnist of *Under the Gables* published by the museum committee of the Inverness Foundation:

"Even Henry (Jensen) senior was getting the Johnny Walker in, because during the prohibition days I'd row out to the end of the wharf and see these 40 foot boats parked there with twin diesel engines in them that could outrun any 'prohis' and there was always one of them anchored there. I was told not to go near those boats…they'd come in at night and they'd meet the boats so many miles out and bring in the Johnny Walker." By the old timer's account: "Everybody got their cuts."

Over 20,000 acres of established vineyards in the region were ripped out during Prohibition. Of the 256 wineries in Sonoma County whose vines had survived a devastating plague of Phylloxera (an aphidlike pest that feeds on the roots of grapevines) in 1878, less than 50 made it through the 1930s.

Home winemaking was rife — made from backyard fruit of vines grafted in the mid to late 1880s from the smuggled rootstock of early settlers (though Russian colonists had been the first to plant for wine grapes, followed by several thousand vines planted at the mission in Sonoma).

Retired *Petaluma Argus Courier Editor*, Chris Samson wrote an in-depth article on Prohibition in the Petaluma area in the newspaper in 2011, shortly before his well-earned "reinspirement" as a happily travelling minstrel (singer/songwriter).

"Petaluma was no different from most cities around the country during Prohibition," Chris reported. "People who wanted to drink alcohol had little trouble finding it."

Native Petaluman Wes Perry was a year shy of his 100th birthday when he spoke to the *Argus* editor about his experiences with bootlegging, alcohol smuggling and speakeasies in and around Petaluma during the 1920s. "If you knew where to go, it was no problem," he revealed. "It was word of mouth. There were a lot of them (speakeasies) scattered around town."

Wes spoke of barges loaded with up to 900 cases of Scotch whiskey being slipped into Tomales Bay in the dark. His dad's ranch, near Dillon Beach, was a convenient off-loading point for waiting cars and trucks to deliver on to San Francisco and Sacramento.

"His father, Frank Perry, was paid $1 a case for his help in the smuggling operation," wrote Chris. "The elder Perry also had a 50-gallon still to make moonshine whiskey."

Luckily for them, the Perry family was never arrested. "The police knew what was going on," said Wes. "As long as you didn't cause any trouble, it was OK."

Still, there were frequent raids throughout Fog Valley, despite police in the area turning an apparent blind-eye more often than not.

There were arrests. *The Argus* reported in 1926: "Two stills seized in autos. Owner is under arrest here." Officers grabbed two complete stills ready to be installed with much paraphernalia and several jugs of liquor.

"A favorite game was to "leak" news and decoy the Feds," wrote Joan Reutinger in a 1995 issue of *The Coastal Post.* "Say that the news leaked that a truckload of scotch was coming to Drake's Summit Road at 10 pm that night. The agents heard the news and were crouched along the road to make the arrest. But the shipment was diverted to Tomales Bay where a sailboat ran the booze to Marshall and a waiting truck. The next night the smugglers might reverse the procedure, leaving the agents completely baffled."

Fog Valley's Italian, Swiss, Portuguese and Irish immigrants were adept at making their own wine and whiskey and in doing so, most managed to keep out of the tricky business of smuggling.

In addition to the Sacramento-based mafia, Point Reyes had one of its own. According to Joan's article, a formidable Vincent (Pegleg) Lucich went from bad to worse once he started shooting at agents. "Pegleg murdered "handsome" but unfortunate hijacker and supplier to Marin County movers and shakers, Nick Sturtevant, as they sat in a vehicle parked along the road near Dillon Beach."

Jack Mason and Joan each wrote of an infamous black hearse that was used to take cargo to San Francisco. The hearse needed no protection because "a lugubrious looking driver" looked like no one anyone would suspect of transporting illegal booze.

Ranchers rented out remote country property to still operators. Life on dairy farms involved much drudgery, especially in the winter months. Liquor, despite the risk, provided an escape as well as much-needed extra money.

The most famous former speakeasy in Fog Valley is the small hidden bar at the back of Volpi's Grocery, still in business, though presently in operation as a bustling family-style Italian restaurant and bar, on busy thoroughfare, Washington Street, in downtown Petaluma.

John F. Mariani's *The Encyclopedia of American Food and Drink* defined a speakeasy as a place where: "in order to gain entrance, you had to speak in a low voice through a small opening in the back door and tell the attendant inside who it was who sent you to the place. The term itself (which dates in print to 1889) may derive from the English "speak-softly-shop" — an underworld term for a smuggler's house where one might get liquor cheaply."

Silvio Volpi and his mother, Giovanna bought the store in 1925. Ranchers coming into town frequented the bar for its tried-and-tested raid-proof escape door into the alley (still visible today). Volpi's Speakeasy closed early, avoiding common nighttime raids. Although Silvio did not make his own booze, his daughter-in-law Mary Lee Volpi reportedly attested to the fact that he and his brother were industrious distributers, "running booze" around the area.

"Prohibition, with its tremendous impact on the eating habits of the country, also had a great deal to do with the introduction of Italian foods to the masses," wrote Mary Grosvenor Ellsworth in her 1939 book *Much Depends Upon Dinner.*

Of pre-Prohibition and Americanized pasta, she declared: "We had cooked it too much, we desecrated it with further additions of flour, we smothered it in baking dishes with store cheese. Prohibition changed all that. Italians who opened up speakeasies by the thousands were our main recourse in times of trial."

Whole hoards of Americans, according to Mary, were thus exposed regularly to Italian food — developing a considerable taste for it. Nowhere more so than in Fog Valley.

"Food served in the speakeasies — with Mama doing the cooking and Papa making wine in the basement, was not quite the same as the food the Italians had eaten in the old country. Sicilian cooking was based on austerity, but America was a protein-rich country. The immigrants were happy to add these symbols of wealth to their cooking and happy that their American customers liked the result."

Meatballs, rich meat sauces, veal cutlets cooked with Parmesan or lemon, clams stuffed with buttered herbed crumbs, shrimp with wine and garlic, mozzarella in huge chunks and eaten as an appetizer — all foods of newfound abundance, developed by Italian/Americans and common fare on menus in several old-school Italian family-style roadhouses and eateries in Fog Valley.

Leland H. Meyers, who later served as Mayor of Petaluma from 1952 to 1953, made bathtub gin during Prohibition. "I have his recipe," his son, Bob Meyers, was quoted in Chris' *Argus Courier* article.

Bathtub gin was the given name for any sort of poor quality homemade spirit concocted in amateur conditions. Gin was the most popular, a mix of cheap grain alcohol, water, flavorings, juniper berry juice and glycerin. The style of bottle used was tall and thin to be topped off with water from a sink, hence the convenience of the bathtub tap.

Clever flavorings masked more dodgy ingredients.

Home brewed beer was every bit as popular during prohibition as it is today. Four commercial breweries were in operation in Petaluma at the time this book went to press and more are in the works. Dempsey's Restaurant and Brewery, Lagunitas Brewing Company, Petaluma Hills Brewery and 101 North Brewing Company welcome beer lovers from around the country to their popular taprooms. A fifth, Henhouse Brewing Company, moved north to Santa Rosa.

Uncle Sam says food will win the war 1911 to 1920
courtesy, the Sonoma County Library

Chapter 15

I'll be home for Christmas — wartime in Fog Valley

During my winter travels around Fog Valley, a sense of solitary timelessness enabled me to picture myself in this place at any given time in history.

Two of the periods I find most compelling in the past century are those of World War I and World War II. The resourcefulness of those left behind is what fascinates me most.

I spent a lot of time with my paternal grandparents growing up in the English countryside. My granddad, Frank, was a greengrocer by trade and found himself (lucky by comparison) gainfully enlisted as a provisions officer for allied troops stationed on the southern Italian coast in the Second World War.

He left behind his wife, Clarice — my grandmother and my dad, John who was a small boy at the time. Clarice ran the grocery store and delivery business to farmhouses in the East Anglian countryside around their home and business for the years that he was gone.

I loved to listen to their stories, my jolly and larger-than-life granddad figuring out the lay of the land and currency of a warm, foreign land, securing fresh fruit and bounty from the cliff-edged orchards of the Amalfi coastline.

In turn, I never tire of talking to U.S. military veterans who had spent time in the UK and elsewhere in Europe during the Second World War.

After immersing myself in the Gold Rush era of my adopted home, I found it incredible to consider The United States' involvement in World War I having started its bloody course within a single generation's lifespan.

It is staggering to consider that more than 116,000 Americans died in service to their country during the First World War. Over 200,000 more were seriously injured.

Less than a quarter century later, 405,000 more American servicemen (and women) perished in the Second World War. And over 607,000 were seriously wounded.

In terms of deaths per population, the First and Second World Wars claimed more American lives than any other hostility in U.S. history, except for the bloodiest of all — the Civil War.

I wondered what conscription would have looked like in Fog Valley during World War I. *Harper's Magazine* in 1918 featured a telling article, entitled: "Uncle Sam's Adopted Nephews."

A captain in America's new National Army: "went to the great cantonments (garrisons) expecting to see a great body of Americans. I found thousands of Italians, Poles, Russians, Rumanians, Greeks and others-all potential Americans, to be sure, but with a long way to travel yet! In each of several camps of 30,000 to 40,000 men I found 4,000 to 5,000 who understand little English and speak still less."

In 1917, the majority of enlisted men from Fog Valley's southern Sonoma and coastal west Marin were these sons and grandsons of immigrant settlers. The more recent the arrival of their families, the less time they would have had to assimilate to American culture.

There is nothing like a major war to unite a national patriotism. Ranch families had as many as 12 or 13 children. The Irish tended to branch out when they came of age, but the Swiss, Portuguese and Italians stayed put, farming, lighting fires, knitting, waiting for their brothers in the services to return to the fold.

The winter of 1942 was a turning point in World War II. Wistful, soft and melancholic American Christmas music of the era left us with a lasting legacy of an overriding spirit of nostalgia for home and tradition.

Bing Crosby's *White Christmas* was chart topper in December 1942. His next big holiday hit *I'll Be Home For Christmas* followed the next year. Judy Garland's 1944 *Have Yourself a Merry Little Christmas* captured the muted yet undeterred tone of the era.

With so many of the region's men gone to war, women took the reigns on running the ranch lands and businesses. The U.S. Women's Bureau reported that the percentage of women employed in agriculture rose from 8 percent in 1940 to 22.4 percent in 1945, a figure likely reflected in Fog Valley's farming community.

Four months after the Japanese attack on Pearl Harbor, in April 1942, *Farm Journal* reported on "women and children already on the farms of America" being ready "to train small town and city women for summer, seasonal and vacation jobs in the poultry, truck and fruit farms of the country."

The Woman's Land Army was formed in 1943 and never before had Fog Valley's female population known such strength in numbers of those who answered the call for farm as well as factory work.

The U.S. military had no choice but to develop training procedures that took ethnic differences into account.

This was a defining moment for the country and for Fog Valley and as a relatively recent settler it helps me put into perspective a palpable patriotism in the region, surprisingly unlike anything I experienced growing up in Great Britain, where so much of one's heritage and national pride was deeply ingrained and long-since taken for granted.

During World War II, numerous airfields were established in California for the training of pilots and aircrews of fighter planes and bombers. Operational squadrons and anti-submarine patrols were responsible for the air defense of the Pacific Coastline in case of Japanese invasion.

The closest airfields to Fog Valley were Hamilton Air in Novato, a few miles to the south (1947 to 1976) Cotati, a few miles to the north and Napa, a few miles to the east. A flood-zone area known as Denman Flats to the north of Petaluma was used for airplane practice landing. After the naval airfield in Cotati was abandoned after the war, runways were turned into a popular race track through the 1950s and 60s (now a mobile home park, shopping center and industrial park).

Supplies of Japanese-sourced Pacific oysters that had spawned so successfully in Tomales Bay were cut off during the war years. The bay came into its own with yet another use. It was a prime location for regular bombing practice. For years after the end of the war, fisherman frequently dragged dummy bombs from the waters of the bay.

Ranchers were instructed to black out windows along the coast during the Second World War for fear of enemy ships. Just as the motorcar had gained speed and popularity, gasoline was rationed and farmers and coastal dwellers drove around the country roads with their vehicle lights turned off at night.

During the wettest or foggiest months of an El Niño winter in 1942 this must have been a risky endeavor. Coastal roads are narrow and winding to this day, not to mention the steep drop-offs in many spots.

Margaret Matteri leased the Jensen family's dairy in Hamlet during World War II with her husband Tony. She is quoted in National Park records recalling practice bombing in the area: "They used to go by in airplanes and let bombs fall…oh, that was scary," she said. "They let them drop here right in the yard…that was dangerous."

The Coast Guard took over the Bay Hotel in Bodega Bay and patrolled Doran and Salmon Creek beaches with dogs. Tank crews rolling through the region were familiar sights, en-route to maneuvers at Bodega Dunes. Simone Wilson's *Sonoma County: The River of Time* depicts Bodega Bay as "A guinea pig for camouflage experiments."

Glenice Carpenter remembered planes flying overhead, blanketing Bodega Bay with smokescreen and on one occasion: "Deafening sounds of a battle somewhere off Bodega Bay early in the war."

Simone wrote that the shaking from the shore barrage was so intense that Glenice Carpenter's dad, who ran the Bay Hotel, hurried all of his customers outside, for fear the old place would fall down. Though the battle was never officially reported, locals suspected a Japanese submarine might have been intercepted near shore.

Eight hundred acre Two Rock Coast Guard Station currently trains 4,000 coast guard recruits a year. The site began as an Army post with a secret mission of listening for Japanese communications.

In her book *Point Reyes: The Complete Guide to the National Seashore and Surrounding Area,* author Jessica Lage described the impact World War II had on ranching on the Point Reyes peninsula.

She wrote of Drake's Head Ranch, which had started off as a dairy ranch, along with several other remote ranches in the area, having been converted to vegetable cultivation in the 1920s and 30s. First generation Italian and Japanese immigrants grew acres of artichokes and peas. Italian Green Globe artichokes were dry farmed with considerable success until war broke out.

Following the bombing of Pearl Harbor, Japanese Americans in the area were forced into interment camps along with 120,000 fellow Americans of Japanese descent. Their American-born children were put in charge of their families in the camps in what was one of the most fragrant violations of civil liberties in U.S. history.

In 1988 Congress awarded restitution payment of $20,000 to each survivor of these camps.

In the same vein, non-citizen Italian nationals, considered a particular threat along the coast, were banned from stepping foot west of Highway One, or anywhere close to the Pacific Ocean.

Reminders of the war were inescapable. Radio broadcasts, billboards, newspapers, letters and Western Union telegrams. Patriotic homeowners smashed glass holiday ornaments from Japan and Germany and turned to making their own Christmas tree decorations with paper, string and natural objects.

With limited labor to cut down Christmas trees and lumber needed for the war effort, American ingenuity came up with the bright idea of the artificial Christmas tree. At the same time, Corning Glass Company of New York began its manufacture of inexpensive, mass produced glass baubles.

Income was better than it had been for years. In 1940, 30 million dozen eggs were shipped out of Petaluma, peaking at the end of the war in 1945 at 51 million dozen eggs that year. Peddler's wagons were warmly welcomed out on the more remote ranches, hauling whatever wasn't rationed and was still in production — a cargo of pocket watches, denim, dry goods and notions.

Holiday season peddling likely increased the load significantly. Popular wartime gifts included pajamas, slippers, nylons (pantyhose), pens and pencils.

For the children, wooden jeeps and airplanes, dolls and military-themed, cardboard building sets were all the rage. Driving into and out of town was not nearly as convenient during the war years as it would be after the 1950s when multi-vehicle families were more commonplace.

Slogans such as "Food will win the war" urged the avoidance of wasting precious groceries. Any excess of regional fresh fruits and vegetables, too difficult to transport overseas was canned and stored.

"Meatless Tuesdays" and "Wheatless Wednesdays" were popular war time promotions imploring Americans to modify eating habits in order to up the volume of shipments to the armed services. The farming folk and neighbors in Fog Valley had far more access to meat and dairy than elsewhere in the country.

Large ranching families were better equipped to deal with shortages than city folk, already accustomed to hand-me-down clothing and shared shoes. In passing many of the old farmhouses still inhabited today, I thought of how hard these families worked in a time before the brink of the washing machine, spin dryer, central heating, refrigerator and television.

Household linen was turned and patched and used until it was turned into handkerchiefs and bandages. How many of us today take the time to patch a hole in linens or clothing? Who has a clue how to make a dress from parachute nylon, handle a soldering iron to repair a saucepan or kettle, re-web a chair seat?

In town, Fog Valley residents took turn on a 24-hour watch for enemy planes from the top floor of the Petaluma Hotel (built 1934). Special papers were required for workers to enter the silk mill (by then known as Sunset Line and Twine). Its manufacture of silk parachutes during World War II was an important mission for the community.

Between World War I and II home cooked meals were transformed from traditional to the new American norm.

It was the beginning of the end of the olden days in Fog Valley. Trademarked and registered manufactured foods that first appeared in stores in the 1920s grew in popularity — Wonder Bread, Welch's Grape Jelly, Wheaties, Velveeta cheese, Peter Pan peanut butter, Hostess Cakes, Yoo-Hoo chocolate drink, Baby Ruth candy bars, Reese's Peanut Butter Cups — Kool Aid, to name a few.

And yet, many festive favorites made it through the maze of convenience foods appearing on Fog Valley store shelves. Turkey (which was not rationed), ham, beans and chestnut dressing, a casserole of sweet potatoes with cranberry jelly, freshly baked bread rolls and pumpkin pie was every bit as likely to be served for Thanksgiving or Christmas as it is today.

Ladies Home Journal reported: "The Pacific Coast housewife has usually come from somewhere else. She has not established a typical dinner that is native to the coast. Her dinner may be eaten without after effects of discomfort."

One of these enduring holiday traditions remains that of the cookie exchange. I'd never heard of this growing up in the UK and I find the concept, first developed as fundraisers in the U.S. in World War I, all the more charming.

Dutch and German settlers introduced the import of metal cookie cutters in a wide variety of shapes and sizes in the late 1880s. Favorite family cookie recipes were shared in cookbooks across the country in response to these new-fangled baking tools.

Cookie exchanges or "shares" took hold in Fog Valley as they did elsewhere across the country as a pleasant way to gather and decompress during the holidays, to catch up with one another's family news and to take home a wide assortment of festive, homemade cookies. My favorite aspect of a Fog Valley cookie exchange is learning about family recipes from around the world.

World War II brought about even more new methods of food processing as manufacturers developed canned and frozen ingredients. More and more processed foods appeared on the scene seducing a hard working farming community with a promise of time saving convenience from decades of peeling, grinding, cutting, roasting and baking.

I took a closer look on the shelves of The Petaluma Market (my neighborhood store) for examples of familiar processed foods from the 1940s. Many trademarked and registered pantry staples of today were introduced in the war years: Nestles milk; Heinz tomato ketchup; Campbells soup; None Such mince meat; Log Cabin syrup; Rumford baking powder.

"Food Will Win the War and Write the Peace," was the slogan of a Food for Victory edition of the *Kerr Home Canning Book*. The booklet's good food habits very sensibly urged readers to: Eat meals at regular hours every day. Do not nibble between meals. Eat leisurely — chew food well. Avoid eating rich foods. Get plenty of sleep, fresh air and exercise. Drink a glass of water before breakfast and five to seven additional glasses during the day. Basic rules to live by today.

The first of the country's supermarkets opened for business in 1946 — Fog Valley's first full size grocery store was a Safeway built on Western Avenue in Petaluma in 1947 (the building burned down in 1955).

Leafing through the *Knorr Home Canning Book* from the 1940s, my mind boggled at the range and variety of jellies, jams and preserves, canned fruits, conserves, relish and veggies boiled in open vessels and put away for the war.

1946 was not very long ago, reported American food activist and farmer Joel Salatin. "Where was all the food, beforehand?" he asked. "Dear folks, the food was in homes, gardens, local fields and forests. It was near kitchens, near tables, near bedsides. It was in the pantry, the cellar, the backyard."

Farm shops are thankfully abundant in Fog Valley today and along with them, a renewed appreciation and willingness to return to a pre-convenience era for real, slow, honest food, cooked from scratch. I don't expect to see much of a resurgence in wartime staples such as jar packed pig brains, kidneys, heart, fried liver, pickled pigs feet and head cheese, though whole animal butchery has made a come back, teaching us the waste-not, want-not methods of our grandparents.

In our holiday cooking more than any other time of year, we reach back through the mists of time to those who came before us. Here we have come full circle.

"People, when they first came to America,
whether as travelers or settlers, became aware of a new
and agreeable feeling; that the whole country is their oyster."

Alistair Cooke

TWO

the people and their
winter celebrations

Susan Villa, mistletoe hunter

Chapter 16

the holly & the ivy —
English, Irish and Welsh

In 1958 John F. Kennedy wrote in his book, *A Nation of Immigrants*, "a 'typical American menu' might include some of the following dishes: 'Irish stew, chop suey, goulash, chile con carne, ravioli, knockwurst mit sauerkraut, Yorkshire pudding, Welsh rarebit, borscht, gefilte fish, Spanish omelette, caviar, mayonnaise, antipasto, baumkuchen, English muffins, gruyère cheese, Danish pastry, Canadian bacon, hot tamales, wienerschnitzel, petit fours, spumoni, bouillabaisse, mate, scones, Turkish coffee, minestrone, filet mignon.'"

The melting pot of Fog Valley is certainly a microcosm, with its own distinctive blend of cultural groups who came together and began to mix and merge beliefs, experience and ideas to shape its unique regional flavor.

There was an excitement in being a part of the opening of a new territory — "the last frontier." Its ability to absorb these various cultural elements and pass them around is what made it so special.

Each group of nineteenth and early twentieth-century immigrants to the region is as significant as the next. They settled in waves, integrating into a shared new reality in which they were able to preserve their own customs and heritage and, at the same time, thoroughly embrace the idea of becoming American citizens.

Between the years 1841 to 1860, over four million people arrived into the United States from other countries around the world. This marked a staggering 600 percent increase over the two-decade period leading up to the 1840s. The majority of immigrants hailed from Great Britain, Ireland and Germany.

While I've been writing this book the state of the country's current immigration policy continues to worsen. It is a mess. For a nation built on immigration, today's attitude toward newcomers — students, migrants or refugees, is a battle of complex racial, economic, ethnic and political division.

Some of this did, in fact exist during the time period of Fog Valley arrivals that we're exploring in this book. Over time, however, multicultural settlers brought with them an undeniable source of vitality, energy, talent, youth and global connections that serve as a reminder of the longer term, positive implications of human migration.

As a British/American myself, it is fitting for me to make a start with introducing my fellow English transplants and the sorts of winter holiday traditions they brought with them to Fog Valley.

The English have a long history of settling the United States — the first non-natives to settle permanent colonies at Jamestown, Virginia in 1607 and Plymouth and Massachusetts Bay in 1620 and 1622.

Many came to escape religious intolerance, others drawn by inexpensive land and economic opportunity. Two long centuries later, east coast migrant pioneers of English descent were amongst the first to pack their bags and carry their customs and cultures across country, traversing the grueling wagon trail from east to west to the final frontier.

During the 1860s, immigration from England to the U.S. swelled to 60,000 people a year — 75,000 people in 1872 alone. Settlement of the Great Plains, the building of transcontinental railroads and the industrialization of the country attracted all variety of skilled urban workers, miners and building tradespeople to America.

Many ex-miners found their way to places where their families were able to speak the language, settle in easily and comfortably and their children merged seamlessly into the community without any social stigma.

Steamers from San Francisco docked south of Petaluma bringing newcomers into Fog Valley. Stagecoaches carried riders overland into the countryside. Incredible to think of today, with soaring property values in the region, The Homestead Act of 1862 offered a modest farm free of charge to any adult male who built a home on the property and committed to the cultivation of the land for at least five years.

Settlers built basic farmhouses from the same local redwood used for the many ornate Queen Anne style Victorian homes we see so well preserved in Petaluma today.

Winter season called for Christmas decor in the homes of early English immigrants, though superstition dictated evergreens were bad luck if brought in before Christmas Eve. That worrisome thinking has long since gone out of the window, but the idea of bringing in the evergreens on the 24th is a festive one and something I like to do myself.

Holly was and is a favorite evergreen for the English. American holly (Ilex Opaca —the evergreen that gives its name to Hollywood in the south of the state) differs in appearance from the pricklier, red-berried English holly (Ilex Aquifolium) depicted so abundantly on Christmas cards and large, old specimens I've spotted around town in the yards of heritage homes must then have been specially sourced from imported varietals.

Likewise, European Mistletoe, ancient protector from evil, had yet to be introduced to America. It was (Santa Rosa) Sonoma County-based, U.S. "Wizard of Horticulture" Luther Burbank who first planted non-native mistletoe in his experimental farm in Fog Valley's neighboring Sebastopol area, in 1900.

Fossil pollens indicate that American native Dwarf Mistletoe, with its genus name "Phoradendron" — "thief of the tree" has likely been in California for millions of years. A natural component of a healthy ecosystem, all species of Mistletoe is, in fact, a parasitic evergreen shrub that absorbs sufficient water and minerals in severe cases of infestation to rob an oak tree of its nutrients after sending an excess of root like structures into tree branches.

"Burbank made the trip to Sebastopol several times a week," wrote Robert Hornback in the *Sonoma County Museum Quarterly*, 1983-4. "At first, he traveled by bicycle or by horse and buggy. Later, he used his car, a Willys-Knight, with the top removed to let in the air."

Luther's journey took up to an hour and a half each way from Santa Rosa to Sebastopol and the early bird he was, he arrived by five in the morning. New creations in fruits and flowers were offered for sale in a catalog of hybrids that drew attention from horticultural and botanical institutions around the globe.

His magical, marvelous, European mistletoe took hold in the region, reproducing itself on the boughs of prolific black oak, silver maple, apple trees, black locust, red alder and Fremont cottonwood. It is interesting to discover that it never traveled more than a seven-and-a-half mile radius of Sebastopol, due to inhospitable forestry to the west and grasslands to the south.

Luther Burbank's East Coast lineage traced back many generations to Cumberland, in the English Lake District. He would likely have been familiar with the Christmas customs of mistletoe and its romantic overtones, which date back to the Celtic Druids. Its ability to blossom and ripen in the most freezing of winter conditions earned it a reputation of sacred vivacity.

It was servants in the UK who popularized the custom of men stealing kisses from any woman caught standing under a bough of mistletoe decorating the house at Christmastime.

Though the mistletoe berry is not to be eaten by humans or our pets (serious tummy ache at best) it is an important nectar plant for bees. Annual proliferation of mistletoe berries is dependent upon bee pollination during spring.

According to *The English Home*: "The plant's green spheres are found festooned amongst the branches of trees, like nature's own Christmas baubles."

Gathering mistletoe requires a long clipper. If a ball of mistletoe falls to the ground it's considered bad luck.

The intrepid Susan of my visit to the Old Adobe and mushroom foraging in the forest set out with me on a European mistletoe hunt the first day of my having to employ windscreen wipers on my car, in months. Good thing British-born Susan has an encyclopedic knowledge of the region's horticultural history, a pair of instinctive eagle eyes (she was in the passenger seat this time) as well as a little over a half a century of making friends in all the right places when it comes to my more obscure requests for connections.

I'd messaged Susan a couple days prior: "Where might I find Luther Burbank's mistletoe?"

"Give me 10 minutes" she'd replied.

Two days later we set off in the direction of the Sebastopol area to visit a school friend of Susan's, who happened to live not far from Luther Burbank's experimental gardens. A few miles along Highway 116 from Stony Point (past historic 1859 roadhouse, the Washoe House) Susan's antenna detected a road-side preview — dozens of 50 pound mistletoe balls some 60 feet into the skyline, dominating the canopy of a row of untended trees separating some non-descript industrial units.

Despite or in spite of a "No Trespassing" sign, we parked the car a little ways off the road and I trotted along after Susan to take a closer look at her find. "No-one will shoot us," she said. I hoped she was right. My fear of being shot at was a recurring theme in our outings that winter. Mistletoe galore was hiding in plain sight. I might have driven around for months, hiking into parks and properties all around the region before noticing the obvious. Turns out that this quietly invasive species loves nothing more than the Sebastopol area's historic specimens. Apple orchards were particularly potent.

Fortunately for me, as I fretted about being caught in the act of mistletoe theft, this first find was out of reach. Back behind the wheel we drove on to novelist and horsewoman Ellen Wight's ranch home, a few miles out of the town of Sebastopol.

Ellen wrote a book called *Tales of the Express*, inspired by a Gold Rush era stagecoach driven by a woman disguised as a man. Even more compelling, Ellen herself joined Ringling Bros. circus in her early 20s, having hoped to ride a horse in the greatest show on earth. Instead, she'd learned to ride an elephant.

She never gave up on her dream of her own horse act and, after working for long time Hollywood horse trainer and Rodeo Hall of Famer Glen Randall Sr., Ellen developed Storybook Carriage Rides. This unassuming talent also lists amongst her accomplishments, seasoned historic costumer, historic doll maker and secretary of the North Coast Draft Horse and Mule Club, frequently participating in California's historic parades.

We made our way out to Ellen and her husband Martin's backyard. There, at the side of Ellen's home, stood an enormous western maple, most likely a Big Leaf Maple, "Big Daddy" of Pacific Northwest maples. Deep in the canopy several large balls of mistletoe hung from long wooden tubers that grew from the tree's branches.

Standing beneath and looking up into the tree, it dawned on me as to how tricky it is to harvest mistletoe and why beribboned little bunches are not sold on street corners much these days at Christmastime.

Ellen took the lead with an extended clipper, reaching as high into the canopy as she could manage without employing a ladder. The tuber attached to the most accessible ball of mistletoe was at least an inch and a half thick. This took some considerable perseverance in clipping until, finally, after about 10-minutes, the great ball came thundering down to land on a blanket of fallen leaves.

Our mission accomplished, we inspected the evergreen for its berry load. They weren't quite ripe, so we'd have to return in a month. Might the berries ripen in time? I'd read that harvested mistletoe ripens when left outside for a few weeks.

Martin, an artist with his own extensive repertoire of creative talents, showed me a portion of fallen tree branch that he'd carefully saved from a previous mistletoe drop. The section of wood where the tuber had been attached was extraordinarily beautiful in its natural design. He planned to make some sort of carved box from this rare specimen.

Given that Luther Burbank's mistletoe is found on 23 deciduous types of tree within no more than a seven-and-a-half mile radius of Sebastopol, a box from this specific find is treasure indeed.

Native Californians believed that clumps of mistletoe represented the winter retreat of the life force of the tree. Tragically, as much as 90 percent of oak trees in Sonoma County were decimated during the 20th century settlement years.

Unlike the redwood tree, the mighty oak made for less desirable lumber. Clearcutting of the giant redwoods (the ecological trauma of felling and removal of all trees from a given tract of forest) was considered the most economically profitable method of logging in the boom years. Oak in the region might easily have been extinct but for this.

California ivy, especially its berries, is, like mistletoe, poisonous to cats and dogs. As far as Fog Valley evergreen traditions in the mid 1800s, indoor decorations consisted of fragrant fir garlands, trees, cedar and aromatic fruits.

For English folk, Christmas dinner has long since been as grand an affair as could be afforded. Genteel settlers sat down to goose, chicken, a joint of succulent roast beef, or turkey as the highlight of a winter holiday feast. Christmas (plum) pudding was and still is frequently hand made in an English home on Stir-Up Sunday before Advent, allowing plenty of time for the rich concoction of beef, raisins and prunes to mature. Nowadays beef as an ingredient has disappeared in favor of a less savory, fruitier concoction. Each household member takes turns to stir the pudding with a wooden spoon, representing the wooden crib in the manger. Each stirrer makes a wish.

According to custom, a silver six pence or similar is tucked into the mixture during the making. The person who finds it in their portion at Christmas will have luck for the coming year. Stirring of the plum pudding is strictly undertaken in a clockwise direction, for luck. As a child I wished and wished each and every Stir-Up Sunday for a baby sister. As my mother was quick to remind me, I already had one perfectly delightful younger sister and a big brother, but I was quite sure in my heart of young hearts that our family was not yet complete.

One month before my 11th Christmas, my wish came true — the safe arrival of a second sister, Lindsey, as per my wish, 10-years my junior and somewhat of a surprise fourth child for my parents and an absolute joy to the family. I always say: "Be careful what you wish for," though in this case, I'm ever glad that I did.

Mince pies were made in Victorian times with proverbial mincemeat, fruit and spices. As with the plum pudding, actual minced beef has long since gone bye-bye, though traditional mince pies still contain suet (raw beef or mutton fat). Mince pies, baked by someone different each day, are traditionally eaten over 12 days of Christmas, thus insuring 12 months of luck in the coming year.

This explains the familiarity and frequency of mince pies on the menu at holiday gatherings in English heritage households today.

In turn, I hope that I've successfully passed along at least a tolerance of mince pies to my American-born sons.

After dinner, a homespun version of newly popularized English Christmas Crackers provided a spot of tabletop festive entertainment, along with parlor games and carol singing. Christmas Crackers made their commercial debut in England in the 1840s, manufactured by a man named Thomas Smith. These clever adaptations of Parisian bon-bon treats — wrapped cardboard party favors filled with a firecracker, motto, sweets and paper crown are only now becoming more commonplace in the U.S., aside from in the homes of Anglo/Americans.

Each year, non-ex-pat friends ask me "What is Boxing Day?" They wonder what all the fuss is about, the day after Christmas, when most American households are back to work, Christmas trees stripped of festive finery and flung out on the sidewalk for earliest collection.

Boxing Day for Brits is a big deal and given that there is a large ex-pat contingency in Fog Valley today, we have been fortunate, over the years to maintain an American version of this extended holiday celebration with close family friends.

Boxing Day, also known as St. Stephen's Day (the first Christian martyr) has charitable roots dating back to Anglo Saxon times. Charity boxes for collecting money for the needy were given out at church doors in Britain for centuries.

After the Church of England took hold of the country in the 1500s, charitable days previously spread out through the Catholic calendar, were more conveniently tied to this one particular day in the Christmas season — December 26th.

The day after Christmas was a suitable day for aristocracy in the UK to distribute gifts to servants and employees. Servants, who had worked Christmas Day, were given time off to return home to open their "bonus" boxes for their own family Christmas. Boxing Day became a second Christmas Day.

By the time English immigrants arrived in California during the Gold Rush, Boxing Day back home was a day of outdoor activity. Unlike in other European cultures, Christmas Eve was and is not much of a day for feasting or gift giving in England. It is a workday of preparation for the decadence of Christmas Day.

Boxing Day was, in the Victorian era, a time to take in fresh air and to exercise —and for the more affluent, hunting, horseracing and shooting. Though Boxing Day became a national holiday in England, Wales, Ireland and Canada in 1871, Fog Valley settlers wouldn't have had this luxury of a day off after Christmas.

Although it is typically a left-over buffet sort of fare in theory, my son Dom's godmother, Lesley McCullaugh's traditional English/ Irish/American Boxing Day dining table is resplendent with all of the favorite holiday foods from the old country: sausage rolls and cold cuts, greens and pickles, breads, cheeses, mince pies, Christmas Cake, sherry trifle, Victorian Christmas Cracker party favors for all.

More than a million Irish people died of starvation and disease during the potato famine that devastated Ireland from 1841 to 1860. Millions more left Ireland during that desperate time. An estimated 1.6 million Irish men, women and children traveled below deck by steamer steerage to America between the 1840s and 1850s.

Poverty-stricken and ready to work, incoming Irish on the East Coast found employment as laborers and housemaids. Those who came to the west found assimilation into California culture less of a challenge. Irish Catholics in Fog Valley arrived to a culture of greater acceptance than other groups and less prejudice given that many of their fellow immigrant groups were also from Catholic countries.

Irish populations in San Francisco had reached 30,000 by 1880 — 37 percent of the city's population. Political and entrepreneurial, the

Irish launched businesses and newspapers, manned the police force and fire brigades. Petaluma and its surrounding area's developing population was every bit as influenced by enterprising Irish immigrants.

Dublin-born merchant seaman Captain Tom Baylis was one of the founding fathers of Petaluma. Tom was raised in Australia. He came to Fog Valley one year before the Gold Rush began, optimal timing for utilizing his schooner for regular trade with market hunters (deer, elk, ducks, geese and quail), readily supplying San Francisco.

He and his business partner David Flogdell built one of the first permanent buildings, a trading post and store on the west bank of the Petaluma creek and later, the adjoining Pioneer Hotel. After his partner passed, Tom built up a fleet of schooners and steamers to provide service not only to San Francisco, but Sacramento and Stockton, too.

The enterprising Irish/American built three warehouses in Petaluma, the stone wall of one is still visible on the side of the Great Mill, in the heart of the city's downtown river district. Tom was charter member of the city's first hook and ladder fire brigade, amongst many other civic roles of leadership and first president of the library association after donating a substantial two thousand books.

Tom's funeral in 1867 was the biggest ever seen in Petaluma. Stores were closed for the occasion, flags lowered to half-mast. Bells tolled and the streets were quiet except for the solemn sound of the Petaluma Band, horseshoes and marching of militia units, Odd Fellows, a fraternal organization and the entire fire department.

Celtic Christmas traditions are charming and distinctive in their seasonal revelry. Those who arrived in Fog Valley to start a new life had plenty of countrymen and women to celebrate with, making it easier to uphold customs and infuse some of these into local culture.

No Irish home was complete without a display of holiday greenery and an evergreen door wreath especially.

Christmas Eve tended towards more of a religious focus in Irish/American households than in the homes of Protestant English neighbors. Work finished by the middle of the day. After dinner, the dining table was re-set for three, complete with a loaf of raisin and caraway seed bread, a jug of milk and a candle to illuminate the meal for the Holy Family.

At night on the 24th, before the family went to bed, door latches were left unlocked and a fire set to keep holy visitors warm. Candles were placed in each window, lit by a young Mary in the house. If there was no Mary (which would have been unusual in those days), candles meant to guide the Baby Jesus were lit by the youngest child.

Picture, if you will, a scene of flickering candles in the windows of a humble homestead of an early Fog Valley Irish family, lighting a path through the countryside on a dark Christmas Eve night.

Irish cooks prepared and preserved holiday foods weeks in advance. As with the English custom, plum puddings and fruitcakes were made ahead of time. A roast goose Christmas dinner differed with the addition of essential and tasty Irish staples, colcannon (mashed potatoes and greens) and Irish soda bread.

The day after Christmas, St. Stephen's Day, or "Wren's Day" was a second day of revelry for the Irish, as with neighbors in the British Isles. Back in the old country children and adults (Mummers) dressed festively in costumes of straw, visited neighboring homes to tell stories and dance for money and treats. "Wren Boys" knew how to party, rabble rousing on each evening for a full 12 days of Christmas, from December 26th to January 6th.

The soda bread recipe featured in section three at the end of the book is that of the late and lovely Maureen McCullaugh, our Boxing Day host-partner Michael's dear mum.

After being widowed in County Armagh, Northern Ireland, Maureen came to live her golden years with two of her three sons and one of her two daughters and their families in northern California.

When Prince Charles, first in line to the British throne and his wife Camilla, The Duchess of Cornwall, visited Point Reyes in 2005,

Granny Maureen was asked to bake her dense Northern Irish wheaten bread and soda bread for the royal couple's dinner at Manka's Inverness Lodge, where they were staying. Granny Maureen's soda bread recipe is featured at the back of this book.

Margaret Grade and Daniel DeLong of Manka's and now proprietors of Olema's Sir and Star, are friends of Maureen's family. The Prince, apparently, eats only unleavened bread. I don't think Granny Maureen from County Armagh ever imagined a scenario in which her old family recipe for soda bread would be served to the future King of England!

Winter carol "Nos Galan" — "Deck the Halls" is a Welsh melody dating back to the 16th Century. English lyrics were applied in 1862, just in time for the first Welsh on the scene to set up homes in Fog Valley.

Welsh workers had left their homeland in droves hoping to strike it rich in the New World during the California Gold Rush.

"Most Welsh emigrants in this period, were, in today's terminology, economic migrants," wrote reporter Gethin Matthews in an article for *Wales Online*, conveniently entitled "The Welsh In The Gold Rush."

This positioned the Welsh, because they were miners back home, particularly well for the gold mines of California. A Welsh information network was in operation that shared details of good job and mining prospects throughout the Welsh-American community.

To put things into perspective, the entire population of Wales was a mere half a million before the 18th century and a little over 1.5 million by 1881.

Irish emigrants to America in the mid 1800s outnumbered the Welsh by 26 to one and yet the Welsh influence on a modernizing America was significant in terms of the level of leadership its people rose to. It appeared that a staunch approach to sobriety and hard work paid dividends.

There were stampedes of exodus from some Welsh mining towns, a reminder today that human mass migration is nothing new. By the time many arrived in the goldfields, competition was at its most intense and the laws of supply and demand, as well as the high cost of everyday living in the camps, pushed fortune hunters out of the goldfields and into frontier towns such as Petaluma.

According to Sonoma County archives, though first Protestant services were held outside of Sonoma in 1849 with a Methodist circuit preacher from Wisconsin, the Welsh were the first immigrant group to organize and erect a church in Petaluma — built on the northwest corner of Keller street and Western avenue between 1865 and 1874, during the pastorate of one Rev A. J. Nelson.

Christmas in a Welsh immigrant household was (largely) a fairly sober affair, though a family-orientated one. Highlight of the darkest days of winter, an invigorating Welsh Plygain service — a time-old, festive matins tradition, took place from 3 am to 6 am each Christmas morning. While many woke early to attend, the most devout stayed awake throughout the night of Christmas Eve. Unaccompanied male voices sing their beautiful, soul-stirring three-part harmony carols to see in the celebrations.

Clearly, not all Welsh people were without a penchant for a drop of holiday cheer. Staff at the *Glamorgan Archives* in Cardiff published recipes for the sorts of long-lost Christmas feasts I imagined early settlers enjoyed.

Welsh Mince pies were made from cows' tongues with half pints of brandy and wine thrown in for good measure.

"To make mince pies take neat's (cattle) tongue, par boil, mince it fine, 2lb of suet chopped very fine, one pound of raisins stoned and chopped small, one pound of currants, one pound of golden Pippins (apples) chopp'd small, a quarter of a pound of loaf sugar, half an ounce of spice, mace, nutmeg, cloves mix'd together, beat until fine, put altogether in a pan and mix it well with half a pint of brandy and half a pint of white wine, when you make your pies – put in your sweetmeat"– wrote a Welsh gentleman farmer named Mr. Perkins.

It may well be that the Welsh in Fog Valley maintained the charming tradition of the "Calennig," a small gift of coins, given from dawn until noon on New Year's Day.

Groups of boys visited homes in their community for the Calennig, carrying evergreen twigs and a cup of cold water from the neighborhood well. After splashing water with twigs on whoever opened the door, the boys were given coins (presumably to go away and especially if the neighbors were not Welsh).

Irish farmer Patrick Lawler's ranch, Petaluma 1850s

Benjamin B. Sovel by a poultry truck,
Redwood Highway, Petaluma, CA in the 1930s
courtesy, Harlan Osborne Collection at the Sonoma County Library

Chapter 17

Jewish pioneers

Largest wave of Jewish immigrants to the United States was that of eastern European Jews who arrived between 1881 and 1924. One third of the Eastern European Jewish population emigrated during that time period.

The 1881 assassination of Russian Tsar Alexander II escalated the level of violence against Jews and anti-Jewish sentiment in that part of the world. Political and economic conditions created a mass exodus and 90 percent of Eastern European Jews headed for America.

By 1924, the Jewish population of the United States was 4.5 million. In 1920 there were 100 Jewish families living in Petaluma and its surrounds. That number doubled by the 1930s.

Petaluma's Hebrew Ladies Society formed in the fall of 1864 and incorporated as Congregation Society B'nai Israel by the state in 1871. It would be six decades until the Jewish community would have a place to gather in Fog Valley other than in private homes, public halls and the occasional church.

Author and historian Kenneth Kann worked for 17 years on his book *Comrades and Chicken Farmers: The Story of a California Jewish Community.* His insightful work captured a powerful and unique period in Fog Valley's cultural history.

He wrote of the Jewish cemetery as a small enclave in the town cemetery in Petaluma, where tombstones outline the history of the community: Sephardic Jews from Spain and Portugal from the mid-nineteenth-century, Eastern Jews from Russia, Austria-Hungary, and Romania through the twentieth-century.

According to Kenneth, pebbles left on one grave by visitors, were an Old World precaution that the body of the deceased remains in the ground. An epitaph on one particular tombstone — "He believed in justice" — proclaims the modern idealism of the eastern European settler, a community of farmers and socialists who raised chickens.

Fog Valley may have been a sleepy farming region, but it had great appeal to this American Jewish community of socialist farmers. Religious Jews in the area were the minority.

"Petaluma…known as the 'World's Egg Basket'…was also a community drenched in Jewish politics and passion," wrote Marek Brieger in *Jewish Currents.* "A place where secular Jews immersed in Yiddish literature and music and active in union life became a community of farmers, stood their ground with bigoted non-Jewish neighbors, experimented with vegetarianism and anarchistic ideas and assimilated to America without assimilating its more shallow aspects."

These youthful men and women created a new world.

Socialist pioneers arrived on the scene towards the end of World War I. Most had heard of Petaluma and its chicken farming opportunities from their cramped immigrant communities in New York.

With them, they brought their politics, Zionist organizations and newspapers. When prominent Jewish leaders such as Golda Meir

(Israeli teacher, kibbutznik, politician and eventual fourth Prime Minister of Israel) toured the major cities of California, they came to Petaluma, a place that symbolized success for Jewish people who worked hard and who had risen above victimization and the ghetto mentality.

"Like the early kibbutzniks, many of Petaluma's pioneers rejected the bourgeois institutions of marriage and organized religion," — reported the *Jerusalem Post*. "others experimented with vegetarianism and anarchist ideas, growing their hair long and living communally — at least until they started having children."

They settled on chicken ranches where they proudly maintained a world political and cultural perspective. Their children took over the ranches in time, though by the time a third generation was born in the mid 1960s, the chicken industry had collapsed and most left the area.

Political divisions were rife. Sadly, strife between the Jewish Communist left and liberal-thinking Jews would eventually split the Petaluma community straight through its heart. Some of the Zionist families moved on to pre-state Israel. Batya and Louis Menuhin, aunt and uncle of famous violinist Yehudi Menuhin were amongst this group of short-term Jewish Petalumans.

Not all of the Jewish settlers who came to Fog Valley became chicken farmers. Bill Straus, born on the onset of the First World War in 1914 in Hamburg, Germany, set out in 1934, with a group of fellow Zionist agricultural youth to take a series of hands-on agricultural courses in the Czech Republic. He and his mother fled an increasing threat of Nazism, traveling first to Palestine. When he came to the States to visit relatives in California in 1937, he fell in love with the countryside and decided to settle.

Bill studied agriculture at the University of California in Berkeley and Davis and bought a small dairy with 23 cows, on Tomales Bay, near Marshall, in 1941.

It was this innovative dairyman and his Dutch wife, Ellen, who, alongside groundbreaking environmental leadership and stewardship in the state of California, in particularly in west Marin, founded the first organic dairy west of the Mississippi in 1984. The couple's eldest son Albert Straus took the helm with Straus Family Creamery, in 1994.

A Jewish community center was eventually built on Western Avenue in 1925 for the handful of more religiously, traditionally oriented Jews who had managed to maintain customs and rituals outside of the political arena. The synagogue still uses the same "yad" (a ritual pointer used by a reader to follow the text during the Torah reading from parchment scrolls) that the community has used since 1861.

Few left-wingers were likely to have celebrated religious holidays, although the festival of "Tu B'shevat" (the 15th of the month of Shevat — January or February), New Year for the trees may have held more appeal to the socialist farming community.

Roots of this celebration trace back to the date historically chosen for calculating the agricultural cycle of taking tithes from the produce of trees, brought as first-fruit offerings to the Temple in Jerusalem.

Over time, Tu B'shevat represented an ecological holiday that reminded Jewish people of their connection to the earth. During Tu B'shevat seder it was traditional to eat from trays of "shiv'at ha'minim" (seven species endemic to the Land of Israel): wheat, barley, grapes, figs, pomegranates, olives and dates.

Zionist Jewish pioneers in Fog Valley would not have had too much trouble stocking their homes with fruits and nuts.

In the winter, usually December, traditional Jewish families in Fog Valley celebrated the festival of Hanukkah, The Festival of Lights, an eight-day period marking the time when Jewish people (led by Judah the Maccabee) reclaimed the Temple in Jerusalem from the Syrians in 164 B.C.E. (Before the Common Christian Era).

Eight candles of the menorah candle holder represent the Jews having found a small container of oil in the rubble of the desecrated synagogue, enough to give sufficient light for eight days.

Hanukkah starts on the 25th day of Kislev in the Hebrew calendar, between late November to late December in the Gregorian calendar. Celebrations kick off at sundown the day before the first day with the lighting of the first candle.

Early Jewish settlers in Fog Valley gathered friends and family into their homes to light the menora, sing songs, play dreidel (a wooden gambling toy), exchange gifts and feast of traditional foods. The Friday evening of Hanukkah marked, as it does for many more Jewish residents today, a main meal of beef brisket, fried foods such as potato latkes, (ever-present) chicken and an array of homemade Kosher treats.

An emphasis on gifts for children developed over time in Jewish/ American families. For those growing up second and third generation in a culture dominated by Santa Claus and his sleigh load of Christmas toys, Hanukkah's seasonal timing proved ideal in not leaving anyone out of winter's peculiar magic.

Spolini Family at their dairy ranch in Valley Ford, CA, 1910
courtesy, the Sonoma County Library

Chapter 18

an Italian feast

Over 75 percent of Italian immigrants who came to the United States in the late 1880s hailed from Mezzogiorno, an impoverished region of Southern Italy where its people lived mostly in clustered hill towns and villages.

It was these giornalieri (farm laborers) and contadini (share-croppers), living the most meager of existences, who packed their few belongings and sailed for America.

By the 1860s, California had become home to more Italians than in any other state in the country. The vast majority of three thousand giornalieri, contadini and their families in California at that time started off in urban Italian communities, including North Beach in San Francisco.

Many families migrated north from San Francisco to Fog Valley and the coast in search of a more familiar rural turf. This was a "kin and village" migration, as with so many of neighboring European immigrant groups.

This period of mass migration escalated in the 1880s. Between 1876 and 1924, four-and-a-half million Italians arrived through Ellis Island in New York.

Italians arriving in Petaluma in the late 1880s found employment at the one silk mill west of the Mississippi. The Carlson-Currier Silk Manufacturing Company opened its doors in a sprawling, multi-windowed brick building constructed in an industrial area adjacent to the city's old waterfront area.

The building, shuttered in 2006, is listed on the National Register of Historic Places. For almost a decade, several projects designed to save it from collapse failed to find sufficient funding. Finally, in February of 2016, news reports confirmed that most recent plans to transform the derelict mill into a 76-room boutique hotel have been approved.

Immigrant workers (mostly women) walked miles from around the area to take long shifts at machines manufacturing silk thread and fine sewing products for a western market.

Italian families stuck together for solidarity. The heart of the community was undoubtedly "La Famiglia."

"Economically and socially, the family functioned as a collective enterprise, an all-inclusive social world," wrote Leonard Covello, in *The Social Background of the Italo-American School Child.*

In a nutshell: "Parents expected children to assist them at an early age by providing gainful labor and family values, stressed respect for the elderly, obedience to parents, hard work and deference to authority."

Most of the Italians who arrived in Fog Valley during the Gold Rush, had no education beyond eight or nine years old. In fact, my own Italian father-in-law left school in Caserta, capital of the Campania region, in the 1940s, at around that same age.

The people who left southern Italy were frugal and ate simply, based on whatever vegetables and grains they had grown for their natural diets in the specific region of their birth. Establishing a homestead in Fog Valley would not have been as big a hardship dietary-wise for the Italians as it was for other cultures, given the Italian propensity to create a wealth of fresh nourishment from so little.

Family-style Italian eateries in Fog Valley are traditional and date back generations. Yet the menu we have come to expect as the norm is an Italian/American development based on Neapolitan heavily spiced tomato dishes and does not reflect how most Southern Italians ate as new immigrants. Pasta and pizza was nowhere near commonplace amongst many incoming Southern Italians.

Fava beans, peas, corn, onion, garlic, lentils, wild greens, chicory roasted for coffee and olive oil worked wonders in a peasant kitchen. As soon as they arrived in Fog Valley, the Italians set to work, planting backyard gardens. They built rudimentary outdoor ovens, raised cows and chickens and goats. Meat was eaten sparingly. Regional dishes still varied tremendously, especially at Christmastime.

A first Roman Catholic Church for Petaluma was built in 1885 and moved to Baker Street in 1925, to make room for the present St. Vincent de Paul Church in downtown Petaluma, which was opened its door in 1928. The historic Baker Street church building has been well maintained by today's Elim Lutheran congregation.

According to *The Catholic San Francisco* publication, it was the coastal Italians of Fog Valley who were the first to organize a central Catholic gathering place in the region.

"In 1860 the Church of the Assumption was built in Tomales on land donated by John and Kate Miller Keys. Archbishop Joseph Alemany, first Archbishop of San Francisco, dedicated the church that same year with first pastor, Father Louis Rossi."

In 1897, a second, stone church designed by architect Frank Shea was built during the pastorate of Father John Rogers. It was destroyed by the 1906 earthquake and parishioners returned to the redwood frame building (with its Tiffany glass windows) that is still in use today.

Christmas celebrations began for Fog Valley's early Italian community eight days before the 25th with a series of prayers and church services called "Novenas." Long before "spare the air days," a "Creppo" — Yule Log burned in the hearth of each family home.

Christmas Eve called for no meat and no dairy. A seafood meal more than sufficed, served before Midnight Mass. Our modern propensity for traditional Fog Valley Christmas Eve Cioppino and fresh crab suppers hail from this classic Catholic custom.

Types of fish and how they were prepared depended upon regional heritage. The "Festa dei Setti Pesci" — Feast of the Seven Fishes (representing seven days of creation) was popularized in the region in the 1880s when many Italian families moved into Fog Valley and out to the coast as fishermen from San Francisco. This Christmas Eve meal traditionally featured baccala (salted cod), clams, calamari, eel and sardine.

After mass, Italian families looked forward to a slice of festive, airy fruit bread, Panettone (popular today) and a cup of hot chocolate. Panettone is one of my favorite Italian holiday treats, the origin of which dates back to the Middle Ages. On Christmas Eve, a large piece of wood was traditionally placed in the fireplace as three-wheat breads were served to guests by the head of the family. A slice was reserved for the following year as a sign of continuity.

Christmas Day dinner, after the 25th was declared as a holiday, was and still is, in Italy, served in the middle of the day. A typical traditional Italian Christmas Day feast lasts all afternoon, as I have experienced myself on many a joyful occasion with my in-laws over the years and consists of a starter of mama's best cannelloni, lasagna or gnocchi, a main course of roast lamb or stuffed and rolled braciole, green salad, fresh fruit, nuts and cannoli, plenty of wine and espresso with dessert.

Epiphany (January 6th) was and is of even more significance to Italians than Christmas Day. That night, a kindly old witch known as La Befana fills stockings hung on the fireplace, with gifts. In time, the youngest Italian/Americans whose parents settled Fog Valley would come to accept Babbo Natale or Santa Claus as a Christmas Eve substitute over La Befana.

Grapevines that had found their way to Fog Valley as old-world rootstock, smuggled in by the Italians, Swiss, French, German and other immigrant settlers, mostly in the 1880s made for good house wine – zinfandel, barbera and sangiovese, was hand tended, hand pruned and hand harvested, crushed, pressed and bottled (as with syrah grapes grown in my own backyard).

Rocky soils from the region's ancient volcanic activity stressed the vines, producing smaller berries than these rustic home winemakers were used to, but the new world wine was naturally plentiful and good, as was the produce, meat and dairy products.

Fog Valley proved a perfect fit for Italians, then and now. Ask around the region for the most prominent Italian/American dairy family and the Benedettis of Clover Organic Farms and Clover Stornetta Farms is consistently top of the list in local lore as first family of farming.

Company founder, the gregarious Gene Benedetti was the embodiment of an immigrant son, born in the region to Italian parents, Giocondo and Pia Benedetti and raised on the family's Sonoma County dairy farm.

A Petaluma High School graduate of 1938, football star and celebrated World War II Navy hero, Gene was awarded the Purple Heart for wounds and the Silver Star for valor in combat, including his role in the first wave attacking Omaha Beach during D-Day invasions.

When the family patriarch passed away in 2006, he was remembered for his sportsmanship and bravery, his insatiable love of his country, a characteristic style of innovation and tradition in business and also for his pipe, his partiality for martinis on the rocks, his bone crushing handshake and a loud, hearty laugh.

Clover's cheerful mascot "Clo" the cow is the region's most recognized business mascot, cleverly depicted in contemporary cartoon form on billboards, milk cartons and a fleet of distinctive trucks.

Clover was the first dairy in the west to offer milk that was certified free of the synthetic growth hormone rBST that increases milk production and also the first dairy in the United States to be certified (in 2000) by the American Humane Association (AHA) for its animal welfare program, American Humane Certified.

A third generation of the prominent Benedetti clan continues to blaze a trail of social, industrial and political leadership in the region. Clover Stornetta Farms president and chief executive officer, Marcus Benedetti and several other family members within the executive branch of the company are lauded for their unique brand of progressive conservatism (a preference for maintaining tradition) when it comes to product development and innovation while, at the same time, holding tight to their grandfather's legacy.

Clover brand processes a range of milk products (including several new cheeses) from four organic and 11 "natural" dairy farms in Marin and Sonoma counties.

Toscano Hotel bar, Sonoma

Portuguese-style goat cheese aging room at the Pacheco family's
Achadinha Cheese Company, Chileno Valley, CA

Chapter 19

Portuguese dairy farming influx

Portuguese immigrants arrived in the region in the mid 1880s, enlisted by fleets of Yankee whaling ships from Maine, New Hampshire, Massachusetts, Connecticut, Rhode Island, New York, New Jersey and Delaware.

The whaling ships had made their port of call for food, water and supplies in the fishing villages of the Azores islands, a self-governing region of Portugal forming an archipelago in the mid-Atlantic.

During the height of the Yankee whaling industry in 1846, skilled young Portuguese sailors navigated their way around Cape Horn, around the tip of South America in search of whales on the California coast.

The American fleet of ships, barks, schooners and brigs had risen to 742 vessels by that time — big business and a ticket out into the world for Portuguese villagers.

Whales were being harvested (ravaged) from oceans around the world. This global fishing industry employed tens of thousands of people. To serve the fleet American consuls were installed in the Azores and in other key fishing ports around the globe.

Great whales roamed the oceans in search of food. Lookouts kept watch on the mastheads of ships from sunset to sundown, 100 feet up, secured only by brass hoops, scanning the sea for the spout.

This was not only a ruthless and brutal industry, it was an extraordinarily dangerous one. According to The Yankee Whaling Museum: "While it was the business of whalers to hunt and kill whales, sometimes a whale would fight back.

Among the more famous of the several incidents of whales attacking whaling vessels are those of the ship *Essex* of Nantucket in 1820, the ship *Pocahontas* of Tisbury in 1850, the ship *Ann Alexander* of New Bedford in 1851, and the bark *Kathleen* of New Bedford in 1902."

Little wonder the Portuguese who made it to California were quick to settle in scenic and temperate Sausalito, north of the Golden Gate. Its sweeping landscape and abundant waters reminded them of home. Sardine and anchovy fishermen followed the whalers' course, as did boat builders and the largest group from the Azores, dairymen from the cow and cheese famous islands, most of whom had never stepped foot on the mainland of Portugal itself.

Hard working dairy families soon set their sights to the north on the rolling hills of west Marin and southern Sonoma County. By the turn of the century the North Bay dairy industry was almost exclusively built on those who hailed from the long, slender, cliffy Azore island, Ilha São Jorge (São Jorge cheese has long since been the most important part of the island's economy).

In the 1940s there was a popular saying in the Bay Area that a traveler from the Golden Gate to Petaluma would never lose site of a Portuguese dairy.

This culture is still very evident today, despite the emergence of the Central Valley as mass-market dairy production center for northern California. Most of the heritage dairy farms that the Portuguese toiled to develop over the years operate as organic and have stayed within the families through multiple generations.

"This is a lifestyle — we don't take vacations," announced a no-nonsense Donna Pacheco, matriarch of her Fog Valley family's 230-acre pasture-based farm and head cheesemaker of the farm's saving grace — rustic, on-site Achadinha Cheese Company.

Donna's computer system had crashed the morning of my visit to the family's Chileno Valley ranch, a 10-minute drive out west through rolling hills of rural West Petaluma.

With 70 farmers markets to coordinate for sales of her aged goat and cow and goat milk cheeses around the outposts of California that week alone, Donna appeared perfectly calm and collected, poised even, as she welcomed me and a small, wide-eyed crowd of around two dozen cheese lovers, into a barn-like party room that stands sentinel behind her weathered Victorian farmhouse.

I was glad to get a glimpse of the inside of the Pacheco clan's eclectic social center and gathering place, home base for the family, farm hands and country neighbors to relax, kick their muddy boots off, unwind and watch a game on the big screen.

The Pacheco clan's late patriarch emigrated from Achadinha — a small parish in the Portuguese archipelago of the Azores, establishing himself in Fog Valley as the first of three generations of dairy farmers in the family in the 1950s.

Donna and her husband Jim have four children, the oldest farming full time and younger siblings still mostly in school, yet up with the larks for 3:30 a.m. daily rounds of goats, jersey cows, beef cows, horses, pigs, sheep and chickens.

William Pacheco (whom Donna and Jim's oldest son is named for) first farmed in the area out at Bodega Bay in the 1950s.

"He bought this farm for $25,000 in 1969," said Donna. "It was one of more than 300 dairy farms in the region. Today there are only 50."

"Reality today is that if you process your own product, you just might make it," said Donna, who introduced herself as a city-girl and though she'd grown up in the mid-west, she hadn't envisioned life as a farmer's wife prior to falling for a charming and persuasive California dairy farmer whom she'd met in a bar.

Fast-forward two and a half decades and Donna's constant commitment to reinventing the (cart) wheel sorted the wheat from the chaff. Here's a farmer's wife who is by default and determination, leader of the pack. She has successfully managed to keep the family in situ on their beloved land through equal measures sheer grit and unrelenting spirit.

Hers is a story of old fashioned farm family values meets-market savvy, modern technology and constant direct outreach with customers through multiple farmer's markets.

The Pachecos bought goats after selling their prize herd of milking cows in 1997. Small production of cow's milk for co-ops had fallen prey to super sized dairies of the central valley dramatically undercutting prices per gallon. It wasn't long before these same big producers followed suit, producing an increasingly popular commodity of goat's milk. Donna and her family could not compete with 10,000 goat-strong dairy prices. They cut their goat herd in half and set about making cheese.

"I'd just had my fourth child, it was a very interesting ride," said Donna, whose first experimental batches of cheese were not good. "I figured it out over time," she said. "If you're not educated in what's coming up, then you're not going to make it." The family sold off development rights to their land so that it will forever remain farmland or open space to stay afloat and to build out their compact cheese factory.

Donna's aged and nutty pasteurized goats milk, Capricious, won "Best in Show" at the American Cheese Society event in 2002. In 2005 it was named one of *Saveur's* "50 favorite cheeses in the United States."

A seasoned multi-tasker, she talked as she set out samples for later of her prize cheeses on a long, hand-hewn redwood table with mismatched vintage chairs.

Two ducks, seemingly oblivious to our visit, quacked and splashed in a tiny concrete pond in an otherwise unadorned rocky courtyard. Donna led us from the party room over to her cheese making facility, where she'd explain how she and her offspring also make Broncha, a gentle table cheese inspired by a Portuguese family recipe and infused with the subtle flavors of the brewers grains they feed to their goats.

A fresh style Feta soaked in a sea salt brine is delivered to market within four days. Her Fresh Cheese Curd morsels are, by popular demand, sold up and down the state, flavored with herbs for Herbie Curd, garlic for Lonely Goat, Sweet Mesquite for Smok'in Goat and cayenne and crushed red peppers for Hot Hilda.

I was a little taken aback on first impression, as I'd driven up a dirt road into a makeshift parking area by the side of the cheese making operation. It had clearly weathered through decades of winter's mud and summer's dust. As with most ranch properties in Fog Valley, you'd need a pair of rose-colored glasses to paint a glossy, bucolic sheen on the harsh realities of keeping the farm going through a recession, a four-year drought and an ever-changing landscape of fluctuating dairy trends and prices.

I was raised in a farming region in the UK where the fortunate, landed-gentry drove around in shiny Range Rover vehicles, decked out to the nines in tweeds and shirts and ties and felt hats. Their spacious, stone farmhouses appeared, to me, the epitome of country comfort and charm.

I'm sure there was a lot more than met the eye in hard work and business savvy for such a warm and fuzzy farming façade, but here in Fog Valley, farming, since its Gold Rush days, is a visibly hard scrabble lifestyle for those who continue to strive.

"Wash your shoes in the footbath on the way in," Donna informed as we stepped into a contrast in worlds. Inside the cheese making facility all was gleaming and pristine. Shining stainless steel production equipment and temperature controlled cheese aging rooms with floor to ceiling wooden racks elevated the tired-old family farm exterior to state-of-the-art, farmstead cheese factory.

I was smitten and in awe of this hard working visionary who leaves her bed in the middle of the night in her pajamas to check on her cheese. "Don't worry, I get my sleep," she assured. Unlike her husband, who doesn't go back to bed after a daily 3 in the morning start, Donna needs her rest and makes sure she gets it.

Jim was raised attending every farm show. "Instead of playing school sports, he learned how to artificially inseminate cows at age 14," said Donna, who, with her husband, has found time for their four children to participate in both 4H and sports.

Though the family drinks unpasteurized milk from its cows and goats, Donna spoke candidly of current trends. Tension exists in today's market between those who want access to raw milk and current government regulations thwarting that access.

"My children were born and raised here, their immune systems know nothing else, while I promote unpasteurized products, there is no way that I would take the risk of someone else's immune system imbalance by selling to them," she said.

Donna explained to a rapt audience how vital a balanced diet is to our frequently compromised digestive systems. The same thing goes for her goats, who enjoy a regular dose of fermented probiotic Kombucha scoby in their whey trough.

"We all benefit from the symbiotic culture of bacteria and yeast," said Donna. I'm a fairly recent convert to the health benefits and zippy, refreshing taste of a detoxifying fruity Kombucha beverage, but I hadn't thought of the actual scoby, sort of the barrier reef of the probiotic fluid, being so beneficial to animals, especially chickens and goats. "If we alkalize our systems, we are much better off," she said.

Before making our way over to the breeding barn, I learned that aged goat cheese does not have to be refrigerated. The maximum life cycle for a goats' cheese is around 16 months, cow and goats milk mixed cheese lasts around six months. Donna routinely hand-turns her aging goat cheese wheels for eight to 10 months, before scrubbing and coating in olive oil.

Six hundred goats produce milk on a natural cycle. Donna incorporates organic cow's milk from a neighboring farm for goat and cow's milk blended cheeses in order to maintain a steady production throughout the year.

"We don't have all of our eggs in one basket," she said. "We sell to a few select restaurants and through a distributer as well as at farmers' markets."

The Pacheco's goats are dairy animals raised for their milk and not for meat. Morning sun streamed through a large, open sided barn, divided into well maintained areas separating various farm animals. Contented cows munched at troughs as we strolled in. Goats galore — I've never seen as many in one place. Donna explained how to spot an expectant goat, girls who lounged! She said there are one or two prima-donnas amongst them and these were often her favorites.

Over in the milking barn, technology is much the same as in a regular dairy farm. Lactating goats, who can live up to 15 years, are milked twice a day, each producing as much as seven gallons a week. When a goat gives birth, she stays out of the milking barn and with her kid for three whole months.

The family's two Australian Shepherds and a tiny black and white barn cat accompanied us around the farm, corralling the small crowd back towards the party room for cheese tasting.

Of all the immigrant groups that settled during and after the Gold Rush, the Portuguese have held remarkably tight to their traditions while assimilating in a new country.

Petaluma's annual Holy Ghost Festa (after the winter) continues to colorfully reinforce the strength and pride of Portuguese tradition and culture in Fog Valley. Back in the early days of settlement out on remote ranches at the coast, tailoring was in big demand in the weeks leading up to the annual Holy Ghost Festa social highlight of the year.

Ranchers were measured at home and their suits would be made up in San Francisco.

Chickens and cows were donated for Holy Ghost Festivals and their meat broiled over open fires. These large and lively gatherings were discontinued out at Point Reyes after World War II but happily remain popular and highly visible to passers by, for those of Portuguese heritage, at the Holy Ghost Society Hall, in Petaluma, today.

The legend of the Holy Ghost Festa traces back to the late 1200s, when two centuries of poverty and famine ravaged the Portuguese countryside.

Desperate people gathered in churches to pray to the Divine Holy Spirit. The Mass evolved into the Espírito Santo Festa, an annual celebration of thanksgiving for the food for the poor given by Queen Isabel.

Young girls of Portuguese heritage are crowned queens during a special Mass at St.Vincent de Paul Church in Petaluma, today. A parade weaves its way through the city streets, delighting residents and passersby with a living window into the past. Celebrants sing and dance and enjoy a traditional free meal of "carne and sopas."

The first few Festas Do Espírito Santo held in Sausalito in the 1880s were horse and buggy traffic-stoppers. Cattle, bedecked with flowers and bells, led the parade of pretty Portuguese girls in their crisp white dresses and crowns. I don't suppose the authorities would allow cattle to head up a parade through downtown Petaluma today, though it would be in keeping with the city's history and fun to see.

Portuguese settlers in Fog Valley called their Christmas Eve supper "Consoada." Dinner consisted of boiled codfish with potatoes and cabbage. Desserts were a big part of Christmas and were traditionally fried. "Filhoses" or "Filhós," a doughy treat sometimes made with pumpkin, are essential to this tasty feast.

No Portuguese Christmas meal would be complete without a traditional holiday cake called "Bolo Rei," a fruitcake with two surprises, a ring/doll/medal and a bean. Whoever finds the ring, doll or medal was considered safe, the one who scored the bean had to watch out for bad luck during the coming year and would be tasked with making the cake the following Christmas.

On Christmas morning, Fog Valley's early Portuguese children opened their gifts before mass with the family. Christmas lunch was a less elaborate feast than the night before. Porto wine, stuffed turkey and traditional desserts sound feast enough to those who consider Christmas Day a lounging, left-overs day, but compared to the multi-course makings of other feast days, this was relatively low key.

Martin-Dolcini Ranch in Chileno Valley, CA 1890
courtesy, the Sonoma County Library

Chapter 20

Swiss in the mist

Most immigrants from Switzerland in the mid to late 1800s headed straight to established Swiss communities in the Midwest, but many came to northern California to work in the viticulture and dairy industries.

Between 1820 and 1930, 290,000 Swiss emigrated mostly to the United States and primarily for economic reasons. Two crippling famines in Switzerland, first in 1816 to 1817 and later, in 1845 to 1855 made for widespread poverty in a compact homeland of around two million people (today, the population of Switzerland is still only around eight million).

With no work and no income to feed their families, travel to the New World called for desperate measures — leaving friends and extended family and knowing they were unlikely to see them again.

Switzerland is a country with multiple cultures: German; French; Austrian and Italian customs influenced different border regions of a country famous for its delicious milk and creamy, mountain cheese.

Swiss Settlers in Fog Valley assimilated more easily than some immigrants considering that they came from such a "multifarious" culture, themselves. Still, they surely missed many of their old holiday traditions, especially the many parades that took place between Advent and after the New Year.

During the holiday season, Christmas carols are sung in each of the languages spoken by the Swiss. "Star singing" was and still is a popular Swiss tradition, in which children carol sing carrying a large star, representing the star the wise men followed, from the last week of Advent until Epiphany on January 6th.

Advent marked the start of Swiss Christmas preparations. An old custom in some villages created decorated Advent calendar windows in actual homes within the community.

Whoever's turn it was to host an Advent window held a party with mulled wine (glühwein), festive foods and music for their neighbors.

Swiss children received a somewhat daunting visit from a sinister-sounding Samichlaus and Schmutzli, his black-clad henchman, whose visits were traditionally December 6th.

When Samichlaus knocked on the door, the bravest of little children answered. It was the parents' job to produce a cobbled together book of sins for the visitors' gentle moralizing. In order to earn forgiveness, naughty children were tasked with reciting a poem and permitted to reach down into Samichlaus' bag for a handful of fruits, nuts and gingerbread.

I don't know what their American counterparts would have thought to this scary prospect if Fog Valley newcomers attempted to preserve this particular tradition in the New World. No wonder the concept of a ruddy-faced Santa was so widely embraced.

Popular foods at the Swiss settler's table included a Christmas ham and scalloped potatoes with melted cheese and milk. For dessert, a walnut cake and Christmas cookies, of which each family treasured its own recipes.

The origin of the famous Swiss fondue dates back to the eighteenth-century, when peasant families and traveling sheep and goat herders figured out the best way to use aged cheeses and breads when fresh foods were in dire shortage in the winter months.

Isolated Alpine villagers heated their cheeses with wine, garlic and herbs and found to their delight and no doubt, relief, that stale bread actually softened when dipped into a tasty, melted cheese mixture.

Fondue didn't make it big on the U.S. food scene until the 1950s through the 1970s, though it slowly popularized after World War II. The early Swiss to settle Fog Valley likely used heavy earthenware pots that would withstand an open flame, not the funky fondue sets that are easy to find on the shelves of our favorite thrift stores, today.

Numerous Swiss/American dairymen and women have saved their multi-generational family-owned dairies by making artisan cheese to great acclaim in Fog Valley today. The Lafranchi family's Nicasio Valley Cheese Factory is one of the most industrious of those busy making award-winning Swiss cheeses to national acclaim in the style of their ancestors.

The Lafranchi family siblings, led by brothers Randy, Rick and Scott, produce a range of cheese modeled on those that their immigrant grandfather, Fred, ate growing up in the village of Maggio, on the slopes of the Swiss Alps. The siblings took a trip to visit cousins in the village in 2007, when the time came to seek relief from fluctuating milk prices by diversifying dairy operations on their family's 1,150 acre Lafranchi Ranch, nestled in the Nicasio Valley.

The family had been farming that same land since grandfather Fred settled in the area in the early 1900s. Fred's son, Will, had harbored dreams of making the cheeses in the Swiss Alps style, but it took until 2010 for his offspring to bring this dream to fruition.

Siblings remodeled an existing dairy barn on the ranch to house the creamery, invested in state-of-the-art cheese making equipment and recycled old shipping containers for ripening rooms.

Thanks to the mentorship of an expert cheese maker from Maggia, the Lafranchis now make some of the best organic farmstead cheeses in the United States — and all from the fresh, organic milk of their grass-fed dairy cows. Evocative of the area, cheeses include: Foggy Morning (also with basil and garlic); San Geronimo; Formagella; Halleck Creek; Loma Alta, Nicasio Reserve and Nicasio Square.

In a recording for the *Marin History Shed*, multi-generational Swiss/American Anita Dolcini recounted her memories of childhood on a Fog Valley ranch.

She talked of there being no automation on these early ranches. Cows were milked by hand. For food, families kept pigs, grew potatoes and hunted rabbits and venison.

Listeners heard how big breakfasts were cooked early in the morning. Fires started up in wood stoves at dawn. Ranch hands and family members tucked into cooked cereal — big pots of rolled oats that had been pre-soaked the night before. In the winter months, calves liver was on the breakfast menu, as was calf brains some days, served with scrambled eggs, hot cakes, bacon or ham.

As is the case today, during drought conditions, there simply wasn't enough water out on the ranches to grow vegetable gardens. These would have to be bought in town. Fog Valley Swiss/Americans spoke Swiss at home, where there was a constant flow of newcomers, sponsored by their families. Anita remembered walking across the fields to school.

"We ate so much venison I'm surprised we didn't grow horns," she shared.

Swiss birthday party at Plank Hotel, Tomales
photographer Ella Jorgensen
courtesy, the Tomales History Museum

William H. and Anna Bihn,
proprietors of the Bihn Hatchery (1877-1952)
courtesy, the Sonoma County Library

Chapter 21

German settlers & the islanders of Foehr

Around seven million German people have immigrated into the United States since the 1880s, yet when the largest group left their homelands, there was no one single nation known as Germany. These were the citizens of the nation-states in a largely German-speaking area of Western Europe.

A series of uprisings had taken place in 1848, orchestrated by rebels whose goal was for the German states to unify under one democratic, constitutional government. Their efforts were unsuccessful.

Faced with arrest and persecution by German princes, up to 10,000 "48'ers" immigrated to the United States bringing with them a craft guild system that would eventually evolve into the trade unions that we know today.

For over a century, Germans emigrated in the hundreds of thousands. They came from three religious backgrounds: Protestant,

Catholic, and Jewish — many arriving with professional skills and capital to start a new life.

Though the journey by steerage was long and dangerous, German immigrants sought economic opportunity and prosperity in a time when the rural way of life in their homelands was giving way to Industrialization.

While many became farmers here in Fog Valley, others entered the trades, started their own German language newspapers and maintained a strong link to their heritage.

These were not the first German people to settle America. Since the 1600s, hundreds of thousands of Americans of German heritage are able to trace their roots back to thirteen families from Krefeld, Rhineland, who boarded the ship *Concord* and sailed for Philadelphia, where they established a community known as Germantown in 1683.

Today, an estimated 15 percent of Americans are of German Heritage, topping even, the prolific Irish.

It was important to the German, mostly Lutherans who settled in Fog Valley to keep their German language and customs alive through the generations and though they didn't create the typical German-speaking enclave common in many parts of the United States, German/Americans took enormous pride in their children being raised with traditions of their ancestors. Community centers were of paramount importance.

An American-based Order of Hermann Sons was named after Germanic forest tribesman Arminius-Hermann, who united the German tribes in 9 AD and defeated the Roman army to end its domination over Germany. The order was founded in New York by German/Americans in 1840. A first California Lodge to bear its name was built in San Francisco in 1870.

Fog Valley has its own Hermann Sons Hall, built in the Art Deco style in 1930, on Western Avenue in Petaluma. Its strong German community still gathers for regular meetings, Oktoberfest and other social events. Founded on humanitarian principles, this non-political and non-sectarian association prides itself on providing a well-kept, vintage space with a stage for the community at large to hold parties and fundraisers.

In December, I pay an annual visit to the German community's charming Christkindl Market — a popular draw for the public at large. It's a treat to see Fog Valley's German/American decked out in traditional Germanic attire — women in dirndl bodices and contrasting aprons, their menfolk in hats and Lederhosen of short-pants made from leather with rustic shoes and wool socks.

One of the most famous of German holiday decorations featured at these Christmas Markets are made of hand blown glass and first imported to the U.S. in the 1880s. Some of these were made in the shapes of fruits and vegetables. Five-and-dime-store pioneer, the American F. W. Woolworth Company was the first importer of these ornaments, including glass pickles as part of the selection.

No one knows who created the quirky urban legend, but an apparently made-up story spread fast that the Christmas pickle was an old German tradition and the last to be hidden and hung on the Christmas tree. The first child to find the pickle was given an extra gift. Pickles remain popular as ornaments at the annual Fog Valley Christkindl market, as elsewhere in America, today!

German children wrote to Christkindl (a young girl depicted in a long white and gold dress, with long blond curls, a gold crown and angel wings) requesting gifts on paper decorated with sugar glued to the envelope to add sparkles. These super-sweet letters were left on windowsills at the beginning of Advent.

The Star singing tradition of the Swiss was also widely embraced by Catholic Germans between December 27th and Epiphany, January 6th. "Sternsingers" — four children, dressed as the Wise Men, carrying the Bethlehem star on a stick, walked from house to house singing songs and collecting money for charity.

After they finished singing, they wrote in chalk over the door of the house. This traditional house blessing was written in a specific way to mark the year.

Children of staunch German settlers in Fog Valley who arrived in the 1800s likely upheld their parents' tradition of chalking the year and the initials C + M + B ("Christus Mansionem Benedicat"— Christ Bless This House) over doorways of their German neighbors.

Advent was and still is the big build up to Christmas for German/Americans. Advent calendars took several forms, the most popular being a suspended wreath of fir tree branches with 24 decorated boxes or bags hanging from it. Each box or bag contained a small gift.

An "Advent Kranz" is the ring of fir branches bearing four candles that we are more familiar with in church settings today. One candle is traditionally lit at the start of each week of Advent.

The Christmas tree, a major cultural connector in the melting-pot of Fog Valley of old was of German origin from the Middle Ages.

Traditionally, the Christmas tree would secretly be brought into the homes of families with children, once the little ones were asleep, on December 24th. It was the German mother's job to decorate the tree as her children slept.

In the German tradition, December 6th is St. Nicholas' Day. "Der Nikolaus" brought smaller gifts than those anticipated for later in Advent, on Christmas Eve — mostly sweets and chocolate for the children. These little treasures were tucked into the children's shoes, placed by the door on the nights of December 4th and 5th.

Christmas dinners were hearty feasts for early German settlers to look forward to in winter. Main courses typically featured a delicious roast goose with red cabbage, potato salad and sauerkraut. Spritz cookies, strudel pastry and fruit stollen bread for dessert.

Petaluma Museum's "Faces of Petaluma Exhibit" ran in early 2015. I was fascinated by an article in the exhibit written by *Santa*

Rosa Press Democrat's adored long-time columnist, reporter and historian, Gaye LeBaron, in a 1991 "Notebook" column.

Gaye's column featured Sonoma County's many folk of Isle of Foehr heritage. It was the first I'd heard of this tiny little island of sailors, fishermen and farmers, population 8,500, some 10 miles off the coasts of Germany and Denmark. Spelled in its own language as Föhr, it is one of several North Frisian Islands in the North Sea.

Though the island people consider themselves quintessentially Danish, this four mile wide and seven-and-half mile long island has been under German rule since World War I.

A quarter of the people who emigrated from the Isle of Foehr over a 120-year period, came to Petaluma. The rest made new lives for themselves owning delicatessen stores in New York.

There are more descendants of the Isle of Foehr in Sonoma County than the population of its island community today.

The first of the islanders arrived in the 1870s to work as ranch hands in Fog Valley's rural Bloomfield. They labored hard and bought their own ranches, paying passage for more and more of their fellow islanders to travel from their homeland to work with them as ranch hands, until they, in turn, worked off their own debts.

An early Isle of Foehr settler in Fog Valley was a man named A. J. Petersen, son of a sea captain who bought his own ranch on Petersen Ranch Lane, Petaluma, in 1908. He farmed grapes, apples and cattle and was responsible for the passage of many, many more family members and neighbors from his homeland, settling in the area. The name Petersen is widespread throughout Sonoma County today.

I wanted to find out more about the people of Foehr. I asked pre-school teacher and native Petaluman, Karen Peterson Nau, if one side of her family was from Foehr. Karen, who taught all three of my sons in their formative years at Petaluma's Happy Day Preschool, reminded me that her mom and dad's last name was "Peterson," not "Petersen." Still, she'd happily reported — her sister-in-law was one of those Petersens.

Soon after, Karen's mom, Ettamarie Peterson contacted me to ask if I'd like to hear about her recent visit to Germany and the Isle of Foehr.

Ettamarie, better known as "The Bee Lady," a dynamic, now retired teacher and beekeeper in Sonoma County for close to two decades, took in two trainee -exchange teachers from Germany 40 years ago. "We've stayed friends and have traveled extensively in Europe and in the U.S.," she explained. Great-grandparents Ettamarie and her husband Ray are busy bees themselves.

They've slowed down some of their commercial activities on their family farm, in West Petaluma in recent years, but Ettamarie is certainly not calling a halt to her sustainable bee and chicken keeping, her educational work with school parties and 4H as well as advising beekeepers around the world.

A twist of fate intervened during a planned reunion with the couple's old friends in Germany. The Isle of Foehr was a favorite destination for a few days away for a group of extended friends and family and Ettamarie and Ray were invited to join them in a cottage stay that was planned during their visit to Germany.

They took the ferry over to the island after spending several hours at The German Heritage Center, on the mainland. "I researched my daughter-in-law Dodie's family and the ship that they sailed on," said Ettamarie.

Dodie's grandparents, Keike and Willi Petersen sailed to the United States on the *President Lincoln*, on 27th September 1913. Keike was 21 years old and had recently married. She finally became an American citizen after World War II, in December 1945.

"Keike and William's daughter Lillian became city clerk in Petaluma," said Ettamarie, over tea with me in Petaluma. One of her sisters, Minnie, was Dodie's grandmother.

Ettamarie was struck by how similar the landscape in so far as the familiar black and white Holstein/Friesian cows grazing the fields, proximity of (17) villages to the coast, cheese making and comparatively mild climate compared to the mainland. "Everything but the grapevines," she said.

The couple enjoyed early morning walks to the bakery to buy fresh breads for breakfast. "We ate a lot of tasty seafood," said Ettamarie who was delighted by the warm welcome for Petalumans by the islanders. "Everyone is interconnected," she said. "Relationships have been passed down from generation to generation."

Agro-tourism thrives on Foehr as it does today in Fog Valley, uniting the two communities in their evolution from remote farming regions to popular places for food lovers to visit. Reed roofed houses, the oldest dating back to 1617 (with arched whale bones for a distinctive gateway) provide farm and village stays.

"A town crier in full regalia took us on a village tour," said Ettamarie. It was a trip she'll never forget and the couple came home with books for their Petersen grandchildren to learn more of their island heritage.

I interviewed two men for the annual Butter and Egg Days special supplement in the *Petaluma Argus Courier*, a couple of months after reading Gaye LeBaron's column in the museum.

Grand Marshall of the 2015 community parade, Dr. Fred Groverman and previously unconnected, fellow Petaluman, "Good Egg" Steve Kemmerle each told me, during our separate meetings, of their Isle of Foehr heritage.

What were the chances of that, I wondered? According to Fred, organizers of extended family reunions called it a day years ago when numbers ran into the hundreds. He had visited the island himself, several years back. "There is a street named Petaluma Weg (lane) in the town of Alkersum," he said.

The climate is mild on the island due to surrounding islands Sylt and Amrun protecting it from the blustery North Sea. Fog Valley newcomers were dairy farmers and had lifelong experience in the cultivation of oats, wheat and potatoes. No wonder they flocked to a region in which there was money to be made from a fast growing population and economy.

I learned from reading through Ettamarie's books she'd bought on the island that on New Year's Eve, the hard working, yet fun-loving people of Foehr would go from house to house, women dressed as men, men dressed as women, singing funny songs, laughing and toasting the culmination of another year!

On special occasions, women settlers from the Isle of Foehr would wear their traditional black and white costumes with an elaborate scarf folded into a headpiece and intricate silverwork breast pieces, large necklaces that have been passed down from generation to generation on the island as well as in Fog Valley.

*Traditional Christmas tree decked out
in a modern day Fog Valley Victorian parlor.*

Hans Hansen Junior and family, Petaluma, CA in the 1920s
courtesy, the Sonoma County Library

Chapter 22

Danish ingenuity

In 1864 a Dane named Christopher Nisson arrived in Fog Valley and changed the course of the region's history.

"When we hear about Petaluma's past distinction as the Egg Basket of the World, we often think of Lyman Byce and Isaac Dias, who invented the first practical incubator, but where would we be without the first commercial hatchery that a Danish-born farmer named Christopher Nisson constructed on his Two Rock ranch?" asked Sonoma County History & Genealogy Librarian and Archivist, Katherine Rinehart in a 2007 article in the *Santa Rosa Press Democrat*.

Christopher Nisson (spelled Nissen when he left Denmark as a 19-year-old), played a significant role in Petaluma gaining status as the chicken and egg capital of the world.

He settled in the Two Rock area in 1864, first working for nurseryman William H. Pepper and later, as a landscape gardener. There was lots of work for landscape gardeners as houses popped up around a fast developing frontiers town.

According to Katherine's account, the ambitious young man saved up his money and bought 100 acres of land for a ranch of his own. In 1876, he married fellow Danish/American settler Ingeborg Ericksen and together they had five children.

"At first, the Nissons grew potatoes and tried their hand at dairying," wrote Katherine, "but (they) eventually settled on chicken ranching. By 1880, Nisson had bought his first incubator from Byce's Petaluma Incubator Company."

This incubator was such a success, the Danish farmers increased their flock to 2,000 layers. The following year, they started selling artificially incubated baby chicks to neighboring farmers. The Nissons were doubly busy, custom-hatching eggs from these neighboring flocks.

Remnants of the Danes' first colony structures for range chickens still dot the Fog Valley landscape today. Five by 10 feet in dimension and built on moveable runners these innovative, first, lathe-floored colony houses enabled farmers to lock chickens in one day and let them out the next.

Christopher and Ingeborg's Danish/American friends and neighbors found that farming in Fog Valley was similar to farming back in their homeland. New World opportunities enabled them to save to buy their own land. Back in Denmark it was hard to get ahead for mostly tenant farmers taxed by wealthy Danish landowners. The milder weather in northern California was also a big improvement.

Between 1890 and 1910, around 150,000 Swedes, Norwegians and Danes settled in Pacific coastal communities, making a living in lumber, farming and fishing industries.

There were no less than four different Danish organizations flourishing in Petaluma for many years. Two of these in the early days of settlement, were the Danish Brotherhood and the Danish Sisterhood of America.

These lodges were established as part of a Danish/American movement across the United States, in which immigrants were able to strengthen connection with their Danish neighbors and celebrate their customs and heritage. Though these organizations provided an environment in which to bond on social and fraternal levels, re-establishing a religious base was a priority.

Most of the Danes in Fog Valley had been schooled in the Lutheran faith, the predominant religion in Denmark, taught in classrooms by grammar school teachers and church deacons.

A growing population of Danish Lutherans made do with services by circuit preachers of The United Danish Evangelical Lutheran Church Pacific Circle. Danish/Americans were baptized, married and buried in services led by circuit preachers until 1920 when a large Lutheran congregation organized itself in Petaluma.

Although a cornerstone was laid for its first church in the 1920s, the sanctuary of the Elim Lutheran Church on Baker Street was not completed until 1930. There are three flourishing Lutheran churches in Petaluma today.

Danish Christmas season in Fog Valley, as in neighboring Northern European settlers' households, began with Advent and, in particular, the Advent wreath. Wreaths have four candles, as with German traditions, though the Danish version was made with fine spruce twigs and cuttings, decorated with berries and cones, white candles and red ribbons to attach to the ceiling.

Lucia, the saint of light was celebrated on the night between December 12th and 13th. Processions of little girls sang traditional songs. Legend has it that Lucia, to keep her hands free, wore a wreath with candles on her head to feed poor Christians hiding in the catacombs of ancient Rome.

Christmas Eve dinner is still served early in Danish/American homes, featuring roast duck or goose or pork with crackling. Ducks or geese are traditionally stuffed with apples and prunes and served with boiled potatoes, red cabbage, beets and cranberry sauce. For dessert, the Danish holiday table features Ris à L'amande — rice pudding with whipped cream, vanilla and almonds with hot cherry sauce or Risengrød — a hot version. A peeled almond is hidden in the dessert bowl and the lucky recipient given a gift.

The lighting of the Christmas tree was and is a highlight of Christmas Eve, after dinner, the tradition of real candles is still in use by traditional Danish/Americans today. I've been fortunate to attend a Danish/American Christmas party in which we held hands and danced around the tree singing Danish Christmas carols.

My Danish friend Lotte Harild Gonzalez, is, like myself, a newcomer to Fog Valley of some 26 years or so. Her annual multi-course, traditional Pentecost Feast (with a California twist or two) is a highlight of the year for her food-loving friends and family. Some day I hope to visit Denmark with her. I've developed a taste for the delicate flavors of her Danish cooking.

Festive and foraged Fog Valley winter greenery

McNear's Chinese camp, Petaluma, CA 1906
courtesy, the Sonoma County Library

Chapter 23

Chinese contingency

Of all the immigrant groups who settled in California during the Gold Rush era, it was the Chinese who struggled with the deepest cultural gulf between themselves and most all other immigrant groups, in their assimilation to an American life.

As with most other immigrant groups of the era, members of the nineteenth-century Chinese gentry, affluent scholars, landowners and officials, had little reason to move into the U.S. frontier.

It was the struggling peasant farmers of the Chinese masses who were desperate enough to voyage to California to pan for gold, being worked ragged in brutal conditions in mines and on the railroads.

Whatever small amount the Chinese were able to earn in the Gold Rush, this amounted to considerable sums of money over months and years, when sent back to impoverished family in China. Patience was a virtue — if they survived to tell their tale.

Thousands suffered through years of grueling blood, sweat and tears with the sole goal of someday returning to their ancestral homeland to be surrounded by the simple comfort of relatives.

A song from old San Francisco's Chinatown expresses this desire in direct terms: "I am returning home with purses and bags stuffed full. Soon I will see my parents' brows beaming with joy."

While most immigrant groups were focused on fully re-establishing themselves as individuals by putting down roots in their new communities, the Chinese had little inclination to strike out alone.

They established their own camps in otherwise multi-cultural gold fields, keeping themselves to themselves. Racial exclusivity did not sit well with mostly European miners who had no previous experience with the Chinese culture. Prejudice and mistrust set in fairly swiftly. Still, the Chinese were not intimidated. They stuck together. By the late 1870s, a quarter of all of the Chinese people in the U.S. were living in San Francisco within an eight-block radius. The same sorts of crowded quarters existed in Sacramento and even a small Chinatown in Petaluma.

This Fog Valley Chinese community emerged within the fledgling frontier city, with its own stores, restaurants, laundries and washhouses. Most of the Chinese who lived in Petaluma in the 1880s were young men in their late teens or twenties. They held tight to their customs and their hopes to one day return home. Unlike all of the other immigrant groups of the era, the Chinese never really planned to settle in California — their sojourn was a way to make money to take back to their families.

Gold in the mines had become harder to find and competition increased. As the Chinese succumbed to being forced out of the mines, they gravitated to urban enclaves. Those who weren't employed in the washhouses and restaurants of their communities found little competition as laborers on The Transcontinental Railroad.

This 1,907-mile contiguous railroad line from Iowa to the Pacific Coast was built almost entirely by the hands of the Chinese between the years of 1863 and 1869. Before the railroad, known as "The Overland Route," harbors in Sacramento and San Francisco had been linked by steamers.

An open-door government policy set in 1868 cleared the floodgates for Chinese immigrants arriving at the rate of 40,000 souls a year. By 1879, after a quarter century of mass immigration, the State of California put the brakes on, adopting a Constitution in which the government was given power to decide who was welcome and who was not.

The Chinese, after building the infrastructure of transportation to the West, were unceremoniously banned from being hired by the State — by corporations, county or municipal agencies. By 1881, immigration numbers of Chinese dropped from the thousands to less than two dozen a year.

Adding insult to serious injury, The Chinese Exclusion Act of 1882 forced families who had stayed on to hang tight in a new wave of persecution or simply go back to China. Anyone who had arrived in the decade prior to the passing of this act was blocked from becoming a naturalized citizen.

Anti-Chinese violence broke out in Fog Valley and throughout California. American people viewed the Chinese, of all the immigrant groups, as being low-paid workers taking jobs away from citizens. Sound familiar? Despite such extreme animosity, capitalism retained a voice in the form of vocal entrepreneurs who resisted the Exclusion Act. Who, they wondered, would work for less if the Chinese were banished?

A report in *The Daily Alta California* in January 1886 outlined the anti-Chinese sentiment in Petaluma at the time: "Not withstanding the heavy rain, the stores and awnings today contained gatherings of citizens discussing the meeting of last night. The radical element is dissatisfied.

The evening imprint today recommends boycotting and the formation of a league, with the pledge that the Chinaman be not employed in any manner…many of the prominent citizens will dismiss their Chinese help on the first of the month. Good, reliable female house servants can find employment there."

Many did refuse degradation and managed to ride it out. In 1857, Petaluma had three recorded Chinese residents. By 1877 that number had risen to 115, many working by then in railroad labor crews straightening the curves of the Petaluma River, as quarry workers and agricultural field hands. Ah (Mr) Sing, Ah Sam, Ah Quong, Ah Fong and Ah Sung were "Chinamen" who worked for local nurseryman William H. Pepper during the taking of the 1880 Census.

The Chinese Exclusion Act was the first law implemented to prevent a specific ethnic group from immigrating into the United States. This act was eventually repealed by the Magnuson Act, in 1943.

Several Chinatown shanties were torn down in 1911 for the development of the McNear Building on Main Street, now Petaluma Boulevard North. Excavations during the building of Petaluma's "Theatre Square," nearby, in the 1990s, unearthed more artifacts from the edge of Petaluma's small Chinatown. Elders in the community remember a popular "Petaluma grocery" store, nicknamed "Chinaman's Market."

Though largely considered peace loving, industrious, kind and frugal, the Chinese were often vilified for cultural habits among some, those of opium smoking and gambling.

"Special Dispatch" to *The San Francisco Call*, reported in 1911: "A sensational raid was made in the local Chinatown last night when Captain Tomas, a special internal revenue officer from San Francisco accompanied by Deputy Internal Revenue Collector Joseph C. Popley, visited an opium den and confiscated a large quantity of contraband material."

The archeologist whom I'd met to tour the Old Adobe during my early research had talked to me about his experience of the Chinatown excavations. Bill had been adamant that the opium problem in Petaluma had not been on much of a scale. "It likely didn't amount to much more than the habits of a few old men," he said.

Through 1910, Chinese men in America wore their hair in a style imposed by Manchu conquerors in the seventeenth-century. "Queues" was the given name to this particular style in which hair was worn long and gathered into an often-braided ponytail. Hair at the front of the head was shaved off above the temples every ten days.

Though they were few, wealthier Chinese women in Fog Valley in the 1880s continued the cultural practice of foot binding.

Festivals and seasonal events were and still are important social events amongst the Chinese. The Chinese Lunar Year, falling in late January or early February is the main festival of the year.

Each household was and is thoroughly cleaned, debts paid and collected in order to start the New Year with a clean slate. On Chinese New Year's Eve, a decadent dinner symbolized a hope for abundance for the coming year. Gifts of money in red envelopes were exchanged.

The Chinese dressed in their best for New Year's Day, offering greetings to family, friends and neighbors —a dragon or lion parade staged in the midst of thundering firecrackers to chase away evil spirits and bring good luck in the coming year. Colorful lanterns and bright banners abound.

In his journal of 1860 to 1864 — *Up And Down California*, William H. Brewer wrote of his first experience of a Chinese New Year. "The festival lasts two weeks, but the police grant them the privilege of firing firecrackers only three days...I thought I had seen firecrackers before, but became convinced that I had not. All day Tuesday, there was a continuous roar of firecrackers."

He described how packs of large red and yellow firecrackers the size of a man's thumb were lit, hurled in the air from rooftops and allowed to fall in the street. "As twilight comes on, the night becomes more picturesque...such a time they had! They claim their dynasty started some 17,500 and some odd years ago."

Four men at Valley Ford Depot
courtesy, the Sonoma County Library

Chapter 24

there's a train coming

Now that we have traveled around the region in winter and met the people who shaped its character and flavor, let's take a brief, but important look at its future.

A little over 150 years have passed since river transportation and the first horse and wagon trails ferried people around Fog Valley. Who, then, would have possibly imagined the reliance on the automobile that would come into play long before the demise of passenger rail travel in the region, in the late 1950s?

Regretfully, most of my travels around the region for my research into writing this book were behind the wheel of my car. Though I do enjoy a pleasant bike ride on errands around town — or, for that matter, anywhere that resembles the flat expansive miles of the fenlands of my youth, you're not likely to spot me amongst the masses of keen country road bikers hauling my spandex-self around these mountainous parts. I'd like to have ridden on horseback but I don't think that's allowed on major roads, these days.

During my many expeditions I pondered the loss of cross-countryside, town and coastal rail connections that made the region so much more accessible in the 1870s through to the mid 1900s.

The Northwestern Pacific Railroad connected to a ferry route at Sausalito, carrying passengers to and from San Francisco into and around the region with relative ease.

Bus transit services in the region were at their best back in the 1980s, when riders were able to map out a route to the most populated parts of Fog Valley. Government spending cuts have slashed routes and regularity over the years to make the more obscure areas unthinkable of being reached by bus.

Fog Valley is a thriving region with a robust entrepreneurial spirit. I noticed a distinct increase in the number of tour-toting minivans traversing the winding lanes, not only in wine country, inland, out along the craggy coastal west. At first, I was a little irritated by the thought of this last of the unspoiled parts of the region being infiltrated by luxury limos, but then, why not reduce the carbon footprint of individual cars careening through the pristine, coastal air? Isn't this what the narrow gauge rail had brought to the more remote parts of the region back in the early days?

Agri-tourism and national parkland visitors heading north from the city are seemingly quite happy to sit back and let someone else drive as they take in the splendid scenery.

Celebrity tastemakers and celebrated chefs look to Fog Valley today for its rich, natural food shed. It took about 70 years to get back to where we were when we were eating in the wholesome way of our grandparents and great-grandparents in the region. And likewise, we're finally taking a tip from the past in reassessing how we move around the place.

By the winter of 2016, when this book is in print, a fleet of 14 hunter-green, clean-diesel, energy efficient trains, running at a swift 79 miles per hour, will transport passengers on a 70-mile corridor throughout the North Bay to (eventually) connect with a ferry to San Francisco, in Larkspur Landing.

This is exciting! Although Sonoma Marin Area Rail Transit (SMART) trains won't do much for jaunts out to the coast, passengers will be mobile from Cloverdale in the north of Sonoma County, Healdsburg and Windsor (phase two), Sonoma County Airport, Santa Rosa (two stops), Rohnert Park, Cotati, Petaluma (two stops), Novato (two stops), San Rafael (two stops) and Larkspur (phase two). Old track buildings have been replaced, historic train tunnels rehabilitated, crossing gates and station platforms built.

SMART trains, paid for by a voter-approved sales tax, will hopefully take some of the pressure off a notoriously clogged freeway, encouraging a renewed focus on working towards the restoration of a cleaner, greener Fog Valley and its borderlands.

A vibrant web of community non-profits, groups and organizations are working together to protect and preserve the region's unique natural resources and to build on and maintain its thriving, sustainable communities.

Yet, a tug and pull of regional balance in economic growth and a strong economy with protection of open space and farmland is an ongoing concern. Economic threat to unprotected family farms persists.

Thankfully, forward-thinking organizations such as the Marin Agricultural Land Trust and Sonoma Land Trust have, to date, collectively protected around 100,000 acres of scenic, natural, agricultural and open landscapes in Marin and Sonoma Counties, since the 1970s.

Farmers and environmentalists were not always the best of friends in the history of the region. And though, remarkable coalitions formed by innovative leaders have succeeded in forming strong, unprecedented partnerships to change the face of farmland and natural habitat protection, placing thousands of acres off-limits to developers, reducing urban sprawl and providing the scenic buffers that are the backdrop of this book.

Fog Valley's city of Petaluma set a nationwide legal standard for residential growth control in 1972. A population explosion of 77.2 percent in the decade prior (from 14,035 people to 24,870) almost doubled the small farming city's population. Voters approved a Greenbelt Approved firm cap that would limit home building and control urban sprawl by setting development boundaries around the city, whose population of around 60,000 has remained steady for the past few years.

Newcomers gravitate to Fog Valley for its bucolic charm and its careful management of cultural integrity. The city of Petaluma has retained so much of its early appeal that it's hard to imagine a future that might bring more infill and traffic to its streets. Yet, a shortage of housing, coupled with escalating housing costs have made it increasingly hard for working and middle-income people to find homes and make a living in a place that was built on such opportunity.

While European white people have dominated the region's population since its first settlers arrived, demographics indicate a landscape of increasingly diverse cultural heritage in the community today.

When I stroll the familiar streets of Petaluma's historic neighborhood and downtown, I think of those who were a step ahead, a generation ago, two, three, six generations past. And I think of those yet to find this place. The region continues to welcome newcomers. In the words of the late, great David Bowie: "The truth is, of course, that there is no journey. We are arriving and departing at the same time."

Remote Highway One along Tomales Bay,
once accessible by narrow gauge rail

"No-one who cooks, cooks alone. Even at her most solitary,
a cook in the kitchen is surrounded by generations of cooks past,
the advice and menus of cooks present, the wisdom of cookbook writers."

American novelist and food writer Laurie Cowlin

THREE

Fog Valley winter's festive food

Chapter 25

vintage recipes

The holidays, like no other time of the year, turn our attentions to recreating delicious meals from family archives.

As we ponder the agricultural hotbed that was and is Fog Valley, we stand hand-in-hand with those who came before — a time, incredulously, when food cost more than land.

The melting pot has bequeathed us a simple and delicious legacy of how best to eat, live and celebrate in a modern age.

Our kitchens today are appointed with the sorts of myriad modern conveniences we mostly take for granted. We don't have the worry of stoking fires and are able to store food at the right temperature, roast, bake and sauté without the fear of soot spoiling our culinary efforts.

It doesn't hurt to remind ourselves how relatively easy entertaining is for us in this age of food processors, instant gas and electric, fancy outdoor kitchens, state-of-the-art brick ovens and dishwashers. Let's take better advantage of all that we have at hand.

Early Fog Valley domestic scenes consisted of scant (far traveled) dishes, no electricity, a makeshift dining table of an upturned dry goods box, crates for stools, limited cooking utensils and a small oil stove.

Many early settlers considered the climate considerably mild compared to where they'd come from, yet Fog Valley's notoriously foggy mornings and evenings must have called for plentiful wood to keep the home fires (and stove) burning.

By the 1870s, most homes in Fog Valley had the benefit of running water (heated on the kitchen stove). *The Modern Householder — a Manual of Household Economy in All its Branches*, published in New York and London in 1872 captures the essence of the middle class Victorian kitchen.

This model of domestic efficiency records a mind-boggling list of over 100 necessities for the fully equipped kitchen — a far cry from the simple set-ups of the new arrivals. I imagine the hardware stores of the day were well stocked given the amount of new homes being built:

"An open range; fender; fire irons; one (plain plank) deal table; bracket of (plain planks) deal to be fastened to the wall and let down when wanted; wooden chair; floor canvas; coarse canvas to lay before the fire when cooking; wooden tub for washing glass and china; large earthenware pan for washing plates; small zinc basin for washing hands; two washing tubs; clothesline; clothes horse; yellow bowl for mixing dough; wooden salt-box; small coffee mill; plate rack; knife board; large brown earthenware pan for bread and a small wooden flour kit.

Three flat irons; an Italian iron and iron stand; old blanket for ironing on; two tin candlesticks; snuffers; extinguishers; two blacking brushes; one scrubbing brush; one carpet broom; one short handled broom; cinder sifter; dustpan; sieve; bucket;

patent digester; tea kettle; toasting fork; bread grater; bottle jack (for rotating meat on a spit); set of skewers; meat chopper; black tin butter saucepan; colander; three iron saucepans; one iron broiling pot; one fish kettle; one flour dredger; one frying pan; one hanging gridiron; salt and pepper boxes; rolling pin and pasteboard; twelve patty pans; one larger tin pan; pair of scales and a baking dish.

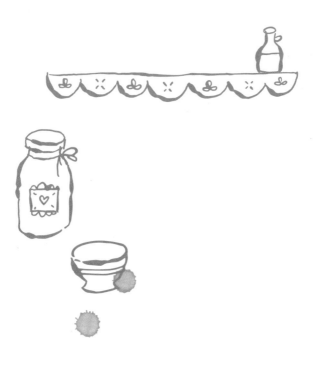

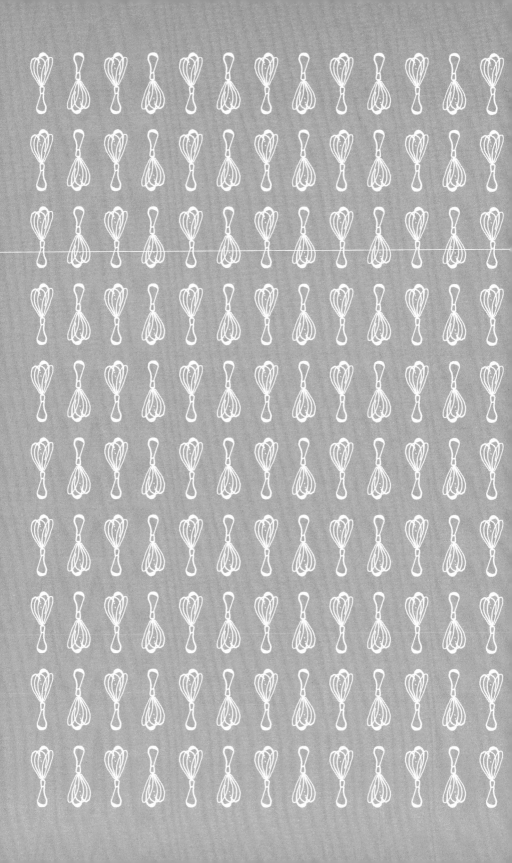

breakfast

X ⋯ X ⋯ X ⋯ X ⋯ X

HANGTOWN FRY

An adaptation of a recipe from Main Street
Placerville's long-lost Blue Bell Cafe

3 raw shucked fresh (live) oysters

1 egg, beaten

1 tablespoon cream

breading mixture (mixture of cracker crumbs and bread crumbs)

1 tablespoon of butter

2 slices of thick-sliced bacon

2 eggs

Pat the shucked oysters dry with paper towels to remove moisture.

In a small bowl, beat the egg with the cream. Dip the oysters in the egg/cream mixture and then the breading mixture.

Heat butter in a frying pan. Add oysters and fry for about 30 seconds on each side or until three-fourths cooked; remove from heat and set aside.

While frying the oysters, fry the bacon in a separate skillet.

Place the bacon (like railroad tracks) in a large frying pan over low heat. Pour a small amount of beaten egg over the top of the bacon. Place the partially-cooked oysters on top of the bacon and then pour the remaining beaten eggs over the top. Cook approximately two minutes or until the eggs are set (eggs are done when creamy, soft and a bit runny; do not overcook). Fold the omelets over the oysters. Place a lid on top and cook just until the steam blends all the flavors together.

Winter Morning
GINGERBREAD MUFFINS

1 egg
1/2 cup milk
3/4 cup unsalted butter, softened
1/2 cup dark molasses
3 cups flour, sifted
1/4 cup sugar
1/4 cup brown sugar
1 1/2 teaspoon baking soda
3/4 teaspoon salt
3/4 teaspoon cinnamon
3/4 teaspoon ginger
1/4 teaspoon cloves
Sprinkle of sugar crystals

Beat egg, gently. Stir in softened butter, milk and molasses. Combine dry ingredients and add to egg mixture, stirring until just moistened. Fill muffin pan lined with 24 paper cases, three quarters full. Sprinkle with sugar crystals. Bake for round 25 minutes at 350°F.

Petaluma Pride

AN EGGSTRAORDINARY OMELETTE
from the kitchen of Susan Villa

6 egg whites
6 egg yolks
1/4 teaspoon cream of tartar
1/4 teaspoon salt
1/2 teaspoon dry mustard (Colemans)
pinch of pepper
1/3 cup milk
2 tablespoon unsalted butter

Cheese Sauce
2 tablespoon butter
2 tablespoon flour
1/2 tablespoon dry mustard
1/8 teaspoon salt
pinch of pepper
pinch of cayenne
1 cup milk
1 cup grated sharp Cheddar cheese
pinch of paprika
fresh, chopped parsley

Separate whites into a big bowl and yolks into a smaller bowl. Warm to room temperature. Preheat oven to 350°F. Beat whites with cream of tartar until stiff peaks form. Beat yolks until thick. Add salt, mustard powder and pepper to yolk mixture. Add milk, gradually, beating until blended.

Gently fold yolk mixture into whites to combine, using a wooden spatula or wire whisk.

Heat a 10 or 11-inch heavy skillet with a heat resistant handle on range top. Splash in a few drops of cold water and add butter to sizzling point. Tip pan to coat. Add egg mixture and spread evenly. Cook over low heat without stirring for a couple of minutes. Place in oven and bake uncovered for 15 minutes or so until top is golden brown.

Make cheese sauce in a small pan while omelet is baking. Melt butter, remove from heat. Stir in flour, mustard, salt, pepper, cayenne and milk. Bring to a boil, stirring to thicken. Lower heat, add cheese and stir until melted.

Loosen sliced omelette with spatula and serve with cheese sauce, a sprinkle of paprika and parsley.

Serves 4.

breads

x · x · x · x

Welsh Miners
BARA BRITH
A Holiday Tea Time Speckled Bread

1/2 pint cold tea

1 pound mixed, dried fruit

6 ounces brown sugar

1 medium size farm fresh egg

2 tablespoons orange juice

1 tablespoon orange zest

1 tablespoon honey

4 cups of flour

2 tablespoons baking powder

1 teaspoon mixed spice

extra honey for glazing

Pour tea over dried fruit in a mixing bowl, cover and let soak overnight. Mix sugar, egg, orange juice, zest and honey and add to the fruit the following day. Preheat oven to 325°F. Sift in flour, baking powder and spice. Mix well. Pour into a buttered loaf tin. Bake for about one and three-quarter hours or until golden in color and firm to the touch. Baste with honey as soon as it is out of the oven. Cool and serve with butter and jam and a cup of tea.

✗ ✗ ✗ ✗

OMA'S CHRISTMAS STOLLEN

1/2 cup raisins

1/2 cup dried citrus peel

1/2 cup dried cranberries

1/2 cup brandy

1 1/2 cups milk

1/2 cup white sugar

1/2 teaspoon salt

2 eggs

2 egg yolks

1 ounce active dry yeast

5 2/3 cups all-purpose flour

3/4 cup butter

1/2 teaspoon ground cardamom

powdered sugar for frosting

Soak fruit in brandy for several hours. Scald milk in a saucepan. Stir in sugar and salt. Remove from heat. When lukewarm, mix in two whole eggs and two egg yolks. Add activated yeast (thoroughly dissolved in lukewarm water with a pinch of sugar for five minutes) to 3 cups of the flour. Mix and allow to rise until double. Add drained fruit, butter, cardamom and the remaining flour. Mix thoroughly, knead and leave to rise in a greased bowl. Cut into four pieces. Roll each into an oval shape, butter tops and fold in half lengthwise. Place rolls onto greased baking sheets, cover and leave to rise until double. Bake at 375°F for 25 minutes. Cool and frost with powdered sugar.

Granny Maureen's
IRISH SODA BREAD
Fit for a King

4 handfuls of plain flour (approximately four cups)
1 teaspoon salt
1 teaspoon baking soda
2 teaspoons baking powder
generous knob of butter
1 cup of raisins
1 1/2 to 1 3/4 cups of buttermilk

Put dry ingredients in a large baking bowl and mix well. Work in butter. Add raisins. Make a well in mixture and add buttermilk until dough is stiff. Knead gently and shape into a large circle. Turn onto a floured baking tray. Make a deep cross in the middle of the dough. Cook at 375°F for 40 to 45 minutes. Toast cooked bread and slather with butter.

X · X · X · X

Fog Valley
ACORN BREAD

European settlers' adaptation of a Native American recipe

1 cup of acorn meal
2 tablespoons of baking powder
1/2 teaspoon of salt
3 tablespoons of sugar
1 cup of milk
1 egg
3 tablespoons of oil

Gather acorns from August to September when shells are soft. Check for cracks, mold and worms and discard any nuts that aren't in good condition. Shell and taste for tannin acid. Leach out any bitterness from tannins by boiling shelled acorns in several successive pots of water. Once the water is clear, the acorns are ready for a gentle roasting in a cool oven — un-boiled acorns for an hour-and-a-half, or two, boiled acorns for one hour. Cool and grind into meal. Heat oven to 400°F. Grease a loaf pan. Sift dry ingredients into a bowl. Combine milk, egg and oil in a separate bowl. Add dry and liquid ingredients together. Stir to moisten. Pour lumpy batter into pan and bake for half an hour.

libations

German Settlers'
WINTER WARMING GLÜHWEIN

1 bottle red wine

1 orange

1 cinnamon stick

16 cloves

4 tablespoons sugar

nutmeg

Pour a bottle of red wine into a saucepan. Peel rind from orange in a single strip. Or zest if you prefer. Add rind (or zest), cinnamon, cloves and sugar to the wine. Heat over gentle flame until not quite boiling. Strain and pour into heatproof glasses. A sprinkle of nutmeg adds optional spice.

Serves 6.

RUSSIAN SPICED TEA

8 tablespoons of black tea leaves
2 tablespoons of whole cloves
3 tablespoons of fresh orange zest
4 whole cinnamon sticks
8 cups of water
1/4 cup of freshly squeezed lemon juice
1/2 cup of honey
Mason jars and ribbon

Place tea leaves, cloves, zest and cinnamon sticks into a cheesecloth and tie at the top. Bring 8 cups of water to a boil, add the bag and allow to steep, covered, for 10 minutes. Add lemon juice and honey and serve. If covered and kept cool, Russian Spiced Tea is good for two to three days. Gift in mason jars with a cheerful ribbon.

Swiss Mountain Herder's
HOLIDAY HOT CHOCOLATE

Etienne Guittard ventured from Tournus, France to the Barbary Coast to strike it rich during the California Gold Rush. He brought chocolate from his uncle's factory to trade for mining supplies. Wealthy miners were more than happy to pay a premium for his treat. He returned to France to finesse his craft and in 1868 returned to California to launch Guittard Chocolate in San Francisco.

Boil three cups of whole milk, turn down heat and whisk. Add three quarters of good quality dark chocolate pieces to pan, stir until melted. Reheat. Add peppermint schnapps to taste.

Out West

WHISKEY OLD-FASHIONED

Muddle one sugar cube with a teaspoon of water and two dashes of Angostura bitters in the bottom of an Old-Fashioned glass until the sugar dissolves. Add one and a half ounces of whiskey (in order of Prohibition era popularity), straight rye, bourbon, Canadian or blended scotch — and stir. Add two to three ice cubes, stir a little more, squeeze a large swatch of thin-cut lemon peel over the top and drop it in. Let it sit a minute or two if you are able to resist.

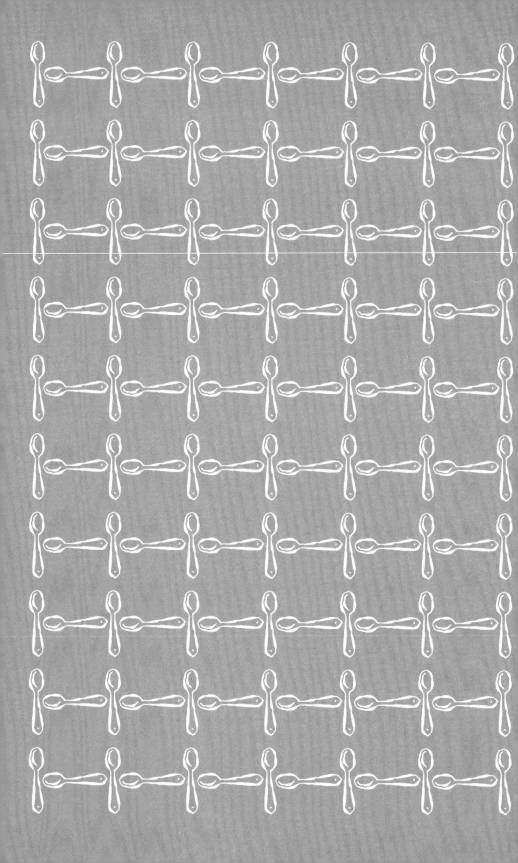

soups, starters and sides

X ··· X ··· X ··· X ··· X

Mrs. George Hyatt's
CLAM CHOWDER

1/2 pound salt pork or bacon

4 cups diced carrots and potatoes

2 medium sliced onions

1 pint clams, chopped

salt and pepper to taste

2 tablespoons of flour

2 tablespoons of butter

1 pint of milk

8 cups cold water

1 pint tomato puree

Dice salt pork or chop bacon and fry over a low flame until stew pan is well greased. Remove from flame. Add a layer of carrots and potatoes, then a layer of onions and then a layer of clams. Sprinkle with salt, pepper and flour and butter. Continue layering. Pour on water and milk. Cover tightly and heat gently until thickened.

Mrs. Will Oeltjen's
CRAB LOUIE

1 fresh crab
1 1/2 teaspoon of Worcestershire sauce
6 hardboiled eggs, chopped
lettuce
1/2 cup catsup
salt and pepper before serving
mayonnaise
lemon

Crab Louie — "King of Salads" reputedly first appeared, at least in its American form, on the menus of the finest San Francisco and West Coast dining rooms at the turn of the twentieth-century. There are lots of versions of this delicious salad, but a true Fog Valley Crab Louie, such as that of Fog Valley housewife Mrs. Will Oeltjen, consisted of crisp iceberg lettuce, a heaping of fresh Dungeness crab meat, slices of hard-boiled egg and a distinctive dressing of mayonnaise, Worcestershire sauce, salt, pepper and ketchup with a twist of lemon.

Lighthouse Keeper's
WINTER WARMING
CHICKEN BROTH

Cut chicken carcass into small pieces and place in a pot with four cups of water and two teaspoons of salt and a bay leaf. Cover and simmer for three and a half hours, or until the meat drops from the bones. Strain into a bowl and when the broth has cooled, remove any grease from the top. Makes one pint.

Petaluma Chicken Farmers' POTATO LATKES

5 russet potatoes

2 onions

3 eggs

1 teaspoon salt

1/4 teaspoon pepper

3/4 cup flour

schmaltz (rendered poultry fat) or olive oil

Peel potatoes and shred with a hand grater. Place in a bowl of cold water until ready to use. Drain thoroughly, retaining the white starchy film from the water in a small jar. Finely chop onions. In a large bowl, add onions to shredded potatoes, beaten eggs, salt and pepper. Stir in enough flour for mixture to stick together. Pour an inch of oil into frying pan and heat over a medium flame. Drop in enough potato mixture, a few at a time, to make 20 latkes. Flatten each latke slightly in the center to cook, turning after a few minutes until golden brown. Drain on a clean towel and serve warm with applesauce.

PRIMARY SOUP

The Chinese Cook Book by Shiu Wong Chan 1893

This soup is always made of equal weights chicken and lean pork: say 1/2 pound of each, for each pint of water. It is advisable to use not less than six pints of water and meat in proportion.

Chop the meat into small pieces

Cook slowly for 2 1/2 hours or until all the liquid has evaporated.

In order to do away with any oil that may exist, put into the mixture a bowl of chicken blood.

Strain through a thick cloth until the liquid is as clear as water. Should there be any oil remaining on top, skim it off. Let the soup cool.

STOVE SOUP

The Chinese Cook Book by Shiu Wong Chan 1893

In cool winter evenings this party is often found in the Chinese House

Put a small stove in the center of the table. Place a pan of boiling primary soup. Cut into thin pieces, six pounds of any uncooked food at all — pike, chicken meat, shrimp, beef, stir until cooked. Serve in small bowls, each one with a well beaten egg, one tablespoon Chinese sauce, 1/4 teaspoon oil and a few drops of sesame seed oil.

WELSH RAREBIT

4 slices hearty whole wheat bread

1 cup shredded extra sharp cheddar cheese

5 tablespoons dark ale

2 tablespoons cold butter

1 tablespoon mustard

1/2 teaspoon salt

1/4 teaspoon black pepper

1 pinch cayenne pepper

Preheat broiler. Lay bread slices on a baking sheet and toast under broiler, turning once until browned on both sides. Remove from heat. Mix cheddar and ale in a small saucepan and heat gently. Add butter, mustard and seasonings once the cheese has melted. Whisk until smooth and heat for a couple of minutes. Cut toast in halves, diagonally. Top with cheese mixture and place under broiler until cheese bubbles and begins to scorch. Remove from heat and serve hot.

Petaluma Gold Rush
BEAN AND FARRO SOUP
from the kitchen of Deborah Walton, Canvas Ranch

1 cup dried Petaluma Gold Rush or cranberry beans

3 tablespoons extra-virgin olive oil plus additional for drizzling

1 large onion, coarsely chopped

2 carrots, coarsely chopped

1 celery rib, coarsely chopped

2 garlic cloves, smashed and peeled

10 cups water

1 large tomato (1/2 pound), coarsely chopped

1/4 cup loosely packed fresh flat-leaf parsley leaves

10 fresh sage leaves

3 sprigs fresh thyme

1 cup whole-grain farro

2 1/2 teaspoons salt

1/2 teaspoon black pepper

Pick over and rinse beans. Soak in cold water to cover by 2 inches at least 8 hours and up to 12 hours. Drain well. Heat oil in a 5- to 6-quart heavy pot over moderate heat until hot but not smoking, then cook onion, carrots, celery, and garlic, stirring occasionally, until onion is softened, about 10 minutes. Stir in water, drained beans, tomato, parsley, sage, and thyme and bring to a boil, then reduce heat and cook at a bare simmer, partially covered, stirring occasionally and adding more water if necessary to keep beans covered, until beans are tender, 2 to 3 hours. Discard thyme sprigs, then blend mixture in batches in a blender until smooth (use caution when blending hot liquids), transferring to a large bowl. Return soup to pot and bring to a boil. Add farro and salt, then reduce heat and simmer, stirring frequently, until farro is tender (it will be chewy like barley), about 30 minutes. Stir in pepper and serve drizzled with additional oil.

main courses

Fog Valley Fisherman's
CLASSIC CIOPPINO

Seafood:

4 fresh crabs

1 pound calamari rings

1 pound raw prawns

1 pound raw clams

1 pound raw bay scallops

2 pounds mixed sea bass, salmon, halibut chunks

Sauce:

2 onions, chopped

3 cloves crushed garlic

1 cup thinly sliced celery

1 finely chopped fennel bulb

1/2 cup chopped fresh Italian parsley

1/4 cup olive oil

4 cups stewed tomatoes (preferably home grown and canned or frozen)

1/2 cup tomato paste

1 cup clam juice

pinch of crushed red pepper

2 cups of water

Sauté onions, garlic, celery, fennel and parsley in olive oil in a sturdy stockpot over a medium flame until tender. Add tomatoes and paste, clam juice and crushed red pepper. Bring to a steady boil. Reduce heat and simmer for an hour or so. Add water to maintain volume of liquid.

Hold crabs firmly to remove the bodies from shell. Split bodies in half and crack legs. Add cracked crab, crab fat, clams, scallops and fish to the sauce. Simmer for a quarter of an hour at least. Add in calamari rings and prawns cooked in a separate pan for the last five minutes of cooking. When all the clams have opened, the stew is ready. Serve with fresh green salad and sourdough bread and a hearty red wine.

COASTAL CEDAR PLANK SALMON

1 untreated cedar plank (6 inches by 14 inches)

2 salmon fillets (up to two pounds)

salt and freshly ground black pepper

5 tablespoons of Dijon mustard

5 tablespoons of brown sugar

2 tablespoons of dill weed

Soak the cedar plank in salted water for a couple of hours. Skin, debone and rinse off salmon fillets. Pat dry. Season fish on both sides with salt and pepper and lay the salmon on the cedar, skin side down. Spread mustard and crumble sugar on top. Chop dill weed and sprinkle over prepared fish. Set a grill to medium high, position the cedar plank for indirect heat, cover and cook for about 20 minutes to half an hour, or until cooked through.

ROMAN GNOCCHI SQUARES

Vintage Recipe From Petaluma High School
(Former) Home Economics Department

1/4 cup butter
1/4 cup cornstarch
1/4 cup flour
2 cups milk
2 egg yolks
3/4 cup grated cheese
salt

Melt butter, add in the cornstarch and then the flour and add milk gradually. Cook for three minutes, stirring constantly. Add yolks and a pinch of salt to one half a cups of the cheese, pour into a buttered, shallow pan and cool. Cut into squares, place them on a platter a little distance apart, sprinkle with remaining cheese and brown in the oven.

SWISS FONDUE

from the French verb fondre — "to melt."

Heat up white wine with chopped garlic, add a grated, nutty cheese such as Gruyère and a little bit of cornstarch, stir while heating in a heavy, flameproof pot, until it's thick and creamy. Transfer to a heated fondue pot. Dip in bread chunks. Try not to drop one in!

Yiddish

BEEF BRISKET IN WINE

2 1/2 pound thick cut beef brisket

1 tablespoon paprika

1 teaspoon salt

1 teaspoon pepper

3 onions, sliced

1/2 teaspoon basil

2 cloves garlic, peeled and minced

1 1/2 cups water

1 1/2 cups ketchup
(F & J Heinz launched its commercial tomato ketchup in 1876)

1 1/2 cups red wine

Preheat oven to 325°F. Trim brisket of excess fat and rinse. Pat dry and place in a roasting pan. Season with a rub of paprika, salt and pepper. Sprinkle onions, basil and garlic over the meat. Mix water, ketchup and wine and pour over the brisket. Cover pan with enough room for the lid to not touch the meat. Bake for around three hours or more. The longer the meat cooks, the more tender. Reduce heat for slower cooking.

Serves 8.

⊹ ✗ ⹁ ✗ ⸳ ✗ ⸳ ✗ ⹁

Danish Settlers'
DUCK WITH APPLES AND PRUNES
And Med Aebler Og Svesker

1 duck

1 teaspoon salt

3 apples

5 ounces prunes

3 cups water

Sauce:

3 tablespoons duck fat

2 tablespoons flour

salt and pepper

Rub duck with salt. Fill with sliced apple and prunes. Use meat pins to close. Place duck back upwards on a rack in a deep pan and place neck and giblets in the pan. Roast for two-and-a-half to three hours at 325°F for 45 minutes. Pour away fat and add water.

Crisp for another 10 minutes at 375°F. Use a meat thermometer to test that the duck is fully cooked. Rest meat for 20 minutes before carving. Skim fat from juices and reserve liquid. Melt duck fat in a saucepan, stir in flour and juices. Boil briefly and season.

Serve with boiled potatoes, red cabbage and pickled cucumbers and halved steamed apples.

Serves 4.

Mission Christmas
EMPANADAS DE CARNE

1 teaspoon aniseed
1 tablespoon sugar
1/4 cup water
2 cups flour
1 teaspoon baking powder
1/2 teaspoon salt
3 tablespoons lard or vegetable shortening
1 farm fresh egg

Add aniseed, sugar and water into a small saucepan and bring to a slow boil for around three or four minutes. Sift flour, baking powder and salt in a bowl. Mix in lard or shortening, beaten egg and the aniseed liquid. Knead until dough is pliable. Divide into three balls. Roll each at a time and use a cookie cutter to cut dough into four-inch circles.

Meat Filling:
1 pound rump beef, cut into small chunks
1 tablespoon lard
2 green onions
2 tablespoons sugar
1/4 teaspoon salt
1/3 cup seedless raisins
1 cup cured black olives, chopped
1 farm fresh egg

Sauté meat in lard until tender. Chop and sauté onions until golden and add in meat, sugar, salt, raisins and olives. Simmer for half an hour. Remove from heat. Add beaten egg. Fill the four-inch pastry circles. Fold over into turnovers, using a fork to press edges together. Prick the tops with a fork. Bake on cookie sheets at 400°F until golden.

Timo's

WILD BOAR RAGÙ

1 pound wild boar shoulder or leg,
cut into 1 inch chunks

2 sprigs of rosemary

1 tablespoon of mixed peppercorns, whole

4 cloves of peeled garlic

2 cups of Syrah

3 tablespoons of olive oil

1 carrot, finely chopped

1 stalk of celery, finely chopped

1 cup of whole tomatoes, skinned, with juice

2 cups vegetable stock

gnocchi or tagliatelle

Place chopped meat in a bowl with rosemary, peppercorns, garlic and wine. Cover and chill in the refrigerator overnight. Remove rosemary and garlic. Drain meat in a colander, reserving wine. Heat oil in a Dutch oven over a medium flame, add carrot and celery and sauté for 5 minutes. Brown meat. Remove Dutch oven from heat. Add tomatoes and vegetable stock and slow cook in a low oven for six hours or more. Serve over freshly made gnocchi or tagliatelle noodles and grated parmesan.

✗ · ✗ · ✗ · ✗

sweets

Mrs Will Oeltjen's
NEVER FAIL PIE CRUST

1 cup of flour
3 tablespoons of lard or shortening
1 tablespoon of vinegar
3 tablespoons of water
1 tablespoon of baking powder
pinch of salt

Makes one crust for an uncovered pie.

Mrs. Hardin's
CHRISTMAS APPLE CAKE

2 scant teaspoons of soda
2 teaspoons of cold water
1 cup of sugar
1 cup of butter
1 egg, well beaten
1 teaspoon of vanilla
1 cup of raisins, chopped
1 cup of walnuts, chopped
1 1/2 cups of chopped apples
2 cups of flour
1 teaspoon of cinnamon
1/4 teaspoon each of nutmeg and cloves

Put soda in water and let stand one hour. Cream sugar and butter, add egg, vanilla, fruit and nuts. Sift dry ingredients together several times and add soda and water. Beat thoroughly. Bake for a quarter of an hour to 20 minutes in a moderate oven.

Mrs. Hardin's
GINGER COOKIES

2 to 3 cups of sugar

2 to 3 cups of molasses

'2 cup of butter

up of boiling water

:easpoon of soda

ɪg teaspoon of ginger

salt

add creamed butter, sugar and molasses to

sheet in a quick oven.

ERRATA

p 299

PRINTED AS

2 to 3 cups of molasses

SHOULD BE

**2 to 3 cups of flour
3/4 cup molasses**

Nonna's

ALMOND BISCOTTI

2 eggs
8 ounces sugar
14 ounces plain flour
2 1/2 teaspoons baking powder
a few drops of orange essence
pinch of salt
5 ounces lightly toasted, skinned almonds

Preheat oven to 350°F. Beat two eggs and sugar. Add flour, baking powder, orange essence and salt. Mix well. Stir in almonds. Form dough into a long roll on a lightly floured surface. Place the dough roll onto a greased and lightly floured baking tray. Glaze the top of the roll with beaten egg yolk. Bake for around 15 minutes. Remove from oven and cut diagonally at finger width intervals. Return to oven for six more minutes. Remove from oven and transfer onto a cooling rack.

Filhos de Natal
PORTUGUESE CHRISTMAS FRITTERS

1 package of dry yeast

1/4 cup of warm milk

4 cups flour

1 teaspoon salt

4 tablespoons brandy

5 eggs, lightly beaten

vegetable oil

3/4 cup honey

1/2 cup hot water

Dissolve yeast in warm milk and let it stand for five minutes. Sift flour, add salt and pour into yeast mixture, brandy and beaten eggs. Knead into a smooth elastic dough. Place in a greased bowl, cover and let it rise in a warm place until doubled in size. Punch down the dough and toll onto a floured board. Cut into strips 1/2 inch wide and 2 inches long. Fry in hot oil for two to three minutes until crisp and golden brown. Drain onto paper towels. Dissolve honey in hot water and dip fritters in mixture until coated. Serve warm or cold.

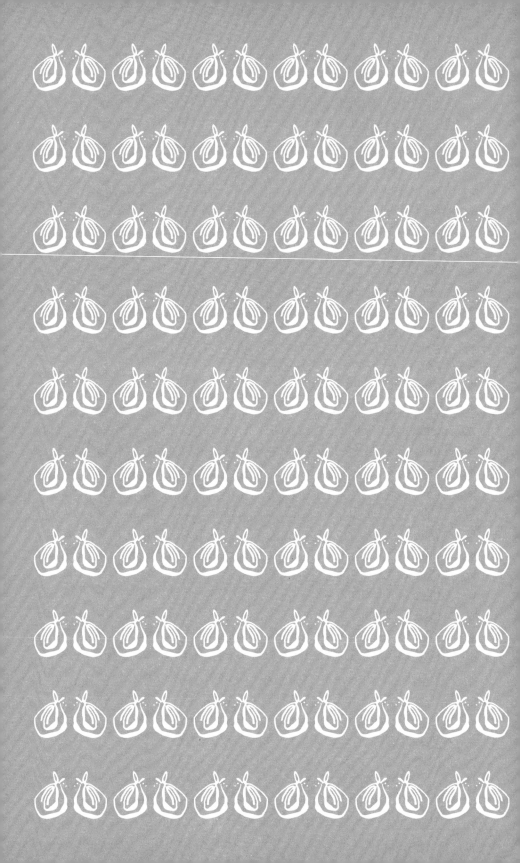

family feasts
and full dinners

X ··· X ··· X ··· X ··· X

A Proper Victorian Christmas Dinner
ROAST GOOSE
WITH SAGE & ONION DRESSING

9 pound goose
2 teaspoons coarse salt

For the dressing:
3 medium onions, peeled
4 large, tart apples, peeled, cored and chopped
2 tablespoons loosely packed dried sage leaves, crumbled
1/2 teaspoon freshly ground black pepper
1 tablespoon of butter, cut into small dices
sliced apples, parsley or watercress to garnish

For the Brown Gravy:
gizzard, neck, heart, liver and wing tips of goose, chopped
1 onion
1 carrot, sliced
2 tablespoons of rendered goose fat or cooking oil
3 cups beef stock
1/2 bay leaf
3 springs parsley
salt and pepper to taste

For the port wine sauce:
1/2 cup port
1 teaspoon mustard
pinch cayenne pepper
salt to taste

Preheat oven to 450°F. Rub inside of the goose with salt. Parboil and onion in boiling water for five minutes. Remove with a slotted spoon and when cool to handle, chop finely.

In a large bowl, combine onions, chopped apples, sage, pepper and butter. Stuff cavity of goose and sew or skewer the openings. Pierce the skin with a trussing needle to help release fat but not juices.

Pour a little water in a roasting pan so that the fat won't burn as it releases. Place the goose on a roasting rack in the pan. Roast at 450°F for 15 minutes, then turn the goose to its side and reduce heat to 350°F for one hour, basting regularly. Turn to the other side for another hour. Turn goose onto its back for the final 15 minutes.

Prepare gravy while goose is in the oven. In a large saucepan, brown the goose parts, onion and carrot, in fat. Add stock and seasonings. Simmer, partially covered, for an hour. Skim. Strain, degrease and pour gravy into a warmed gravy boat to serve.

For the port wine sauce, mix all ingredients in a small saucepan. When serving the goose, split open the breast and pour the sauce on top.

Serves 8.

Petaluma Jaycee Wives'
TURKEY DINNER FOR 250

The United States Junior Chamber was established in 1920 to provide opportunities for young men to develop personal and leadership skills through service to others. The Jaycees later expanded to include women (also known as Jayceettes and Jayceens — clearly a sociable crowd).

17 roasted turkeys

75 pounds of cooked, mashed butternut squash

20 large cranberry rings

75 pounds of cooked, mashed potato

10 bunches of celery

44 pies

Acknowledgements

I am indebted to a small, yet formidable circle of people who have gathered with me around my kitchen table in all aspects of the writing and production of this book. I'd like to extend my deepest thanks to concept editor and fellow Fog Valley adventurer, the ingenious Elaine Silver. Editorial cheerleader since the start of my Fog Valley rambles, Elaine's gentle guidance once again makes for an immeasurably better final form. Cover, inside page and recipe illustrator extraordinaire, the intuitive and sublimely talented Nicky Ovitt transformed my Fog Valley imaginings into images even more beautiful than I'd dared to envision. Book designer and print maven, Lorna Johnson glided through this monumental process with masterly skill and her trademark professional poise over multiple refills of the teapot. I'm forever grateful to have had the chance to work with such a terrific team to bring this book to life. Susan Villa, stalwart friend, neighbor and former president of the Petaluma Historical Library and Museum is a fountain of knowledge on Fog Valley of yesteryear. Susan's unwavering support with research, in the field and as an early reader has been a life force in the substance and shaping of this book. Very special thanks to dear and devoted girlfriend and early reader Lesley McCullaugh, for keeping me from going completely stir-crazy over the past year and a half with frequent mini-trips and theatre outings with fellow Fog Valley "glampers" Gail Foulkes and Jane Sell.

My husband, Timo has been my rock throughout. Long days at the keyboard were rewarded with evening meals and bottles of homemade wine! Our strong and steady partnership has, without a doubt, been a defining factor in my writing life. A large part of this book was written at the kitchen table where most everything else in its production took place, often in the company of a menagerie of household pets and one or (occasionally) more of my three beloved sons — Rocco, Luc and mostly, Dominic, my youngest, whose senior year of high school has been flavored with a constant barrage of hometown history.

Sources

A Nation of Immigrants by John F. Kennedy

Angelisland.org

Artisan Cheese Trail

Bay Nature Magazine

BBC History Magazine

Bon Appétit Magazine

Buckeye Cookery & Practical Housekeeping 1877

California Department of Fish and Game

California Digital Newspapers

California Missions Resource Center

Celebrating Petaluma
by Petaluma Sesquicentennial Committee/Petaluma Visitors Program

Chief Marin, Rebel and Legend by Betty Goerke

Christmas in the Gold Fields — Journal of Sierra Nevada History and Biography

Coastal Post

Dewey Livingston's 1993 *Historic Resource Study*

Farm Journal

Fisheries and Aquaculture Department — United Nations

Guardian of the Lights — Stories of U.S. Lighthouse Keepers by Elinor D. Wire

Glamorgan Archives

Godey's Lady's Book

Harper's Weekly

Harry Potter books by J. K. Rowling

History of Dungeness Crab Fisheries in California
by Walter A. Dahlstrom

Historic Legends of Sonoma County by Fred Cook

Historic Photos of Sonoma County by Lee Torliatt

Historical and Descriptive Sketch of Sonoma County, California
by Robert A. Thompson

Household Words by Charles Dickens

Inside the Victorian Home by Judith Flanders

Jerusalem Today

Jerusalem Post

Jewish Currents

Journal of Sierra Nevada History and Biography

J. P. Munro Fraser's 1880 History of Sonoma County

Knorr Home Canning Book

Learning Journey on the Red Road by Looks For Buffalo

Letters of Note by Shaun Usher

Lighthouses and Lifeboats of the Redwood Coast by Ralph Shanks

National Geographic

North Coast National Public Radio

National World War II Museum

Native Technology and Art

North Bay Bohemian

Marin Agricultural Land Trust

Marin Journal

Marin Story Shed Project

McEvoy Ranch.com

Much Depends Upon Dinner by Margaret Visser

One Hundred Mushroom Receipts by Kate Sargeant

Petaluma Argus Courier

Petaluma Historical Library and Museum

Petalumans of Yesteryear

PBS *The History Kitchen*

*Point Reyes: The Complete Guide to the National Seashore &
Surrounding Area*

Point Reyes, The Solemn Land by Jack Mason

Point Reyes Visitors Center

Portuguese Historical and Cultural Society

National Park Service

New York Times

North Coast Heritage Grain Alliance

Roughing It by Samuel Clemens

Santa Rosa Press Democrat

Sacred Sonoma by Beth Winegarner

Sonoma County Historical Library

Sonoma Magazine

Sonoma County Master Gardeners

Sonoma County Museum Quarterly

Sonoma County Mycological Association

Sonoma County: The River of Time by Simone Wilson

Studies of American Fungi by Sarah Tyson Rorer

Sunset Magazine

County County Parks Association

The Californian

The Catholic San Francisco

Tales Of The Fish Patrol — Jack London

The California Indian Museum and Cultural Center

The Coastal Post

The Encyclopedia of American Food and Drink

The English Home

The Pew Research Center

The Social Background of the Italo-American School Child
by Leonard H. Covello

The Social History of the American Family
by Marilyn J. Coleman and Lawrence H. Ganong

The Women Suffrage Cookbook by Hattie A. Burr

The Yankee Whaling Museum

Tomales History Museum

Under The Gables, Inverness Foundation

University of California Ag and Natural Resources Department

Up And Down California, The Journal of William H. Brewer

U.S. Department of State Office of the Historian

Wales Online

World Wildlife Organization

For each new morning with its light,
For rest and shelter of the night,
For health and food, for love and friends,
For everything Thy goodness sends.

Ralph Waldo Emerson